DEFY GRAVITY

OCT , 2021

FROM THE FANS

Tianna's inspiring and insightful memoir is essential reading for anyone wishing to gain a deeper understanding of what it means to be a female elite athlete. Tianna represents a powerful and essential voice in the world of athletics; she's a leader and role model who embodies what it means to be a champion and whose story is sure to inspire the next generation of girls in sports.

~Alexi Pappas, Olympian, actress, filmmaker, and author
of the bestselling book, Bravey

Early in high school, Tianna had promise on the track, but she did not yet have the courage to push past her fears. Once she learned how to do so, she applied these and other skills to become an Olympic champion and an inspiration to many. Tianna's willingness to speak out with great insight on today's key issues both inside and outside the sports world make her story one not to miss.

~Michael Repetto

Tianna's raw honesty and genuine reflection on what it feels like to know what you are capable of, but not quite in touch with yourself to reach that potential, is like looking in the mirror. And to be let the fear of this potential get in the way of pursuing potential success is something every reader—athlete, career woman, mother—can relate to. But then to be encouraged to face this fear and step up to the challenge by the fierce and loving voice of Tianna is a reminder of what we can all achieve.

~Katie Wanket, Editor

The destination maybe unknown but the hard work and dedication makes Tianna's story relatable, inspiring and badass. The honesty of the struggle, laying bare the disappointments and knock backs only add to the admiration of this amazing human.

~Amanda Husband

I was hooked by the first page, wanting to know what was going to happen. She gives such an honest and raw view at her life and I am in awe of her courage and strength. Her story is captivating and she is downright inspiring as an athlete.

~Shannon Czimskey

Tianna's wildly honest and deeply motivating personal narrative highlights the inevitable highs and lows of an athlete's life while elucidating what it means to fall down, get up, and fly beyond expectation.

~Alysia Puma, high school cross-country coach and English teacher

Tianna took me on a wild ride through her experiences running track in high school. From laughter to remembered teenage angst, I feel like I was right there with her., up to and including the moment she owned up to her inner demons and the voices of self-doubt that sabotaged some of her performances. I want to get acquainted with that Tianna B.

~Phoebe Potter

Tianna's writing is gritty and inspiring—especially when she describes those moments when she shrank back from her goals due to fear, thinking it would be okay, only to have it be anything but. Tianna's vulnerability and unwavering commitment to honesty capture something inherent in the human spirit: resilience. Tianna's work will influence you to make the best choices you possibly can, aim high, and realize your dreams by doing the real work that few among us are willing to commit to.

~Stefanie Frank, Entrepreneur, Co-Founder, Frankly Good Coffee,
Former Online Copywriter, Estate Planning Attorney

A cross between a page turning story you can't put down and a lyrical masterpiece, Bartoletta's words acknowledge the messy truth of being human who is striving for greatness. Survive & Advance gives us a behind the scenes look at the winding path towards being a champion, studded with lessons and revelations that can apply to anyone. With every poignant and relatable sentence, Bartoletta proves that her dominance extends further than her decorated athletic background."

~Sarah Tanza, Doctor of Physical Therapy

"More please!" Your writing style brings the pulling hooks for inquisitive minds. Very raw and real account.

~Good Mood Mike, U.S. Government

As a track fan for 60 years this book took me into the physical and emotional challenges of elite track competition at a level I could only imagine.

~David Potter, M.D. Retired Physian

Her words have a way of bringing the reader into the space/place you are describing, as if we are there with her - whether it's at the track meet flirting and accepting the new moniker of Project or hearing her own voice on the answering machine at home or getting inside her head and heart at the state meet.

~Kathy McGroddy Goetz

"Reads to me like your blogs do... sincere, sensitive and from the heart, but also with space and pace to be taken on by the reader and to be understood."

~Rob Covell Photographer

As a track & field coach who began his career by starting a track club for age-group girls, and ended it by starting a collegiate women's t & f / xc program from scratch, I stumbled onto Tianna's Blogs via social media and became instantly enamored with her ability to be the voice of female athletes who have been through the trials and tribulations faced by females in both athletics and society.

~Jim Hiserman Retired Coach

Tianna is a delight to discover. She's a vinyasa of experience, emotion, and enlightenment, quivering, but breathing. Her writing uncovers wordings that were meant to be.

~Jeffrey Kane

Like the Olympic jumper and sprinter that she is, Tianna is an exceptionally talented writer as well. When she chooses to weigh in on something, she elevates the discourse of any given topic with her perspective, shaped by her life's experiences and pursuit of excellence. Whether it's about the world of track and field, or life in general, Tianna speaks truth to power in a way that deeply resonates with anyone who reads her words. She is able to identify and convey the universal truths at play within our societal dynamics and break it down into easily digestible nuggets of wisdom. Whether or not you follow the sport of track and field, the value that Tianna Bartoletta adds to the sport and to this world as an athlete, yogi, and a person, is immeasurable.

Sonya Alcocer-Charles, TB's Breakfast Club member, Twitter follower,
Track and Field fan, and overall huge fan of TB

Since I first knew her as a teen, Tianna had always been thoughtful, intellectual, and insightful. And that has carried through adulthood with her blog, and I am excited to see her journey continue with her memoir.

~Jeremy Secaur, Tianna's high school Physics teacher

Tianna Bartoletta is a tremendously gifted writer among her many talents. Her words are amazingly candid and always thought provoking. Tianna never fails to strike emotional chords in her readers, and her life story she shares in this book will do the same.

~Jack Viera

Tianna Bartoletta is one the most raw, real, and powerful persons ever. I say that because she hits life straight in the face. She trains like a military beast yet is humble and pliable like rhe spirit of a flower. She is one of the most honest and self correcting through life's experiences and has probably the best adaptation skills needed to get through anything. Tiana seeks balance through her goals and her experiences. Her love for learning has also shown over time shes a great teacher. I have found Tiana to be most honorable. Given support this girl can conquer anything!

~Tamara Hayes, Holistic Health Practitioner and Life Coach

As a huge fan of track and field, I am always fascinated to read the stories behind the amazing athletes I watch on my TV screen or in the stadium. They seem so calm and focused and almost super human. As a viewer, it is easy to take for granted that this is just 'what they do' and not appreciate the very human struggles, challenges and setbacks that all these athletes have to overcome to get to where they are. It is incredibly inspiring to read about the reality behind the performances, the hard work and the struggles, both mental and physical that athletes go through. I found reading about you both inspiring—it made me think, yes come on, work hard and I can get where I want to be too—and touching—your honesty and self-reflection and capacity to make yourself vulnerable by opening up are very admirable. The funny details and anecdotes give an interesting insight, and made me engage with you as an author and want to know more.

~Jane Salvatori

In her new memoir, Tianna Bartoletta artfully takes back her narrative in a way that is honest, daring, and heartening. This book is incredibly raw and not to be missed.

~ Malissa Rodenburg, Women's Running

Survive & Advance is a story of a life spent running. My life has not been an easy one to live, and so Survive and Advance is not an easy story to tell. Some of the subject matter may be difficult to read, could be upsetting, or triggering.

It is the honor of my life to share this story with you. All I've ever wanted for myself was to be truly seen; heard when I spoke; and supported when I was struggling. Through all the ups and downs I relay in the pages ahead, I want you to remember this one important truth:

I survived.

Survive & Advance

Author: Tianna Bartoletta

Editor: Marla McKenna

Associate Editors: Lyda Rose Haerle, Griffin Mill

Cover Design: Nicole Wurtele
Graphic Designer with The CG Sports Company

Interior Layout: Michael Nicloy

Cover Photos: Anthony DiPasquale
Interior Photos: Mario Bassani, Dwight Phillips

Published by: CG Sports Publishing
Head of Publishing: Michael Nicloy

A Division of The CG Sports Company
www.cgsportsco.com

ISBN: 978-1-7359193-1-7

Produced and Distributed by Nico 11 Publishing & Design

Quantity order requests can be emailed to:
matt@cgsportsmanagement.com

Printed in The United States of America

To Mom

Because you made me.
You are one of my greatest teachers.
Because of you and all we've gone through together,
I have become a woman I can finally be proud of.

And I'm proud of us too. I love you.

SURVIVE & ADVANCE

RUN

I'm standing in a tunnel staring into the light. My shoulders slightly slumped from the weight I'm carrying, my chest tight from the gravity of the moment. I will my right foot forward, and then my left, and then the right again. But I stop.

I'm standing at the mouth of the tunnel now, having stepped fully into the light. I shift the weight I'm bearing between my shoulders. My chest readjusts its grip on the tightness it insists on carrying. Again, I will my left foot forward, and then my right.

I'm walking now, escorted by a person in uniform to a front-row seat—to my fate. They ask me to lift my shirt. They check my number, what I'm wearing, and they make sure I am who I say I am, while they run a finger down a roster of names. They write a checkmark next to mine. As I walk away, the process is repeated with the next in line. The person in uniform occasionally looks up from a worn clipboard to monitor our movements.

I'm handed a tiny block; it's the only thing I am allowed to possess out here, beyond myself. A large clock just outside my periphery begins counting down. It tells me that I have 30 minutes left…now 29. I'm in London at the IAAF World Championships. This competition will begin right on time, so I straighten the bib number I have safety-pinned to the front of my uniform. I ask for help readjusting the one on my back.

My spikes are on, and my sweats are off. I take the tiny block I was given by the official and place it at the spot where my approach will begin.

The competition commences.

I'm up. I take a deep breath. I rock my weight backward as I step my right foot behind me. I hinge forward and close my eyes.

"A person is always running," I hear the voice of one of my former coaches say in my head. "You're either running from something or running toward something, either way you're running. It's just best you know which it is."

I reopened my eyes. I know which it is as I throw my left arm forward with the violence of a boxer's knockout punch in a championship round. I know which it is. I drive out with the kind of force one can only generate with wrath mixed with flammable desperation. I know which it is as I reach my top speed on the runway.

I'm running for my life.

TRACK OR FIELD?

I was born in Elyria, Ohio, a small, unassuming city about 20 miles or so west of Cleveland. My dad, Robert, was born and raised there too. My mom, Jo Ann, was in Bessemer, Alabama. They found their way to each other when my dad ventured out of the city to go to college.

"You went to college?" I asked him once. I'd never heard him talk about school beyond high school.

"Yeah, I went!" A sly smile bloomed across his face, "I knew I had to go to college to find a wife!"

I expressed my disbelief that one would pay for college simply to find a wife.

"Noooo, I went up to the college!" he said, dissolving into a fit of laughter thoroughly amused with himself.

My mother, tall and slender, spent her time studying and dancing. Graceful, yet stern, her demeanor was of a royal air. One would never know she was one of twelve children who grew up in a two-bedroom house.

Me, on the other hand? I was an average but active kid. My only brushes with adversity involved being left-handed in a right-handed world and being an older sister to Christina. Even with a martial artist for a father and a dancer for a mother, none of us had any reason to believe that I'd become anything spectacular because I was incredibly ungraceful, uncoordinated, and unaware of my body. I was a multi-sport athlete starting in middle school. I played volleyball in the fall and basketball during winter. When spring arrived, the two sports available were wrestling and track.

I chose wrestling—naturally.

I grabbed a flyer with the interest-meeting information on it for my parents. My dad, a bit of a hometown hero, was memorialized on the walls of the high school for his wrestling ability. We had heard tales of epic matches while looking at old newspaper clippings and photos. I had my father's wrestling singlet and wore it often. I was a daddy's girl and didn't think twice about following in his wrestling footsteps.

Mom did though. My father and I appealed. We explained that, even though I would be wrestling boys, we'd be similar size; that I was freakishly strong for my frame; that dad would be there the entire time; and that he'd teach me so much and so well, matches wouldn't actually be a match for me at all. Mom refused to budge on her position; and so, I found myself walking by the wrestling mats to attend my first day of track practice in the school parking lot.

Miss Hersman, our social studies/history teacher, was our track coach. Most of us, myself included, only knew of track from seeing it on television during the 1996 Olympic Games in Atlanta the year before. Fascinated by gymnasts like Dominque Dawes, I could hardly be bothered to watch anything other than gymnastics during my childhood. But there I stood, prohibited from joining the wrestling team, waiting to join the track team.

Trackless, we gathered in the school parking lot where we had practice.

"Everyone, stand on that white line," Miss Hersman barked at us.

We quieted down and rearranged ourselves for her. After all, she was one of the "cool" teachers—she drove a Thunderbird and ran a snack and candy shop out of her cupboard at the back of the classroom. With no access to candy at home I used my allowance to satisfy my sweet tooth during school hours.

"Welcome to the track team. I'm now going to divide you up between track events and field events, and we'll divide you up further after that."

I raised my hand, "Miss Hersman, when you say track over there and field over here, does that mean the 'track' side is just running?"

She looked hard at my face and found that I was completely serious.

"Yes, Tianna."

That was all the information I needed to declare myself a field event athlete. Who runs for fun?

I stayed put while my other non-running classmates coalesced around me. Eventually, Miss Hersman made her way back to us. She explained the different field events we could do. We didn't have much by way of equipment in this junior high parking lot that would serve as our training ground, but we did have a rectangular pit, filled with a suspicious-looking combination of sand and dirt, that resided at the end of a poorly marked parking space.

She explained the elements of the long jump which, for our purposes, simply consisted of lining up with your back against the school's brick wall, running through the parking spaces, and launching yourself into the air once asphalt turned to sand. We'd figure out approaches and make acquaintance with the long jump takeoff board at our first meet.

It took out-jumping one of the boys on the team at practice that first week for me to fall in love and begin a decades-long obsession with traveling farther, faster, and higher.

IT'S GOTTA BE THE SHOES

"We're not buying you spikes," my mom said without looking up from her reading.

My first track meet was midweek, and I did not own any spikes. Specialty shoes were expensive. I had been flipping through Eastbay magazine, which sold a whole gamut of sports apparel and equipment, for my first pair of spikes. I circled my favorites and headed down the stairs to show them to my parents.

"Those are nice," my dad said, disinterestedly, as he handed the magazine to my mom.

"We're not buying you spikes," she said again, after looking at what I'd circled. "We don't even know if you're gonna stick with it, or if you're good. We bought you a violin and what did you do? Barely got through Hot Cross Buns."

It was true, they had shelled out a hefty sum of money on ankle braces, volleyball knee pads, Adidas snap pants, and anything else I swore I needed to perform well. They weren't buying my lines anymore.

"Let's not get ahead of ourselves. Let's just see how it goes this week," my mom said.

As certain as I was that I'd be the only one at the meet without spikes, I was determined to earn some. My mother inadvertently had issued me a challenge that I fully intended to accept.

On meet day, before leaving the school, we were issued our uniforms. Like Kleenex, our coach pulled old, worn jerseys from broken down cardboard boxes. I sniffed my jersey but immediately wished I hadn't. The random number I was assigned was peeling at the edges. Even still, I was excited to have it. I slipped the baggy top over my sports bra and waited for the distribution of our T-shirts and warm-ups.

After everyone had their gear, we boarded the bus, fighting for the "premier" seats at the back. I chatted away happily with my teammates. Some slipped headphones on while they flipped through the plastic sleeves of their CD keepers. I looked on longingly. I didn't have a CD player, or spikes, and my shoes were from the athletic section of Payless Shoes. We were headed to a tri-meet with two middle schools in Lorain, a neighboring city. We jogged a lazy two laps and stretched sloppily to prepare for the first race, the 100-meter dash.

I was in the first heat, lined up in the middle of the track. Our coaching staff had shown us starting blocks, mounted on slabs of wood. earlier that week. But I still hadn't learned how to use them. The official placed the blocks in my lane. I knew that my left foot was meant to be forward in the blocks because, at our last practice, coach had us all cross our arms in front of our chests. Then she walked past us one by one and shoved us from behind, noting which foot we shot out in front of us to keep from falling. I bent down to slide the left block forward; I slid the right block back to some arbitrary position making sure it wasn't even with the left; I at least knew that much.

I stood upright again as we were told to strip out of our warm-ups. I watched the girls to my left and right slip down to nicer uniforms and better shoes. They all had spikes. I attempted to swallow the lump that had developed in my throat. I shifted my gaze to the track as my eyes traced the lane lines. There were so many lines. There were lines that extended straight from where I was standing, but there were also lines that intersected the straight lines and curved right before straightening out again. We had no such lines in the parking lot at Northwood Junior High.

The official took his place on the step ladder and raised the gun in the air.

"Runners, take your mark!"

I knew this meant it was time to place your feet on their respective pedals, and once you did you needed to be still.

"Set!"

This means you raise your butt in the air from what Coach Hersman told us at practice.

BANG!

The gun went off louder than I expected. I jolted straight up and began to sprint. I approached the line and wondered if I was meant to continue running straight or veer right with the other lines. I veered right. I ran as fast as my Payless shoes would allow me and won my first race!

At the finish I turned to look back toward the starting line. Red flags waved furiously as the remaining runners finished their races and gathered at the finish line. My dad ran to the infield and spoke enthusiastically to the opposing teams' coaches and officials. We were excused by the line judges, and I walked over to my father feeling happy with myself for winning. I wondered if that showing was good enough to earn my first pair of spikes.

"Good job, T," my dad said as he acknowledged my approach, "but they are going to disqualify you."

I stood in stunned silence wondering what I did wrong.

"Did you run out of your lane?" my dad asked me.

"No, I followed the lines," I replied in my defense.

"Which lines?" my dad asked me again.

"The one that turns and then goes straight," I said as if everyone else was stupid.

"I see," my dad said as he walked back over to the huddle of coaches and officials.

"It's her first track meet, and they've never been on a track before. They practice in the parking lot. She beat the others by so much, you can't really say that she interfered with anyone," my dad argued on my behalf.

"Coach, she was running in the same lane as my athlete!" a coach responded excitedly.

"Yes, but she was already 10 meters behind. You can disqualify Tianna, but your athlete still got beat. DQ'ing her isn't going to change that," my dad responded in turn.

"Now, now, we're going to let this go this time because it's her first, and we don't want to go and discourage the kids," said one of the officials.

It was now official. I had just won the 100-meter dash, after a little advocating, and a lot of waiting. I smiled big! Later that season, I'd lose the 100-meter dash at the Elyria City Championships to Maria Whitely who attended junior high at Eastern Heights. I carried that loss with me for an entire year, until we lined up against each other again at City Champs the following year. I won that race, in my new spikes!

BLACK LOVE

I was always in love. I had embarrassing, debilitating crushes. Loving hard from afar and to the point of paralysis up close. I remember convincing my mother to buy me a specific First Down jacket because my crush had one, only to arrive at school and find out I hadn't gotten the color right. This same boy and I ended up in computer lab together on large, colorful, Apple Macintosh computers where we played *Oregon Trail* and *Mavis Beacon Teaches Typing*. One day, as we were packing our things to prepare for the end of class, he spoke to me.

I froze and waited forever for him to speak again.

Eventually, he said, "You know what's interesting about you?"

"What?" I asked, barely keeping my voice from shaking with the excitement of being engaged.

"Your back looks EXACTLY like your front!" He burst into an obnoxious laugh as other members of the class joined in.

I looked into his hazel brown eyes one last time and exited the classroom.

Crushing on him was much more fun when I didn't know him, I thought.

There was a reason I didn't know him.

Windsor Elementary was a predominantly white school on the north side of town. I spent seven years being the only black kid in class. To be completely honest, I didn't know I was black. Or, at least, I wasn't aware of what it meant to be black.

Until then.

It was the first week of seventh grade at Northwood and I was completely overwhelmed at the number of students, at the size of the school. I was at my locker practicing taking my lock on and off as quickly as possible because I had the added pressure of switching classes, and if I didn't want to lug my textbooks around all day, I had to get better about making the swap between classes.

Turn the dial 3 times to the right and stop
Turn the dial to the left, pass the first number stop on the second number.
Turn the dial to the right and stop on the third number.
Voila!

I checked my class schedule which I'd written and rewritten a dozen times. My textbooks were covered in paper grocery bags from Apples, the local grocery store, and I'd doodled on each one, in glitter gel pens, the name of the class, and on the inside flap the time of the class.

I was most excited for lunch. I already knew that I had the same lunch period as a lot of my friends from Windsor; comparing schedules was the first thing we did at orientation once we were in possession of our schedules.

I was in the G.A.T.E program, which stood for the Gifted and Talented Education program. This meant that my schedule was full of honors classes and large blocks of time where we'd converge on the G.A.T.E. classroom and commence with non-traditional learning.

For example, while other students were learning how to write five paragraph essays, we were writing screen plays. And the best received screenplay (as voted by the class) would be put on by the class under the direction of the winning screenwriter. When other students were tackling word problems in math class, we were doing logic and rebus puzzles for time on a stopwatch. I loved every minute. And for me the best part was that all but one or two of the students in the program came from Windsor Elementary School.

I made it to the lunch period without incident, a little late because my fingers fumbled the combination at my locker where I stopped to drop off my books and grab my bagged lunch. A creature of habit, especially when it came to food, I ate the same lunch every day, a peanut butter and jelly sandwich, a Ziplock bag of whatever potato chips we had in the house at the time, a baggy of fig newtons, and a Capri Sun, a napkin that usually had a handwritten note on it from my mom that said, *Love You* or *Go make a difference.* I entered the cafeteria slowly. It was exasperating walking in alone and searching frantically for familiar faces to sit with, all while outwardly playing it cool.

I located my Windsor friends sitting at a table in the back corner of the cafeteria. As I approached, I noticed that they all still had bagged lunches too. I found this comforting. It was nice to know that, even surrounded by all this change, some things could stay the same.

I was at the table now.

"Hey!" I said as I set my bagged lunch on the table and pulled out a chair.

"Hey," they said back to me in melodic unison.

They seemed surprised to see me, which was confusing because we all compared schedules and had known we'd have lunch together.

No one was saying anything. I was focused on extracting my smashed pb&j sandwich from its wrapping when someone finally spoke up.

"I just thought you'd go sit over there now," one of my oldest friends said to me.

"Where?" I asked, not bothering to look up, intent on freeing my sandwich from its plastic prison without getting peanut butter or grape jelly on my fingers.

"Over there," she said.

Again, I didn't bother to look up, instead I settled on asking her why she'd thought that.

"Because you're black," she said.

"Oookaaay…and?" I said back.

"Aaannd…I figured, we figured…you'd be more comfortable with people like you."

We. All of them. My oldest friends.

"Like me." Absently, I repeated the words as my now free sandwich sat lamely on the table. I must have dropped it; no matter—my appetite had dissipated anyway. "I don't know anyone here. You guys are my friends," I said, hating the pleading I could begin to detect in my tone.

"Yeah, well it's probably time anyway."

I stood slowly, packing the remnants of my lunch back into the brown paper bag. I tossed it into the trash and walked zombie-like to the girls' bathroom. I sat in an empty stall reading the graffiti on the stall door until the class bell rang.

The following day, I entered the cafeteria, bagged lunch in hand, eyes forward. I found an empty table. And I sat alone…for an entire week.

D.A.R.E. DEVIL

On the first day of the beginning of my second week of eating lunch by myself, a girl I did not know approached the table.

"Come sit with us. We're tired of seeing your sad ass eat by yourself," she said flashing her pearly white teeth at me in a beautiful smile.

"Okay," I said without resistance or hesitation.

I was sad. Every day, I had watched my Windsor friends laugh and giggle together over bagged lunches with their name brand snacks, while I sat and ate alone. Banished. Nibbling the corners off of Fig Newtons. Pathetic.

I pulled out a chair and made myself comfortable at the new table, where I was no longer "other." They asked me my name, and where I had gone to school, and why none of them had ever seen me before.

I told them.

"Why you talk like that?" someone asked me.

"Like what?" I asked in return, confused.

"Like a white girl," someone else said.

I shut my lips tightly, opting to shrug my shoulders in lieu of speaking again.

They all laughed. But this group laughter felt less like being made fun of and more like benign amusement at the new girl they've allowed into their lunch circle. In my first of two weeks, I learned two lessons. The first was that black meant something, and the second was that a person could *sound* white.

Speaking of sound, Mr. McKitrick, Northwood's wrestling coach, health teacher, and our lunch period's cafeteria monitor, bought a device that measured the cafeteria noise level in decibels. If we reached levels higher than his predetermined allowances, he would eliminate the à la carte menu. That meant, no pink frosted cookies. And, even though I brought my lunch to school every day, I almost always spent part of my allowance on pink cookies or strawberry eclairs. The à la carte menu was a treat we did not wish to lose.

But on this particular day, the entire cafeteria seemed riled up. It was loud, perhaps because it was Papa John's pizza day, or maybe it was uncomfortably hot. Whatever the reason, we were smashing the decibel ceiling, and Mr. McKitrick was pissed. The angrier he got, the more he yelled, the redder he became, the more the cafeteria descended into a raucous chorus of laughter and yelling.

Not loud by nature (although I can be), I sat quietly at my rowdy table of new friends, amused by the chaos taking place around me, until a police officer entered the cafeteria.

The noise level decreased noticeably as the officer caught our attention and approached Mr. McKitrick. He and the officer looked in the direction of our table. I dropped my head, knowing somewhere deep within my DNA that to make eye contact could be to come across as aggressive to a law enforcement officer.

This officer wasn't a stranger to any of us. He was at the school all the time on behalf of the D.A.R.E program, the Drug Abuse Resistance Education curriculum that was popular in the '90s. Still, a cop. We were less intimidated by him when he was giving his "just say no to drugs" spiel than if we would run into him in any other situation. Huddled with Mr. McKitrick, both men continued to look up at our table and then back at each other. Whatever they were discussing seemed to be serious, and we seemed to be the topic of conversation.

My new friends were from the south side of Elyria. Seemingly segregated, a majority of the African American population seemed to reside either there or on the west side of Elyria. They were bussed in to Northwood. And when my mother could not take me to school herself, I caught the bus from my aunt's house on the south side too. My mom would drop me off at my Aunt Pat's house early in the morning where I'd wait and pass the time watching *Hey, Arnold* until I saw kids gathering at the corner to catch the bus.

Part of me felt like the gig was up, that everyone must have known that I lived on the east side, which was zoned for a different school, but claimed I lived with my aunt so I could attend Northwood. Maybe this time, instead of picking on my new friends, which happened far too often for no particularly good reason, it was me who was going to get it.

The officer slapped Mr. McKitrick gently on the shoulder as he took his leave. The officer headed over to our table. All of my new friends were looking him in the eye with expressions that said, *What are you bothering us for today?*

"Come with me please," he said.

When no one moved, I dared to look up and see, to my horror, he was addressing me. A collective "oooooo" rumbled through the cafeteria as I, trembling, gathered my things and followed the officer out of the cafeteria.

He led me down the hall and to the principal's office where he asked me to take a seat.

I waited, for God knew who, for God knew what.

After what felt like an eternity, the guidance counselor appeared from behind the desk and asked me to join her in her small office. I did.

Once I was seated, I asked her why I was there.

"We've been made aware of troubling activity you're involved in. Possible gang activity. And your teachers are concerned," she said.

"Who!?" I demand to know. "What gang? And who's concerned?"

She didn't answer the questions.

"Call my mother, please. Now," I insisted.

The counselor tried to calm me by explaining further, "We've been told that you are making fun of students who get good grades, as if to say that being a good student is something to be bullied for."

"I'm sorry, do you not realize that I, myself, am an honors student, that I'm in the G.A.T.E. program? How does that make any sense? Is my transcript in this file cabinet? Pull it." I was livid. "Call my mother!" I said again, but louder this time.

The only thing that had happened to me up until that point in my middle school career was that I'd been banished from my lunch table by my white friends and embraced by a new table of all black ones. And for that, Mr. McKitrick, who knew of me because he and my father were on the wrestling team together "back in the day," raised the alarm.

I refused to answer the counselor's probing questions with anything other than, "Call my mother." So she let me go. I'm unsure if they ever called my mother, but I did.

There's no telling what happened when my mother visited the office the following day. The school administrators never bothered me again, and I never asked my mother. If the incident with Mrs. Brown (my former kindergarten teacher) seven years prior was any indication, I knew that it was handled.

The cafeteria, the police officer, and the counselor's questioning was too much for my increasingly fragile psyche. I had been completely comfortable not being tied to race as my primary identity. But these events made me want to fully reject the parts of me that could be identified as white, like how I spoke (according to my new friends). After all I was banished from that table, and then all but arrested for joining another. Was I being radicalized by the trauma? It felt like it. They had made me feel foreign in my own school, among my own friends, in my own skin, and I was furious about that. One big question remained unanswered: what does it even mean to be black?

I didn't know what it meant to be black, but I did know that being black was complicated. I ruminated on this as I sat alone at lunch for that first week of school. And yet I would learn that my blackness was an asset in certain settings. Like, during volleyball and basketball games. I'd yet to be on organized team sports before I got to middle school, so it was peculiarly polarizing and confusing for me; the way my friends both sought to isolate me from their peer groups in social settings while embracing me on the court.

I escaped this confusion with music. I believed that music would be the perfect introduction to a culture I didn't know much about. Not allowed to watch the Black Entertainment Channel (BET), MTV, or listen to rap, I began to take blank tapes and record songs off the radio. I experienced stress and anxiety waiting and waiting for the right song to come on, making sure my cassette was recording over blank tape and not over another song, hoping the radio host or a commercial didn't interject before the song's conclusion. Once I had my song, I'd look it up on lyrics.com and proceed to memorize it. Once I had done so, I'd find a way to share my new and hip knowledge during lunch. With no street credibility to fall back on, I used my knowing the lyrics to every song and my ability to duplicate the beats with my fists, fingers, and pencils on the lunch table, to secure my spot in my new peer group.

GYM CLASS AND LANE VIOLATIONS

I was not prepared for high school. On the very first day of freshman orientation, after meeting en masse in the largest of Elyria High School's two gyms, the students were given their schedules and told to find their classes. The parents, seated in the bleachers like students attending a pep rally, stayed behind.

I walked timidly through the double-wide corridors of my new school, all too aware of my jean skirt riding up as I walked.

"You fine as hell," said a boy I didn't know. It happened so quickly I could barely register the exchange before he was gone.

Me? Fine? That was a first.

Ever since my run-in with my junior high crush, I'd been praying to become pretty and full-chested, but nothing happened. Instead, I was blessed with even more acne and a complexion so uneven my own mother called me "Meeko" after the raccoon in Disney's Pocahontas.

Flattered didn't even begin to describe how it felt to hear that about myself. I walked taller as I made my way through the halls locating my classes ahead of my first day of high school.

Northwood Junior High was one of three middle schools in Elyria, but each of those middle schools all fed into the one and only public Elyria High School. If I thought Northwood was a culture shock, Elyria High was like a different country. With one exception, my dad's side of the family all attended Elyria High before me. And the family's reputation preceded me in every way, especially when it came to sports.

Freshmen had their own gym at Elyria High, and although that sounds fancy, it wasn't. This gym was decrepit, and it featured a basketball court that transformed into a volleyball court. Suspended above was a dangerously square-ish running track. Paint peeled from graffiti-stained, once-upon-a-time white walls, and large swaths of the track rolled in on itself like carpet.

We had all feared high school gym class. Far too many '90s movies detailed how embarrassing dressing or showering in front of other people could be. So, we were all relieved to learn that showering wasn't mandatory or expected. All lined up on the basketball court's sideline, we listened to Coach K. give us the typical first-day-of-class rule briefing. We were anxious to play though. Gym was an excellent place to let off some of the pressure of self-consciousness I allowed to build to unhealthy levels as I navigated the halls of the school.

This I could do, I always thought. Academically, I was challenged in ways that kept me completely engaged in my full course load of AP and Honors classes. But the hallway...navigating the hallways in high school was like rowing upstream on the River Styx.

Relief would wash off me in waves once I'd changed into my gym clothes and joined the class on the baseline. For the next hour, we'd forget we were supposed to care about being cute or cool, and together we screamed, shouted, laughed, talked shit, and escaped from what it meant to be in high school—little fish in a very big pond.

Gym was the only class I had that wasn't part of my accelerated learning or honors program. As such, it was the one time of day I interacted with students I wasn't already in class with. In fact, none of the people in my gym class were in my other classes. In my other classes, I was often the only black student. Here, in gym class, it was a more diverse group of students. It was nice to get a break from being the "only" or "other." And on dodgeball days, nobody cared who you were anyway; you were going to get a rubber ball to the face before you left. Equal opportunity.

During one gym class, as we were setting up for a version of kickball I had never heard of before, a new student sauntered into the gym. He was short but handsome; his hair was short but gathered into perfect waves; a thin but well-groomed beard framed his square-ish face. He looked like a grown-ass man.

We stopped our fussing over the equipment to watch this new person who was approaching Coach K. Turns out, he was older than all of us; but he was a freshman, having failed to progress beyond the ninth grade a couple times. So intrigued were we by his face, we never noticed the bracelet monitor he had around his ankle.

Darryl was hilarious. We all got a kick out of laughing at him trying to play anything while holding up his sagging pants that were three sizes too big or watching him attempt to run to first base without creasing his Air Force Ones. He'd flash us a huge smile with his perfect teeth and laugh with us. He knew it was absurd, but he didn't care. Darryl was going to do Darryl. That also meant Darryl could not and would not be rushed.

One day, our gym class gathered on the baseline together before making the trek back up to the main gym. Occasionally, we'd make the trek as a class, from the small gym to the varsity gym on the main level, to participate in activities or games that required more space. Coach K. began to head out when I realized I had something in my pocket that I'd prefer to put back into my locker for safekeeping. I ran back to the locker room and then jogged to catch up with the class.

Out of the stairwell and into the main hallway, I saw Darryl and the tell-tale wide-legged walk of a person trying to keep their beltless pants on. I jogged by him, wanting to catch up with the class, when he reached out and grabbed me from behind as I passed him.

I was whipped around by the strength of his grip and found myself inches away from his face. He smiled that pretty smile and flashed his perfectly white teeth, but his eyes held a glint of something I had never seen before. Something that felt…dangerous. I removed my arm from his grasp, claiming that I didn't want to be later than I already was. Darryl continued to saunter not bothering at all to pick up his pace. I jogged away wondering, not for the first time, what infraction led to the house arrest bracelet on his ankle. From that day forward, I made it a point to avoid Darryl as much as I could. I would sprint to be at the front of the line, or the first out of the gym, being careful to stay well beyond his arms' reach.

We had made it to the table tennis unit in gym, and I could not be more excited. We had a ping pong table in our basement, and my father (don't tell him I told you) played in underground tournaments. He had a custom paddle in a zipped, nylon carrying case and a collection of his "good" ping pong balls that we weren't allowed to touch. My sister and I would watch my father practice like Forrest Gump with one side of the table folded up so that he could volley with himself. Marveling at the speed with which the ball and my father moved, we grew more and more excited to play with him. The problem was this: we sucked.

After growing increasingly annoyed at our high-pitched begging to play with him, my father decided to stop saying no. He was going to allow us to play him on one condition: we had to learn the game. Having gone to the library, Dad returned with a VHS tape titled, "Table Tennis: The Sport." As we sat in front of the television in our basement, holding our own paddles, we learned the rules of the game and practiced our back and forehand swings and mimicked slams. After sitting through the video and running through a few drills, we were permitted to play our father. We still weren't great, but we became good enough to practice with, and he always blessed us with a slam so hard the ball would bounce off our faces to mark the conclusion of play.

He'd say, "Oops!" in an innocent falsetto as he zipped his special paddle back into its case.

"Daaaaaaaad," my sister and I would say in exasperated unison. Giggling we'd head back upstairs, longing for the day we'd beat him.

I couldn't beat my father, but all of that practice at home made me impossible to beat in gym class. By this point in school, I was known as the "track star." After winning all of my events at the city championships the year before Coach K. and my classmates were caught unaware by this secret talent of mine. None of my female classmates wanted to play me; all of my male classmates wanted to beat me. Even the coaches hopped on tables to play me. A sudden-death tournament began to form around my table and me. I'd looked up between games and spotted Darryl. He was the only one in our class uninterested in playing table tennis, but all too interested in me.

I was so much better at table tennis than my classmates that the other gym teacher, whose class met the time block after ours, secured permission for me to skip study hall to play for his class too. All too happy to play for an extra hour every day during this unit, I came home to brag to my dad. Proud of me, he sent me back to school with an upgraded paddle and my own zippered carrying case. You couldn't tell me anything.

Day after day, I stayed back while my classmates returned to the small gym to dress and head off to their next classes. I'd play and defeat challengers for the next hour after which I'd make the trek back down the main hallway and dark stairwell into the small gym and on to the locker room. Having played overtime one day in order to secure the win, I sprinted through the hall and took the stairs two and three at a time, when I ran smack into Darryl.

"Don't be in a rush," he said as he crowded me into the corner like a skilled boxer cutting off the ring.

He used his body to back me into the corner and moved from side to side to block my attempts at slipping by him.

"I'm late," I said in a strangled-sounding voice, straining to wiggle my body in any way possible to escape from the trap I was in.

When I couldn't free myself, I looked at him. Again, he was just smiling that beautiful smile, showing off his perfectly white teeth. His eyes sparkled with barely restrained mischief.

"Where are you going?" he asked as I managed to create a sliver of space between us.

"To my next cla…" my words got caught as Darryl clasped his large hand on my neck.

He wasn't hurting me yet, but the shock of this unwanted touch paralyzed me. His grip on my throat tightened as he pushed his body, and his weight sunk into mine. I could feel his penis through our clothes against my leg. I was disturbed and disgusted, angry, and ashamed.

Darryl, liking this interaction, applied so much pressure to my neck I was lifted up to my toes. He leaned in to kiss my lips, and I turned my face so quickly that his lips planted an unwelcomed kiss on my left cheek. Amused at my efforts to resist him, he chuckled into my cheek, his lips still on my face. His hand squeezed tighter around my neck, and my cheek grew hot and then moist as he licked the entire length of my face as his thumb dug deep into the soft skin beneath my jaw.

Blowing into my ear, he darted his tongue inside, and he whispered, "You shouldn't be so beautiful."

Grabbing my crotch, he pulled his other hand away from my neck so quickly I nearly lost my balance as my feet flattened back onto the floor. Embarrassed and ashamed, I ran all the way to the locker room without looking back. I washed my face with the harsh pink antibacterial soap that's a staple in public restrooms and changed into fresh clothes. I paused at the locker room door, opting instead to open it inch-by-inch. I wanted to make sure that the coast was clear and that Darryl wasn't still lingering around waiting on me. Taking the stairs two and three at a time, I swung open the double doors and disappeared into the mass of students hustling to get to their next class.

AFTERMATH

There's a strange thing that happens after you've been violated, or at least after I've been violated. Unfortunately, I know, because it has happened to me *multiple* times. The first time was in the first grade when my classmate, Justin, grabbed my face and kissed me on the lips as we both searched for a specific book that was located on the shoulder-height bookshelves. They separated the reading corner from the rest of the room.

I punched him in the chest. He told on me, and I got in trouble—admonished for breaking the class rule that demands we keep our hands to ourselves. It didn't occur to me to challenge the absurdity of a rule that punished me for using my hands but not him for weaponizing his lips. Instead, at eight years old, I began retracing my steps and my conversation wondering where I gave Justin the impression that I wanted to be kissed. Guilt rushed through me as I found a way to take responsibility for Justin's behavior and for punishing him for something I caused.

My dad was informed of the situation when he picked me up from the after-school program. I told him that Justin kissed me and that I had punched him in the chest for it. I explained that, in addition to being mad that I was the one in trouble and not him, I'd have to administer a cootie shot too. I began the incantation of "circle, circle, dot, dot," while my father waited patiently for me to finish.

When I had, he said quietly, "You did right."

Good, I thought, *if my dad says it was right then it was right.* And yet, I locked a small piece of myself away…the part I felt was responsible for this violation. We spent the short drive home discussing where you should hold your thumb in a clenched fist when throwing a punch.

My incident with Darryl left me with a similar aftertaste. I spent the remainder of the day questioning every move, body expression, and word spoken to identify where or at what point I had waved the flag signaling my openness to such an act. I couldn't find blame in my behavior, but my mind would not stop playing his last words to me, *you shouldn't be so beautiful,* over and over. Something shifted in my thought process and settled hard into my consciousness. *Did I bring this on myself?*

All summer I had been praying for my period, praying to become a woman, praying to become pretty. And, although I wasn't convinced that my prayers had been answered, Darryl was what people mean when they say,

"Be careful what you pray for." Darryl was what I got for not being satisfied with myself.

How do I make peace with this? I asked myself.

This feeling that my prayers were so powerful that I brought this violation on myself, or the feeling that God, who's supposed to be omniscient, could have simply not answered this particular prayer, knowing what would happen. I didn't have an answer to that question, nor could I sit with those increasingly intolerable feelings, but there was one thing I could try. A memory came to mind. A girl named Sonja, who was the granddaughter of one of the elders at my church, visited one Sunday. Her arms were wrapped in gauze from her wrist to her elbow. I asked her if she had had an accident.

"No, I cut them," she said to me. She rolled the gauze down a bit and I could see fresh red lines against her caramel skin.

"Whoa, you okay?" I asked her, confused.

She shrugged.

Now, in my bathroom I grabbed a pair of scissors, my super sharp Fiskars seemed to be able to cut through most anything. I rolled up the sleeve of my right arm. With a shaking grip I slid the blade of the scissors against the smooth virgin skin on the inside of my wrist. Nothing happened. I needed to apply more pressure. I took a deep breath, deciding which hurt I could tolerate more, the hurt inflicted on me by others, or the hurt I inflicted on myself. I slid the scissors across my wrist with more pressure and watched as my skin seemed to unzip beneath the blade. I watched as blood beaded and dripped down my arm temporarily distracting me from the pain of private shame. I rolled my sleeve back down. I had track practice.

THE LAST SUPPER

Unlike Northwood Junior High, Elyria High School did have a track. It was a mile away from the school on the south side of town. You could either catch a chartered school bus after the last bell or get your own ride, walk, or run to practice. Ely Stadium was a decrepit arena, with barely functioning facilities, but it was the only track we had access to, so we loved it.

It seemed as if there were hundreds of people who thought they were cut out for the track team. I saw Darryl laughing with my mother at our first track meet. She was in the stands with her cooler full of snacks for the team and me. My heart leaped up into my throat, then sank heavily into my gut. Darryl's beautiful smile and pearly white teeth seemed to catch the sun and render me momentarily blind. My mother sat next to my torturer, and she has no idea. I decided that as long as he was in the stands, then he wasn't down on the track and I didn't have to worry about him getting too close to me. I won my events, and after the meet my little sister and I piled into my mom's mini-van and headed home.

On the drive home, Mom told us about the nice young man she passed the time with in the stands, and she invited him over for dinner later that week; we'd have lasagna. My mother, the youngest girl of 12 siblings didn't learn to cook the way her older sisters could, but lasagna she could do. We loved it. Now, I'd have to share my favorite meal with one of the worst humans I knew.

Riding in the car, my stomach did cartwheels and backflips. When we pulled into the driveway, I was green with nausea. I stumbled out of the car staring at our home's façade—our white and black, two-story home that we had custom built just for us. I'd had a say in what my room looked like, I was there when we settled on the crown molding and the berber carpet for the high-traffic areas. I remember the look on the Dale Yost Construction team member's face when Mom insisted on a particular shade of red for her front door. From childhood, her dream was to have a black and white house with a red door. I preferred a nice stone or brick façade, but I wasn't writing the checks, so I settled on offering input on the interior.

A feeling of foreboding washed over me as I took the first unsteady step toward the front door. Saliva coated my mouth in preparation for the arrival of an upsurge of vomit. *I cannot let him violate me again*, I thought, looking at my home as I walked to the front door. He cannot know where I live, he can't know where I sleep; he cannot cross this threshold. He cannot violate the safety and security of my home here. I decided that I had to tell my mom.

I stepped inside the screen door that had a glass window where a screen would have been. I began to strip off the layers required to navigate an early outdoor meet in Ohio.

"Mom?" I called to her tentatively, my voice breaking along with my courage.

"Yes?" My mom answered as she made her way back through the foyer from the kitchen waiting for what I had to say next.

"You know that boy? The one you were sitting with and talking to at the track that you invited for dinner?" I couldn't look up at her. My eyes darted back and forth around the floor. I never raised my eyes above knee level. The shame seemed to make me collapse inward like an imploding star.

"Yes, what about him?" my mom asked in a tone that revealed she was losing her patience with me.

"He touches me at school." I forced the words out of my mouth so that I would not have time to choke them back down.

"What do you mean?" she asked.

"I mean," I continued, "he touches meeeee." I dragged out the word hoping she could interpret what I was saying, without actually voicing that I let that boy lick my face and grab my crotch without even uttering a sound of dissent. I was disgusted with myself all over again.

"What do you mean, T? Where?" She inched closer as if getting physically closer would get us closer to the end of this awkward conversation.

"He licked my face," I said, still not ready to talk about being grabbed by the crotch, "and grabbed me so hard he ripped the pocket on my jeans. I don't want him here; I don't want him to know where I live or where I sleep."

The silence between us stretched on for so long, I looked up to see if she was still standing in front of me.

Quietly, she had begun to rearrange the coats in the front closet. *Like me,* I thought, *she is attempting to distance herself from the conversation.* After fixing the coats, my mom proceeded into the family room, a large unused room that featured my dad's 100-gallon fish tank, my mother's heavy marble chess board, a telescope, and a couch none of us had ever sat on. I stood frozen at the door, eyes fixed on my mother's back as she continued through the family room and headed into the formal dining room. She was speaking to me, but her words sounded like they were traveling to my ears through water. I couldn't make them out, and I did not ask her to repeat herself. No one does.

Instead, as I began to head up the stairs to my room after kicking off my shoes, I asked her another question, "So, can you tell him he can't come?" I waited an impossibly long moment for her answer.

"You know, T," she said without looking up, "even Jesus ate with sinners." I knew what that meant. My mother rescued people like other people rescued pets. Not judging them for their circumstances but simply offering what she could to give them a way up and out. Sometimes it was moving into the guest bedroom, or renting them an apartment, taking them shopping, or buying them groceries. One of her favorite quotes, which she learned from listening to the Christian radio station, was, "At all times preach the gospel, and only when absolutely necessary do you use words." So that was that; Darryl would be coming to dinner. I closed the door to my room softly to avoid further confrontation and sat down hard on my black futon trying to decipher the feeling of deep betrayal coursing through my body.

LASAGNA

The day Darryl joined our family for dinner was my last day as an extrovert. I passed the school day half-conscious. The countdown to when two worlds, which I did not want to ever meet, would collide, was ticking by—both slowly and at the speed of light. I spent the day wondering what my dad knew. Because he was a third-degree black belt, I often kept him in the dark about stressful interactions I had with peers which I thought would upset him. God forbid he would see fit to hop in his car and physically do something about it. Someone, I don't remember who, told me that a martial artist's hands could be registered as weapons, and if they were to get into a fight, it wouldn't just be assault (which was bad enough), they could be charged with assault with a deadly weapon too. This terrified me; so much so, that my personal rule was to protect my father, even as I was unprotected.

Once, my dad took me on a drive to North Ridgeville, a city between us and Cleveland. It was just the two of us; I often craved alone-time with my dad. Even though it was just the two of us, I was buckled in but stretched out in the back seat, conversing with him and making eye contact on occasion through the rearview mirror.

"You know, T," my dad said, "you're a lot like I was, growing up. I didn't really fit in anywhere really. It's not that I didn't have friends or wasn't well liked, like you are. It's just that I always felt a little on the outside. Do you feel like that?"

He glanced in my direction through the rearview mirror.

"Like I don't fit in?" I asked.

He raised his eyebrow as a response.

"I don't know, I mean I don't NOT fit in, but I'm not one of the popular kids, I'm not in the in-crowd or anything, but I'm not an outcast either. Guess I have sports to thank for that."

I could see my dad either nodding in agreement or acknowledgment of what I'd said…I couldn't determine which.

"You'll always be on the outside, T," he said when he spoke again. It was a hard truth to hear but felt true and had largely been my experience. "You have been chosen and set apart. So don't try to fit in. It will only make you miserable."

I stared out the window, watching the little brick bungalows of North Ridgeville's quiet neighborhoods pass by.

"And, T?" he asked snatching my attention back into the car. "People will be drawn to you."

I looked up at him and sat forward so that I could lean my forearms on the armrest between the driver and passenger seats.

"What's that mean? Drawn to me?" I asked.

"It means you'll find that people will want to be around you, to be near you, to involve you. Boys will want to get close to you."

I rolled my eyes. "Dad, are you trying to give me THE TALK? Because mom handled that years ago," I said, amused.

"No," he said as he chuckled. "I'm trying to give you a heads up about what life could feel like for you as you get older. We're a lot alike—maybe you'll handle it better because I've told you. But most importantly, all I'm trying to tell you about the boys is this: I have a gun."

I sat back hard, smiling and shaking my head at my father. We were laughing, but I took him at his word. And his words, "You'll always be on the outside," snapped into place, like a final puzzle piece that completes a complicated picture.

If Dad knew about Darryl, I'd not only be embarrassed, but I'd have failed…failed to insulate him from my issues. I did not want to ask my mother if she told my dad. In fact, I hadn't uttered more words than I absolutely had to her since that fated conversation at the front door a few days earlier. The school day passed in a blur, as did the track practice that followed. We came home from practice to a house that smelled of red meat sauce and Texas toast. Involuntarily, my mouth watered, and my stomach grumbled. I kicked off my shoes and walked up the stairs to my bedroom. *If Darryl stands right here*, I thought, *he'd be able to see the door of my bedroom.* My room was situated at the top of the stairs, as was the bathroom I shared with my sister. My door was to the left of the stairs, the bathroom straight on. The door to my bedroom was so close to the staircase that I had actually fallen all the way down the stairs just from exiting my room too quickly. The idea that just hours from now Darryl would not only be in my house, but could possibly know where I slept, made me sick to my stomach. I masked my vomiting with the sounds of the running shower. It felt wrong to shower and clean up for this; it also felt wrong not to. Everything was wrong. I showered quickly, and mindlessly got dressed.

I heard the front door open from my spot on the futon under my window which faced the street. I parted the slats of the horizontal blinds to peek out at the red taillights of the car that delivered my molester to the front door of my family home. My heart raced faster than I thought was possible without exploding. I could hear the rush of my blood coursing through my veins. As if on autopilot, I rose from my futon and exited my room. Assaulted by the smell of garlic, I paused at the top of the stairs preparing myself for the sight of my molester breaking bread with my family. I stepped into the hall bathroom to look at myself in the mirror. My acne-scarred face stared back at me with sad eyes. I'd spent the last few days grappling with the fact that my mother did not believe me. It wasn't as though I was a pathological liar or had a history of "telling stories." Compounding my feelings about my mother's disbelief was the reality that Darryl was downstairs waiting at a dinner table with my family, and he was there because my mother refused to rescind her invitation to him...because Jesus, whose life we were striving to model, also ate with sinners.

For the first time, the table in the formal dining room was set for a meal. As a family, we never sat in there except for one time when our family hosted Thanksgiving. We set the table then, along with two other 6-foot folding tables to seat everyone. Otherwise, my sister and I did our homework there, or my mom balanced the family budget there as the light from the hanging chandelier centered in the tray ceiling provided some of the best light in the house. Now, that same bright light lit Darryl's face and amplified his smile tenfold...the smile that disarmed me for the first time in gym class...the smile that charmed my mother...the smile that belonged to the boy who terrorized and violated me.

I took the seat my mom asked me to take, located directly across the table from Darryl. *At least she didn't also ask me to sit next to him*, I thought as I straightened the plate and silverware on my place setting. Against my will my mouth watered as my mom set the plates of Texas toast in front of us. The lasagna was resting on the stove. My dad, who was seated at the head of the table, made small talk with Darryl. I could tell by the ease of the interaction that he didn't know what Darryl had done. That, at least, brought me some comfort, and my shoulders melted down away from my ears just a bit as I had one less thing to worry about.

My mom entered the room again smiling. She carried the lasagna, in its glass casserole bowl, with towel-wrapped hands. She set the dish down in the center of the table on pot hoders and stood proudly. "Looks good," we all said in unison. One of the youngest of 12 children, my mom was often shooed out of the kitchen growing up, and as a result didn't learn to "throw down" in the kitchen like her older sisters could. That night the menu was Mom's homemade lasagna, corn, and Texas toast. I chose the slice that seemed to have the most garlic as my dad cut the lasagna into serving-sized squares with a spatula. We each passed him our plates to slide our slices onto as my mom settled into her seat at the opposite end of the table.

I nearly dropped my plate. I jumped so hard at an unwelcome touch from beneath the table that I momentarily lost my grip on the plate as my dad passed it back to me. My eyes darted to Darryl's face only to find him sitting peacefully as if nothing was currently happening. His socked feet ran the length of my leg. The lower half of my body remained paralyzed as I regained my grip on my plate and set it down gently in front of me. My appetite was gone, but I took another bite of my toast. I didn't want to give Darryl or my mother the satisfaction of any sort of spectacle, and I damn sure didn't want to tip my father off that something really horrible had happened between Darryl and me before and now. I held my fork sideways, using it to slice my lasagna in half. At the same time, my little sister took her first bite. "Eww. What's different?" Christina asked looking down at her fork, which she used to dissect and inspect the lasagna more closely. She had no filter. If she wanted to say something, she did.

"It's ricotta cheese!" my mom said cheerfully, sitting up taller in her seat.

"Oh," Christina said with obvious disappointment. Mom's lasagna doesn't have ricotta cheese. She only uses mozzarella, a ton of thick, gooey mozzarella. Darryl's socked foot slid further up my leg.

"What made you try ricotta?" I asked in a much higher-pitched voice than was normal. My dad's eyebrow twitched up in response. My mom made a sound that served as the answer to my question. I took a bite. Christina was right, it was different. But most importantly, it wasn't as good.

Darryl's presence at dinner could not ruin Mom's lasagna because Mom didn't make Mom's lasagna. That thought scrolled like ticker tape through my consciousness. Darryl's socked foot stroked my leg from knee to ankle continuously. I sat my fork down gently on my plate and pushed myself away from the table. I excused myself before standing and returning to my room. Darryl said he'd see me at school. I walked past the fish tank and our untouchable marble chess set and vowed to never speak to my mother again.

WHO'S GOT NEXT?

My run-ins with Darryl ended once a new quarter began. That baton passed to Kevin. He was a new student at Elyria High and in one of my elective classes. Before Kevin became one of my abusers, he was, like Darryl, charming and funny. He wasn't particularly handsome, but what he didn't have in looks, he made up for in charisma. He towered over me at six-feet-tall and had the muscular frame of a high school wide receiver, although he couldn't be bothered to commit himself to team sports. The confidence and ease with which he roamed the halls; the way he leaned casually against lockers, one foot planted on the wall, while in conversations that he always only seemed half interested in, intrigued me.

I intrigued him too, with my *otherness*. We exchanged phone numbers, and even though I knew I was not permitted to date or even call boys, I began to plot ways in which I could pull this off. The key was the guest bedroom, which doubled as an office, and had its own phone line. All I'd have to do was sneak into the guest room, crouch between the daybed's frame and the wall, keep my voice low, and I'd be in business.

It took me a few days to gather the courage to call him. Not a fan of sneaking around or breaking the rules, I poked my head outside my bedroom door and listened. I could hear the TV blaring from the family room; my parents' bedroom lay in a shroud of darkness, and although Christina's bedroom light was on, she had to have been downstairs too. I had no idea how long I'd have before someone ascended the stairs. But my spending all of my time in my room became the norm ever since the "family" dinner with Darryl. My family now saw so little of me that my dad put a TV in my room. I didn't have cable, but I had everything I needed between PBS and playing tapes on my VCR, only emerging for food and water, school, or track meets. Confident I could sneak into the office undetected, I felt my way through the room in the dark and located the landline phone. Tilting the phone's keypad toward the window for more light, I dialed Kevin's phone number. I imagined that whoever picked up the phone would hear my heartbeat first.

"Hello?" a woman asked.

"Hello, may I speak to Kevin?" I asked in my most confident voice.

"Hold on," she said abruptly. "KEVIN! Some little white girl is on the phone for you!" It took all the strength I had to not hang up right then.

"Hello?" Kevin's deep voice filled the silent spaces on the call.

"Hey, it's Tianna. You know I'm not white right?" *What I stupid thing to say*, I thought.

"I know you're not white, what kind of shit is that?" he asked, words dancing between his laughter.

"Anyway, what you up to?" I asked, not knowing the art of small talk or even what we were on the phone together for in the first place.

"Chillin," he answered, giving me nothing to work with in terms of furthering the conversation.

"My mom's calling. I gotta go, I'll see you in school."

But my mother wasn't calling. In the span of two minutes, I learned something about myself. As much as I longed to be like the girls who blushed and curled the cord of their bedroom phones between their fingers in the Disney movies we'd watched on double-feature Friday, I did not enjoy talking on the phone…at all. If Kevin wanted to talk to me, he could do so at school. I put the phone on the receiver and returned it back to its designated spot on the windowsill. I felt my way back out of the room and returned to mine. As much as I had not enjoyed the phone call, I did take pleasure in my disobedience. I had not only called a boy, I had gotten away with it.

I rarely saw Kevin during the school days with my schedule being a full course load of honors and AP courses. After school, between the end-of-the-day bell and the start of basketball practice, was when I'd mix and mingle. I was not a particularly good flirt, but Kevin and I exchanged quips and brief touches that broadcasted we were into each other—a hand on a shoulder, a brush of a finger on the back of a hand. Each little touch sent jolts of electricity through my body. The memory of Darryl's unwanted touches were overridden by each desired one from Kevin.

Before basketball games, some teammates and I would walk downtown to McDonald's for a pregame meal. If we had enough time, we'd eat in, but typically we'd eat on the walk back. Ungloved fingers freezing as we unwrapped double cheeseburgers and fished out fries from the bottom of grease-stained brown paper bags.

"Fuck!" I shouted after taking a bite into my burger.

"What?" one of my teammates disinterestedly asked.

"There's onions on my burger, didn't I say no onions?"

I didn't expect an answer. We continued walking on as I continued to eat my burger, between the onions and my thumb breaking through the bun, I was deeply unsatisfied with my pregame meal. I was thinking, *I should have just gone to Mr. Hero's across the street,* when we ran into Kevin on the way in.

"Yo!" he shouted, as he reached out to give my teammate, his cousin, a big hug. He moved towards me with anticipation. I stepped towards him prepared to also give him a hug. He towered over me and bowed his head so that his face was closer to mine. I opened my mouth to speak but before I could utter a single word, Kevin jerked away and took a step back.

"You've been eating onions or something?" he asked, revolted.

The taste of the unwanted onions still lingered in my mouth, so I could only imagine what my breath smelled like.

"Yeah, they put onions on my burger this time by mistake. I'm sure I asked for no onions," I explained.

"You knew I wanted to kiss you today, and you go out and eat a mouthful of onions."

This was news to me. I hadn't yet been kissed, and I didn't count Justin's unwanted sloppy kiss he planted on me in the first grade.

"How was I supposed to know tha..." My snarky reply was interrupted and expelled from my mouth as Kevin cocked his arm back and slapped me across the face.

A swift, yet unfamiliar well of anger bubbled to the surface, turning my face hot. My eye watered like flowing tears, their salt stinging my cheek that felt as though some surface blood vessels had been ruptured from the blow.

Shocked and angry, I gathered myself; my teammates were silent but looking on anxiously.

Kevin's cousin, the point guard of our team, looked at me with her mouth agape, shaking her head, and mouthing the words, "I don't know what to do; he's my family."

I turned to face Kevin, who seemed to have shed his anger from a few moments before and was inching closer to me yet again. I drew my left arm back, not once breaking eye contact with him. When he was within range, I balled my fist and landed a left hook just below his last rib. Kevin doubled over, and from his weakened position, it was me who had the upper hand. I stepped forward without thinking, prepared to follow my left hook with a right jab, when my teammate, Kevin's cousin, grabbed me from behind around the waist and dragged me backward.

"He's my cousin!" she shouted into my ear.

"He fucking slapped me!" I screamed in a voice that sounded as though I'd swallowed glass. "Fuck you and your cousin!" I screamed in her direction as my other teammates dragged me to the locker room.

My eye was bloodshot red. I stared at myself in the mirror wondering how to explain this when my parents arrived. Breathing deeply, I managed to calm myself enough to put the incident aside and table the disappointment I felt towards my teammate in order to focus on the game.

"What happened to your face?" my mom asked me in the car on the drive home.

"You didn't see me get elbowed in the face when I went up for that rebound? When that big girl thought she had boxed me out, I jumped over her, and she elbowed me on my way down?"

"Oh, yeah," my mom said, glancing at me through her rearview mirror. "Ice it when we get home," she said.

I nodded my head, yes, as I stared out of the window wondering, yet again, what it was about me that invited this into my life.

I think I need a boyfriend. That was my final thought as I laid my head on my pillow, staring up at my ceiling—home to its own galaxy of glow in the dark stars that I had precariously balanced on my desk to apply. *Maybe then I'd be safe.*

DAMSEL IN DISTRESS

How to get a boyfriend, the cursor flashed in the Yahoo search engine box. I tapped delete until the only word left was *how.*

How do I do anything? I thought to myself as I logged off the family's shared PC in the family room. I wasn't allowed to date; I wasn't allowed to call boys on the phone. The situation was precarious. I wanted to feel safe and protected in the halls of my high school, but it would require disobedience. My mind was spinning with calculations. How will I effectively date someone with enough of a reputation that it offers *me* cover? How will I make sure the relationship is well known enough to provide such cover without my parents finding out? Especially my dad?

Dad was one of the coaches on the track team; I wouldn't be able to control who said what in front of my dad when I wasn't around. My stomach flipped with the reality that I was going to attempt to live this double life to better protect myself. I thought of the Carl fiasco. Poor Carl.

Carl was the only other black kid at my elementary school. Occasionally, new families would move into the school district. They seemed to just be passing through; they never stayed long. So, the arrival of Carl raised the number of minority students in my class to two. Naturally, my two friends, Julie and Desiree, felt Carl and I belonged together (it wasn't until I was much older that I realized their only criteria for this was that we were both black). Turned out though, Carl actually did have a crush on me. And I did like the attention that was directed at me. On a bus ride from a grade-wide field trip to Ashland University, Carl presented me with a teddy bear. I loved stuffed animals.

How could he have known that? I thought as I stroked the soft and glossy fur of my new bear. The bear was wearing a t-shirt that said, *Somebody in Ashland loves you.*

"Oh, really?" I asked Carl with a raised eyebrow. Love? Really?

He nodded his head. Light reflected off the lenses of his black-rimmed glasses as the frame rested gently on his chubby cheeks. He wore a gold rope chain around his neck and a ring on his pinky finger. I didn't know any other kids my age, least of all boys, who wore real jewelry. I had seen Carl's father before too, when Carl's dad came to pick him up from school. He had had a similar rope necklace, but where Carl kept his hair short, his father had a well-shaped afro. I decided that their family must have had more money than my family. I often categorized my friends that way at Windsor: Megan

37

and Marielle—more money. Julie and Desiree—less money. Lindsey and Chad—about equal. These categories were how I decided who could come over to my house. If peers were in the "more money" category, I'd accept invites to their homes, but extended none to mine. The other categories were free to come hang out with me whenever my parents allowed it. I understood socioeconomic status long before I understood race.

"Yeah, so, will you be my girlfriend?" Carl asked, snapping me out of my ruminations.

"Sure," I said absentmindedly.

My friend Lindsey smiled widely. "Guess you should sit with your boyfriend then," she said while shoving me out of our shared seat.

I flashed her a slight frown as I rose to change seats, unsure of what I had truly gotten myself into. I was now somebody's girlfriend. I now had a boyfriend. Carl stood to let me slide toward the window.

"Sit down!" the bus driver yelled from the front.

Carl, still standing, stood and faced front as if to talk back to the driver. I pulled him down into the seat by his arm. Carl shot me a look so full of something that looked like love that I physically recoiled deeper into the seat, hoping I'd melt into the window. As I was pulling my hand away from his arm, he grabbed it gently and interlaced his fingers between mine. I was sitting next to a boy on a bus. I was holding a boy's hand. Beyond the initial jolt of electricity that ran through my body when our palms touched, I was underwhelmed by the "hand-holding." His hand still in mine, I turned to face the window and watched as the landscape passed lazily. *I am someone's girlfriend,* I thought as the bus pulled into the school's parking lot. *Eww.*

"What's that?" My mom asked as I was getting into the car, pointing to the teddy bear that she knows full well she did not give me enough money to purchase.

"It was a gift from Carl," I offered as a true but incomplete explanation.

"Oh?" she said in a way that means I need to keep talking. I didn't though. So, she continued. "He didn't just give it to you?" she said suspiciously.

"Yes, he did." I said, doubling down on my desire to remain tight-lipped about my new relationship.

"Okay, let's say I believe that. What did you say? Why did you take it?" she asked.

"I said thank you. And I took it because I like stuffed animals," I replied.

"Okay, then I'll buy you a stuffed animal, and you can return that to him tomorrow." She looked over at me to note my reaction. I had none. "No man, or boy gives a girl something for nothing." She exhaled loudly as we drove the rest of the way home in silence.

I was somebody's girlfriend, and I was already dreaming about the breakup.

It'd been three years since the embarrassment of returning to school, returning the bear, and breaking up with Carl the day after we became a couple. He cried, and I stared back at him with emotionless eyes, embarrassed for the both of us. That situation prompted the "talk" (the takeaway was to "save yourself for marriage"), and conversations about dating (the takeaway was that "you're not allowed to for now, but perhaps at 16 there will be a review of the terms"). I was between a rock and a hard place…I could risk the ire of my parents for this blatant act of disobedience or endure the uneasy vulnerability that came with being "unattached" in those high school hallways.

I still wasn't sure how to get a boyfriend, but I made the decision to do it. I had no idea how much power there was in a reputation—how your reputation enters crowded rooms before you do. I was unaware that the entire athletic department had been holding their breath for my arrival at Elyria High School; athletes across all Elyria High's sports knew exactly who I was.

That would be enough. By the time my first track season rolled around, Tianna "the track star" was the girlfriend of the captain of the football team. He asked if he could kiss me in the side hallway by the art rooms. It felt good to be asked. I stood on my tiptoes to get my lips close to his. Just like I had seen in the movies, every hair seemed to stand on its end as our lips touched. My heels seemed to float gracefully back to the floor when we parted. I slid an intricately folded note into his hand and told him I'd see him later. I waited as he sauntered away into his art class, his tiny and always empty backpack slung over his right shoulder. He disappeared into the classroom, and I skipped down the hall to my class. I was somebody's girlfriend. I had just been kissed. For a moment, I stopped caring about how I'd get away with it.

I had another problem though. That captain of the football team had had girlfriends before and had expectations of what it meant to be doing the whole boyfriend/girlfriend thing. Things like visiting each other's homes, calling each other on the phone, going out on dates. None of which I was allowed to do. I passed notes to him like my life depended on it, singing his praises in stanzas of unearned adoration. He had no way of knowing that I wasn't actually interested in being his girlfriend, just in being able to say that I was. I had made a miscalculation, though—two miscalculations, actually. The first one was that some classmates would be jealous enough about the two of us that they'd go to great lengths to "force a breakup." The Captain's inner circle, a gaggle of girls, did not appreciate that they had to compete for his attention with a girl they did not grow up with, who lived on the opposite side of town, and whom people spoke of as if she were the second coming of Christ the Lord. They'd follow me to my classes and step on my heels so that my next step forward would be right out of my shoe. They'd tell me how weird I was and how the Captain was too good for me. The second miscalculation was that I didn't plan for the possibility that I'd develop feelings for him beyond gratitude. I thought I was just using him for self-preservation. But that damn kiss changed everything.

I was largely okay with the parameters my parents had set for me when it came to dating. Not calling boys wasn't an issue, I didn't call girls either. I hated speaking on the phone. But I had a loose understanding of the Captain's dating history, and I desperately wanted to keep him happy. Especially since my experience at school *had* changed for me when we became a couple. The harassment stopped. I liked the ease with which I could navigate the halls, I no longer felt the need to shrink myself under the gaze of a boy passing by on his way to class. I felt protected. But, if I didn't figure out how to make calls and go on dates, that security would be short-lived.

I was still no closer to figuring out how to give the Captain the "girlfriend" experience, when the Homecoming Dance was about to take place. Where I had previously been ambivalent about my upbringing, I was now thoroughly embarrassed; enough so, that very few people knew anything about my life after the school bell and beyond sports. Even my new boyfriend had no idea about the rules I was trying to circumvent to stay with him. Naturally, he asked me to Homecoming. And naturally, as captain of the football team he was voted Homecoming king. *Damn it,* I thought. *How do I pull this off?*

My answer definitely would have to involve my high school friend Marita. Marita was a biracial beauty with long curly hair. She was the daughter of coaches, both of whom coached multiple sports on the junior high and high school levels. Her father, Tom, was the man who encouraged my dad to use the summers to develop my track and field skills further. Our friendship evolved along the lines of our fathers'. She was one of the popular girls at school, and my having a friend like her granted me temporary access to a world I'd been locked out of since the first week of seventh grade.

On evenings before track meets, both home and away, we'd gather as a group and eat at the Applebee's located in the parking plaza of our struggling

Midway Mall. Once I got dropped off at the front door, I knew I'd have two hours of unsupervised and unstructured social time, during which I'd say what I wanted and eat what I wanted, as long as I had enough of my allowance saved to cover it. My go-to pre-race meal was always the same, the buffalo chicken wing appetizer, medium heat, all flats with sour cream on the side; all washed down with an unlimited supply of raspberry lemonade.

Eventually team dinners at Applebee's turned into sleepovers at Marita's house, and it was at one of these sleepovers the problem of Homecoming was solved. With very few dining options available to us in Elyria, Applebee's was already the designated pre-Homecoming dinner spot. I loved this because I could pitch this to my parents as nothing out of the ordinary. I would get dropped off at Marita's where we would get dressed and ready as "each other's date." So, as far as myself or my parents were concerned, I was attending Homecoming with Marita as her date, you know, "just us girls." But Marita was never without a boyfriend, nor was she raised with any such rules governing what she could or could not do. She was my cover, but she could and would do what she wanted. Her true date (and mine) would pick us up at her home, and together we'd drive to Applebee's, dine together, and then head back to the school gym for the dance. I was satisfied, every step of the way, that if something were to go wrong or seem suspicious, I could successfully wiggle my way out of it—using my mastery of semantics, a skill I'd developed when I all but stopped speaking at home and began writing, after that unforgettable lasagna dinner.

Confident that I'd be able to pull this off, I put Homecoming logistics on the back burner as I shifted my focus to what would happen once we got to the dance. I decided to risk it with my parents; I felt it would be easier to ask for forgiveness than for permission. It was settled then. Tianna, the odd girl out, would be going to Homecoming with her boyfriend, the captain of the football team and Homecoming king. My chest swelled with pride as I realized I was in control. I was the puppeteer pulling the strings of my life, preparing to dance.

"You ready!?" My parents yelled up the stairs as I put the final touches on my appearance in the bathroom mirror. Not well-versed in makeup at all, my entire collection was made up of foundation I purchased at Walgreens, which looked like the best match in the fluorescent white light of the pharmacy; a black lip pencil which I used for both my eyes and my lips (It didn't occur to me until college why that's disgusting.); and a clear lip gloss. My hair, that featured a few spiral curls and crimps, held the familiar yet fading burnt smell of the curling iron. A spritz of body spray from Bed, Bath, and Beyond put the finishing touch on my preparations, and I descended the stairs in my gown. I meant to be preparing at Marita's house but decided to arrive dressed to avoid any embarrassment that having such a lame beauty routine could cause me on what would already be a stressful day.

Mom and I went over the evening's plan and schedule on our drive over to Marita's house. My mom had never been a fan of Marita, largely because of the way Marita treated and talked to her parents. Once, Marita lost her temper with her parents so badly, even I tried to melt into their wood-paneled walls. When she was finished and had calmed down, I gathered the nerve to ask her, "How do you do that?" balancing both admiration and shock at her disrespectful assertiveness.

"It's not my fault that they're fucking stupid!" She looked back at me, her light-colored eyes twinkling.

Makes sense, I thought as I settled in on the couch.

Not too long after witnessing Marita punking her parents, I was in my own home bouncing around the kitchen looking for a bowl. My mom, who had noticed there were clean dishes in the drying rack waiting to be put away, told me to take care of them.

I channeled Marita and shot my mother a look that said, *how dare YOU ask me to do ANYTHING for YOU.* Ever since Darryl and that gross lasagna, this thought would actually cross my mind first, whenever she asked me anything. Common sense had kept me from relaying that through words or body language. But not that day. On that day I channeled Marita and pushed back, first with the look, and then with words.

"I'll get to it." I said, not bothering to look in the direction of my mother who was sitting on the couch in the family room. It was a clear line of sight because of our home's open floor plan.

"Excuse me?" she said to my back from her seat on the couch.

Knowing I was flirting with danger, I kept my lips sealed and turned towards her, but only to make my way to the pantry to grab the bag of chips I wanted to snack on. My hunger was the only reason I'd left my room in the first place. Her face disappeared as I opened the door to the pantry, but I couldn't help but register how rigid she'd become at my abhorrent behavior. By the time I closed the pantry door she was standing there, exactly like an antagonist in a horror movie that seemed to appear out of nowhere. It took all of my self-control to not jump out of my skin in fright because of her sudden appearance; instead, I turned away from her and walked back to the counter that held the plastic bowl that I hoped would hold my chips if I got out of that interaction alive. I felt her following me across the kitchen.

"What did you say?" she asked me.

I said nothing.

"I asked you to put the dishes away," she said again, her growing anger barely controlled as she spoke.

"And I said I'd do it, but not now," I said with a delivery that displayed more gall than I actually had. I picked up my bowl to return to my room. My mother's long arm cut the distance between us to nothing in a split second. I was not prepared for that. My mother didn't hit me; and lately, because we barely spoke to each other, we didn't exchange hugs either. Her hand closed, her fingers gripped and bunched the fabric of my shirt.

"I don't know who you think you are, but I asked you to do something."

I pulled away from her and yelled, "I hate you!"

A brief crack in the stern expression she was wearing on her face betrayed how hurtful that was for her to hear. The downward tug of my bottom lip betrayed how close to tears I actually was too. We stood in stalemate silence as we both reflected on how we got here.

"Go to your room," my mother said to me in a barely audible whisper.

I grabbed my bowl of chips and left. Ascending the steps, I couldn't help but notice that, although scary, that brief moment of saying exactly how I felt, exactly the way I felt it, had felt good. I was no longer carrying those words in my cells. Out in the atmosphere now, the emotions I felt towards my mother that I was carrying within me each and every day, alleviated just a little. And that was relief I felt I could use more of.

Finally satisfied with the plan for Homecoming, my mom dropped me off at Marita's house and pulled away. A few moments later, the boys arrived. I tried my best to avoid being in any pictures. It was difficult to settle into the spirit of fun when I was overcome with obsessive thoughts about getting caught. We piled into my boyfriend's car and together began the drive across town to Applebee's. I was in the passenger seat; my left hand held his right as he steered with the other. We were approaching a light. Just one more turn and we'd be in the Applebee's parking lot. My head sunk heavily into the headrest relaxed and happy that one of the trickiest parts of the plan was being executed without issue. I looked over at my boyfriend and smiled at him, his face lit up as his wide grin spread across his perfectly groomed face. I smiled back before turning away to look out the passenger side window and right into my mom's wide eyes.

"Fuck! Fuck! Fuck" I said turning away from the window. I turned to face Marita who was currently in the backseat making out with her date.

"Bam!" I called her by her nickname to get her attention. "That's my mom! Right there!?" I shouted.

"Oh! Mrs. Madison!" my boyfriend said from the front seat, waving at my mom as he began to make the left turn. My mom switched lanes like a stunt driver on *The Fast and The Furious*.

"Oh, shit," Marita said from the backseat.

"Late much!" I yelled at her, irritated that she had been so busy sucking face that she had played a useless lookout.

"Get out of the car," my mom said, knocking on my window.

"I'm sorry, guys, I have to go." I said, mortified.

"What? Why?" my boyfriend asked.

"It's a really long story that none of us have time for. Please go eat. You're the Homecoming king. Go to the dance; I'll tell you about it later. Who knows, maybe it will be funny, but not now."

I grabbed the door handle to open it slightly, then gathered the flowing fabric of my Homecoming gown in sweaty palms and kicked the door the rest of the way open with my high-heeled foot.

"Just wait until I tell your father," my mother said, pulling out of the parking lot.

I can wait, I thought as I slumped as far down into the seat as I could. I couldn't bring myself to look back at my friends, unsure if it would make me happy to see them enter the restaurant laughing and smiling, or if it would break my heart.

KINGS AND THINGS

"Oh, T," my dad said to me after my mom explained what she saw. My little sister, always thrilled to witness someone else getting in trouble, sat alert and quiet in the corner of the room. I also sat quietly, still in my Homecoming dress. My mom looked angry, but my father looked sad. It was his sadness rather than her anger that made me regret what I had done...or had tried to do.

The discussion seemed to happen around me as both parents tried to work out a punishment suitable for that level of manipulation, lying, and disobedience. I asked to be excused to go change out of the dress that I no longer needed to be wearing, when the doorbell rang.

"Go upstairs," both of them said in unison.

In my room I walked over to my window that faced the street and looked down over the driveway.

"Oh, no!" I whispered. It was them, the boyfriend, Marita, her date, and another one of their friends. I collapsed down to my futon unsure if it was possible to feel any worse than I already did.

Another conversation was happening without me as my friends lobbied for my freedom. Feeling much like a princess locked away in a tower, I heard my parents tell my friends to drive safely and to have fun at the dance. Dramatically, I placed my hand on the cool glass of my bedroom window as I wished them well from the cover of my darkened bedroom. In sweats, I made my way back downstairs to grab something to eat and drink. My mouth and throat had been dry since my mother and I locked eyes at the stop light in front of Applebee's, and having never made it to my pre-Homecoming dinner, I was starving.

"Those are some good friends you got there," my dad said to me as I attempted to pass silently through the kitchen. "Get dressed, I'll take you up to the dance. But I'm picking you up too."

I stared at my father and looked behind him searching for my mother and sister, but they weren't there.

I shrugged my shoulders. "I don't really feel like going anymore," I said.

It was true, any ideas I had had of what Homecoming was supposed to look and feel like were shattered. What's more, I was really starting to hate high school. The hits just kept on coming.

"Come on, T, it's Homecoming. Let's go, I'll be in the car."

Begrudgingly, I climbed the stairs again, slid off my plaid flannel pajamas, and pulled on my Homecoming dress.

"I never ate," I said to my father as I piled into the front seat.

"We'll stop at Burger King then."

I ate my burger on layers of napkins spread across my lap, and a bib tucked into the top of my dress to avoid the inevitable ketchup and mustard splatter as I bit ravenously into my burger.

Dad talked the entire ride to the school. I was lost in my own thoughts. His words, *Come on, T, it's Homecoming*, replayed over and over in my head and made me wonder if I had been wrong. Perhaps I *should* have spoken up about wanting to go and who I wanted to go with and perhaps they would have allowed it because Homecoming was special. *Perhaps.* A cynical voice in my head reminded me that, not too long ago, I did take an extremely uncomfortable step of putting myself out there; I did speak up, and I did ask for what I wanted. And look where it got me. Darryl still came over for dinner.

We pulled up to the side of the school near the bus drop-off zone. My father told me I was beautiful as I smoothed my dress and prepared to exit his car. I gave him the small slight smile of an exhausted soul and made my way toward the school. I walked in, just as my boyfriend led another girl by the hand to the middle of the dance floor.

I knew that this would have to happen. I didn't know how to dance, so my original plan was to force him to take his dance as king with somebody else anyway. The Homecoming queen maybe? I didn't know. Once I understood I'd end up back at the dance anyway, I began to hope that that part of the night would have already transpired while I was still playing the role of damsel in distress, locked away in my "tower." I watched from the shadows of the gym's bleachers as my boyfriend box-stepped and drew his dance partner closer and closer. My heart was breaking in the same slow, treacherous way that ice cracks when giving way to more weight than it can bear.

What did I expect? I could only be a "girlfriend" during school hours anyway, I thought as I stared on. *Is it me, or is this the longest song ever?* Another thought skipped through my mind like a flat pebble skimming the surface of a still pond, *This is what you deserve. You can't do anything any of these other girls can do. Look at him. Look at you.* That was the final thought that crossed my mind as the song came to an end. My boyfriend and his partner rocked to stillness in the center of the floor, stared into each other's eyes before he leaned in and kissed her. As soon as their lips touched, the gym erupted in cheers. A re-creation of a scene that I've seen time and time again in movies whose characters' lives I've coveted.

I dug my flip phone out of my little purse and called home.

"I'm ready," I said, when my father answered the phone.

"You sure? So soon?" he asked.

"Yep!" I said, more chipper than I felt. I snapped my phone shut debating how to pass the fifteen minutes it would take for my father to get back to the school from the house. New, complex, and confusing feelings bubbled up and swelled in my chest. I wasn't sure if I had been betrayed or if I had been cheated. I wasn't meant to be there; he didn't know I was there. If I had been home, I wouldn't have seen it. I would have likely heard about it but would have probably opted to not believe it in exchange for maintaining the feeling that being paired with someone like him gave me during school hours. But even knowing that that was my reason for having that relationship in the first place couldn't dampen my disappointment. I couldn't help but question his motives. Were we using each other? I was traveling down a rabbit hole that only seemed to grow darker as each question begot more questions. I walked toward the exit to spend the remainder of my wait in fresh air; I waved hello and goodbye to classmates. I flashed fake smiles to everyone I encountered. The lights of my dad's new Chrysler 300 dimmed and brightened as he navigated the speed humps in the parking lot.

At home and in bed, a thought floated through the landscape of my fading consciousness: *if your mom won't save you, your dad can't save you, and boys can't save you...who or what is left?* I went to bed that night staring at the glow of the dark stars I affixed to my ceiling. I rolled onto my side as a passing car's headlights briefly illuminated the corner of my room where I kept my track bag. Light reflected off the metallic finish of my spike plate which dangled by its laces from a loop on the bag.

That's pretty, just like stars, I thought as I drifted off to sleep.

A LITTLE TASTE

I tried the boyfriend thing, which was a doomed endeavor since I wasn't actually allowed to date. So, I began to look forward to track season instead— more time outside the home, more time focusing on myself. Having gotten a small glimpse of hometown glory after winning all of my events at the previous year's City Championships, I was excited, if not a little scared, to venture into the world of high school track. Maria Whitely, the only sprinter to hand me a loss, was now going to be a teammate. I wondered how easy it would be to drop the competitiveness that existed between us in favor of being good teammates.

We gathered for track practice at the back entrance of the high school. Dozens of would-be athletes talked excitedly while filing into the yellow school bus. It didn't take long for us to segregate ourselves. The distance runners without cars or the desire to run to the track, sat toward the front, and the short sprinters crowded in the back of the bus. The track was just a mile away from the school, and we had the option to walk as long as we arrived before the official start time. The bus let us off at the general admission entrance, and we stepped into the stadium. The gate that led to the track was straight ahead. To our left, built up under the grandstand seats were dungeon-like bathrooms and locker rooms. Their dinginess, lack of light, and signature cold, stone floors and walls certainly didn't offer inspiration before a race. Paint peeled back from the walls, revealing past layers of peeling paint. The red, grated lockers were the newest additions to the locker room, having been slid into place over the summer. The away football teams used this locker room, and I often wondered if the accommodations were a deliberate attack of psychological warfare.

People who had opted not to change into their practice clothes before boarding the bus did so in these locker rooms under the grandstand. After the first week of practice, my feet were so chilled by the bare floor that I changed before boarding the bus, in a better-appointed locker room at school.

I had never seen a track team bigger than our team was on the first day. I made this comment to Marita, who was ahead of me in school and had been around the sport her entire life.

"Just wait. Every day the team will get smaller and smaller and smaller," she chortled; and she was right. By the time our team began to travel for its midweek meets and weekend invitationals, there were no more than 20 people on the track team—down from 100 bodies on day one.

I loved to travel by any mode of transportation. At that time in my life, the back row of the bus was the most coveted seat. I finally had a CD player, and my parents had recently bought a PC that could burn CDs. I spent most nights searching and looking up songs that would take almost 24 hours to download on LimeWire. I'd make lists of songs I'd heard on the radio and seen listed on the backs of those AOL free trial CDs that we seemed to have an entire drawer of. With headphones on, I sank back into the brown, faux leather fabric in our bright yellow school bus.

We were traveling to Lakewood, a well-off high school on the east side of Cleveland. My mouth fell open as our raggedy bus pulled into their pristine parking lot. The field was flawless. Having never seen turf before, I wandered out onto the infield to touch the grassy carpet which made up their football field. The D-shaped zones punctuated the infield and made the track look huge. I was on the hook for the long jump, the 100-meter dash, the 4x100-meter relay, or the 4x200-meter relay; the coaches would make that call as the meet progressed. I walked with my gear over to the long jump pit which was set up in the D-zone. The runway ran parallel to the infield, and jumpers would be jumping towards the finish line. We typically jogged a lap or two as a team before breaking off into our own warm-up routines and rituals. I pulled out my sprint spikes. I had finally earned sprint spikes by proving I was committed to the sport. But when I asked for long jump specialty spikes the answer was essentially, "You can't jump in those?" Not wanting to push my luck, I lusted over *Eastbay* magazine's selection of long jump spikes in private.

A whistle blew to get the jumpers attention, and we gathered around an official at the pit he called out our names . After listening to the official explain what "up, on deck, and on hold" meant, we rearranged ourselves to prepare for the start of the competition. In meet settings like this one, the best jumper is the last jumper. But with multiple events to contest on the same day, it usually means running straight out of the long jump pit and right to the starting line of the 100-meter dash.

My dad walked over to the pit. He wasn't my jumps coach at the time, but he was Dad, and I hated jumping without seeing his face somewhere within the vicinity. I stood at the board with my back to the pit and walked "heel-toe" the number of shoe lengths of my approach. It hadn't occurred to any of us at that point to find a tape measure and record the actual length of my run-up. But that wasn't an unusual sight to see at meets of this caliber. The long jump began without delay, and the officials moved through the roster of jumpers efficiently. My turn came, and I looked for my father as I stood readying myself at the top of my approach. Left foot forward, right foot back. I ran as fast as I could and took off at the board. I folded myself into the go-kart position my jumps coach, Mike Lugar, had drilled into me. The jump seemed to take forever, but, as always, I met the sand with an ungraceful thud. I popped out of the pit with carried on leftover momentum I'd built from the run up. Brushing coarse sand off my arms and legs, I made my way over to my father as the officials extended their tape measure.

"NINETEEN FEET, ELEVEN INCHES!" The official shouted. I screamed and threw my hands up. It was a new personal best—by a foot.

"See what happens when you ride the go-kart?" Coach Mike said.

"See what happens when you're obedient," my father said to me.

He was referring to the boyfriend I had, but should not have had, and my Homecoming deception. I eventually told my dad that things fell apart between the Captain and me not too long after Homecoming, although seeing him still gave me butterflies in the pit of my stomach. He wasn't my boyfriend anymore, and it was true that I felt burdened by my little deceit, but it was worth it in the face of the alternative, about which my father knew nothing.

"Yeah, I do feel *lighter* I guess," I said to my father who was smiling down at my sandy face.

"T, we're physical people. When the Lord wants our attention, he'll affect us physically. Maybe its sickness, injury, whatever it is—it's the Lord trying to bring you in line," he said with the surety of someone unshakable in their faith and beliefs.

In that moment, I did believe that I was being rewarded for "good behavior," but I also recognized that I was not the "woman of faith" my dad thought I was. I resolved to do better as I made my way over to the 100-meter dash.

It was a successful freshman season. I qualified for state in the 100-meter, the 4x100-meter relay, and the 200-meter relay. I made the podium with my third-place finish in the 100-meter dash. I ran 12.04 seconds to finish behind sprint phenom Khalilah Carpenter and another sprinter from Columbus. Khalilah delivered me an ass whooping unlike any I had ever experienced. Stepping to the line with Shirley Temple-like curls in her hair, I had never met a more beautifully lethal female in my life. She scared the shit out of me. I had heard (or read on dyestat.com) that she ran 11.33 in the 100-meter dash. Having never broken 12 seconds in the 100-meter dash, I walked to the starting line like I was a condemned death row inmate walking the "Green Mile." Khalilah ran 11.59 seconds in the prelim and came back and ran 11.75 in the final. After her prelim run, she probably realized there was no reason for her to work that hard. Second and third place were 12.03, and 12.04 respectively. She was in her own lane, running her own race. Meanwhile, 10 meters back, the silver and bronze medals were up for grabs.

I licked my wounds and bounced back in time to anchor my team's 4x100- and 4x200- meter relays to fifth and sixth respectively. My efforts contributed to our team finishing fourth overall—our highest finish. It was a respectable showing for a freshman navigating the district and regional qualifiers to make it to the state meet. And even though first through eighth place got medals, I was proud of my haul.

Not only was my first trip to state pretty special, I also loved how it felt like a great big giant slumber party at the hotel with the conjoining doors unlocked and propped open between rooms; and I loved the per diem we got for going. Before we were loaded into the minivans that would transport us south to Dayton, Ohio, we were each handed an envelope of cash. It was our food allowance; I had never had as much cash in my possession as I did then. I loved the power that seemed to flow from the green bill into my hands, as things that weren't previously accessible to me, now were—like springing for the Sobe in the glass bottle instead of the Fruitopia, or ordering an extra side with dinner, just because. I decided then that this was an experience I wanted to have again and again.

SCHOOL PROJECT

After getting a taste of the state championships and the podium, I worked hard and looked forward to making another trip back to Dayton, Ohio. I wanted revenge for not making it to the state meet in the long jump as the number one seed. The previous year, the officials at the district meet in Amherst, Ohio, were uncertain if not unwilling to accommodate my heavy event schedule on that day. On the starting lists for the long jump, 100-meter dash, 4x100-meter relay, and the 4x200-meter relay, we were hoping that the long jump would be complete before the 100. If that happened, the rest of the day would be manageable.

But there seemed to be a countless number of girls ready to jump for their chance to advance to the regional meet. I was not aware enough of meet management to be concerned but had I been, I would have known I was in trouble. I hadn't taken a single jump by the time the starter at the 100-meter dash made their final call. My coaches scrambled over to inform the officials that I'd be checking out and would return after the race. The officials said, if I weren't back before it was my turn to jump, it would be a foul. That seemed unfair to me, but the 100 was more pressing business, and I jogged over to the starting line. I won my heat.

Somehow, in the time that I checked out of the long jump to go race in the 100, I missed two jumps. With my warmups and sneakers in hand, I jogged from the 100-meter finish line back to the long jump. An official greeted me with a smile.

"Perfect timing, you're up!" he said cheerfully.

"What! Now? I don't get a few minutes?" I asked between gulps of breath as if this would help me recover more quickly.

"You have the minute you're allowed to have on the runway. If you can't take the jump, you can pass," he informed me.

"If I pass this jump, I have no other jumps! I don't make the final!" I began to sound hysterical. The official gave me the same smile that airline gate agents do when you're complaining about your seat selection on a full flight.

"It's your decision," he said to my back as I threw my clothes off to the side of the runway and walked back to my mark where I initiated my approach.

"T!" My dad yelled to me from the fence.

I looked up and gave him a weak smile and slight nod of my head. *It's not happening for me today*, I thought to myself. But we're here now, let's see what's what.

I felt heavy on the run. Each of my legs felt burdened by lead shoes, although I was still jumping in sprint spikes. I took off, landed, and looked into the pit at the jump. *Oh, not bad*, I thought to myself with some surprise. I looked up at my dad, expecting him to match my pleasure at overcoming exhaustion and giving the effort I had to produce this result. Not my best, but the best I had. But my father's face relayed none of those emotions. I looked at the official, red flag. I had fouled my last and only jump. I would not be going to state in the long jump.

That memory left a bad taste in my mouth. And I was ready to rinse it with successive successes the following season. As soon as basketball season ended, I went into tunnel vision mode for track and field—spending extra time in the basement lifting on my dad's Bowflex, rolling back and forth with my mom's ab roller. I'd occasionally hit my dad's heavy bag he had suspended from a beam in the far corner of the basement. I have always loved watching my dad make the speed bag sing and dance, and the ferocious grace he displayed pummeling his heavy bag. I'd try to imitate that art when I was alone in the basement, but I was not committed to being good at it. You can't play boxing, and I respected the sport too much to dishonor it by taking my wack blows to the punching bag seriously.

The regular track season went as expected; we were in the Lake Erie League and faced stiff competition from Cleveland-area schools with bigger budgets. Our first trip to Cleveland Heights highlighted the disparity. Their track was real. Their uniforms were new. As girls tend to do, we took a group trip to the bathroom. Unlike the ones at Ely stadium, theirs were well lit and very clean.

"You're about to take a shit, aren't you?" I asked Marita.

"Duh, I'm running the 4, I've got the bubble guts," she replied.

I chuckled. It's a well-known phenomenon to not visit the bathrooms in the warmup areas at running events. That pre-race dump is essential to high performance. As much as we like to deny it happens off the track. We enter our respective stalls.

"Yo, Bam..." I called out using Marita's nickname, "you don't touch the seat with your butt, do you?" I asked as my quads began to shake from the virtual wall-sit I was engaged in.

"No! That's nasty!" she yelled back.

"Just checking" I said as I returned my attention to my quivering quads. The door to the restroom opened, and we fell silent. Whoever had just entered the bathroom decided to occupy the empty stall between us. The door creaked open and closed. We could hear that shiny metal lock slide into place.

"WHAT THE F- SOMEBODY DUN SHI-DOO DOO'D ON THE DAMN SEAT!" The mystery woman bolted out of the stall and out of the restroom. Marita laughed, and my quads gave out. Cold porcelain pricked my skin as my laughter turned into F-bombs. It was time to run.

Although dual meets are scored as team events, we never actually cared if our team won or lost. We were concerned with our individual efforts. After all, if you don't have it together individually your team doesn't stand a chance anyway.

Our next dual meet was against Euclid High School. Again, I was scheduled to run the 100, 200, compete in the long jump, and anchor the 4x100-meter relay. Our team of misfits filed off the bus and into yet another stadium that was a million times better than our own. Euclid's athletes were scattered around the entrance to take quick glimpses of their competition for the day. We must have looked completely nonthreatening, what with our ill-fitting warmups and our mostly white team compared to their majority black one.

Our team warmed up as we always did, and Marita wandered off to fraternize with her friends on Euclid's team. We were debuting new uniforms at this meet—well, new bottoms. Marita had convinced her parents who were the head coaches of the men's and women's track teams that the girls needed briefs. It was also the first time we would be traveling with a massage therapist. We may not have had the funds to get a track worthy of our talent, or uniforms that fit, but we knew the importance of injury prevention.

"Dad, can I ask him to massage my butt?" I asked once we arrived at the track in Euclid.

My dad, with a quizzical eyebrow raised, said, "It's a muscle, ain't it?"

I nodded my head yes.

"Then don't be weird about it."

Relieved because my glutes had been sore for days, I walked over to the therapist and asked if he would work on my glutes.

"GLUTES!?" Marita yelled from somewhere behind us. "You want your booty massaged?" she asked.

"Yes. It's a muscle, ain't it? Right, so don't be weird about it." I said with more confidence than I felt.

"I want my glutes done too then," Marita said, convinced of its necessity.

"Me too," said another disembodied voice as I stripped to my sports bra and briefs and laid face down on the massage table.

"Y'all, look, she getting that booty massaged!" A passing group of boys from Euclid shouted.

With my face smashed into its cradle on the massage table, I couldn't easily crane my neck to see who those voices belonged to. Embarrassment kept me from caring enough to look. When my massage was over, I hopped off the table, slid on my baggy warmup suit, and prepared for my first of four events.

Sometime after the 100-meter dash, when our team was taking a collective breather together in the stands, the same group of Euclid boys meandered by. Apparently, Marita was already familiar with one of them. She flirted shamelessly as their group stopped in front of ours.

"Where they find you at?" one of the boys asked me.

Too shy to respond, and taking a cue from my father, I raised one of my eyebrows.

"Elyria don't have black people. They damn sure don't have fast people. Where they find you at, the projects?"

Shocked, I locked eyes with the boy without speaking. I couldn't decide between being offended or flattered, and as a result I felt paralyzed. I understood then what the looks of disbelief were at the finish line when I crossed well ahead of their fastest runner. The 200 was next on my agenda, so I stood up to make my way down to the field to do an abbreviated warmup on the backstretch.

"Oh, shit! Project is in the 200 meters too. Tell your girl she bout ta get her ass handed to her!" a Euclid boy said to his teammate.

I smiled as I walked away from them and toward the 200-meter start.

"Good job today, Project," another boy from Euclid said to me as I boarded the bus.

A.J. was his name. I told him thanks as I made my way to the back of the bus. I threw my track bag and boom box (which I brought to every track meet) on the seat across the aisle from me. I stretched my legs across the sticky faux leather, my head supported against the dingy glass window.

"I think you have a new name, and a new crush. Ain't that right, Project?" Marita said poking her head over the seat.

A.J. was really cute, and maybe being called "Project" wasn't too bad after all, I thought.

Later that evening, around the dinner table back at home, my mother asked how the meet went. I told her it went well and that I earned a new nickname.

"Oh?" she questioned while moving her food around the plate with her fork.

"Yeah, they said I'm so fast Elyria high had to recruit me from the projects. So, they call me Project now," I said, not without pride.

"Are you serious? And you *like* this nickname?" she asked me in disbelief.

I didn't answer…preferring to slice my Salisbury steak patty in perfect segments on my plate.

"Your father and I have worked so hard to make sure you did not have to live the life that either of us lived growing up. All of this work just for you to embrace the idea that that's where you come from. Who are you?" she asked, pushing herself away from the table.

"There's a reason you don't know," I said under my breath as I too pushed away from the table.

Done with dinner, I returned to my room. I removed a box of chalk from my junk drawer and in large sweeping motions I wrote the name, Project, on my bedroom wall.

Much to my mother's dismay, being granted the nickname, Project, gave me a character I could play for competitions. So, I leaned in, donning crystal-studded bandanas, and rap heavy playlists—you know, my very naive idea of what a person from the projects was like. My mother, who actually grew up poor, rolled her eyes every time she saw me step out of my room as a sheltered and well-off girl playing at "ghetto."

The only time I wasn't playing a part was when it came to the "boys." Marita gave me A.J.'s phone number sometime after the last dual meet. She was dating his teammate Dion and jumped at the chance to make a love connection. I prepared myself to call him. I downed a bottle of water, ran through melodic scales, and practiced saying different variations of "Hello, this is Tianna," "Hey, this is Project," "What's up, A.J.? It's T." None of those sounded particularly smooth to me. With shaking hands, I flipped open my cell phone and dialed his number. It rang forever. Finally, I heard the tell-tale click of an answered call.

"Hello," he said, with what sounded to me like confusion.

His confusion shook what little confidence I had left, and with a shaky voice I said, "Hello? Hey. Yeah, this is Tianna."

"Tianna?" he said, as if struggling to remember where he knew that name from.

"Project?" I replied, trying to jog his memory.

"I thought this was Richard," he said.

"What? Why would you think that?" I asked, my voice rising in pitch.

"Because the caller ID says Richard. No big deal, your phone is in your dad's name. It makes sense," he said comfortingly.

"No, my dad's name is Robert, not Richard."

"Well, you're Richard today," he chuckled either with amusement at himself or me. I couldn't tell which but assumed the latter.

"I gotta go. My mom's calling me..." she wasn't. "I'll try to hit you back later," I wouldn't.

I pushed end, flipped the phone closed, and dropped it on my bed before flying out of my room and down the stairs.

"Did you know that caller ID says Richard is calling when I call someone from my cell phone?" I asked indignantly.

"No, but how do you know it does?" my mom asked me.

Unsure if I was allowed to call boys on my cell phone, I lied and said I had just called one of my girlfriends, and that she told me it said Richard.

"Well, you sound like a Richard." Christina chimed in from her spot on the family room floor.

"Shut up!" I shouted back at her as both parents began to chuckle. I knew what they were laughing about.

Several years ago, at our old house on Abbe Road, we had an answering machine. The kind that required one of those mini tapes. It was located in the den which functioned as the family room and playroom. For some reason, unbeknownst to Christina and me, the answering machine began to record as we were entertaining ourselves in front of the television.

Later, my mom descended the stairs after a long day at work to check the machine. It was flashing the "new message" light, and for some reason my sister and I found this exciting and so we gathered together around my mom to listen. Mom pushed play. You could hear my little sister's angelic voice, barely audible over the sounds from the Disney Channel on the television and the clinking of our Tinker Toy sets spread out on the floor. Christina's voice was so sweet. But why was it on the machine? We shot confused looks at each other as the tape continued to play. All we could hear was the faint sounds of the Disney Channel playing in the background. But then there was a loud grunt followed by what sounded like a body being pushed to the floor. Next, we heard a boy say, "Stop! You know my back is already hurting!" Except…there was no boy in the house. We were baffled listening to this recording. My mom's eyes narrowed looking from my little sister to me, and then to my father, almost wondering when exactly during the day we snuck a boy into the house.

My mom slowly turned to face me…"Tianna, was that…you?" she asked me. I could hear the mixture of disbelief and barely contained laughter in her voice.

"T," my dad jumped in, "your voice is deeper than mine."

The three of them burst into a fit of giggles, while I zipped my mouth shut feeling very embarrassed.

Back in the family room of our new house, I relived the same scene. Both parents and my little sister laughing about my voice. I turned to leave.

"Where you going, Richard?" Christina's cute little voice called after me.

From Project to Richard. *What's in a name?* I pondered as I climbed the stairs back to my room.

SOPHOMORE SLUMP

The rest of that track season went well. Another year of getting stronger and faster saw me qualify for state in the 100, 200, 4x200-meter relay, and the long jump. The previous year it was Khalilah Carpenter of Brookhaven High School in Columbus who put the fear of God into me by handing me a butt whopping of which I had never experienced before. Khalilah was a senior, and it would be her last year embarrassing the girls who tried to run with her. After the last state championships, I was somewhat resolved to take my loss to her, bide my time, and take my run at the title after she was gone. My plans were disrupted, almost as soon as they were put in place, by a new girl on the block, LaShauntea Moore of Firestone High School in Akron. All season she had been walking down girls on relays and dropping them after 20 meters in the 100 and 200. I lined up against her earlier in the season at an invitational and knew firsthand how close to impossible it would be to beat her. I was grateful I did not have to see her until we made that trip to Dayton. I progressed through districts and regionals without incident.

The long jump was the evening before the division one state championships began. My competition was a girl named Cobie Carlisle. She was also a sprinter jumper, and we had battled against each other at the OHSAA regional meet in Amherst, Ohio, a few weeks before. It was so cold that evening that the long jump was contested. I wore my flannel pajama pants as warmup bottoms. That decision was almost too much for my mother to bare. She had finally just warmed up to the idea of "Project," and now had to deal with her daughter, the number one long jumper on that side of the Mississippi River, showing up to the meet in her pajama pants and wearing a Swarovski crystal-studded bandana peeking out from a beanie.

Cobie jumped 18 feet 10 and a half inches that day. I stood on the runway in my sprint spikes looking down at my feet and the anklet that reminds me which foot to start on. Much to my father's amusement, it took me a long time to quickly identify left from right. For whatever reason, I had to think for a moment before saying whether something was to the left or to the right, using my hands as reference. I'm left-handed, raised in a family of right-handed people. I do almost everything as a right-handed person except write. I jump off of my left leg. Most left-handed jumpers take off from their right.

I checked my stance and rocked back. I stepped forward and rocked back again. This pre-jump ritual was dramatic but served as a distraction to anchor

61

my mind to something that wasn't about nerves, or medals, or distance. I count my lefts. Every time my left leg touches the track, I count. I start with my left foot forward and so the first step is a right. I fix that by counting that step as zero. When the left comes back that's one. I knew that when I got to six it was time to jump. Counting for me was another way to anchor my mind to something practical rather than leaving it in idle. Counting also kept me from looking for the board, from chopping my steps, from worrying about anything at all. I took off from the board perfectly, pulled my knees to my chest, extended my legs, and pulled them up toward my chest to ride in that go-kart position I had been practicing. My arms were extended forward and out, stuck in space as I travelled through the air. I landed on my feet and my remaining momentum catapulted me out the back of the pit. The official watching the board waited for me to exit the pit before tossing up his white flag. Two more officials unwound the tape measure. The entire crowd waited with bated breath as the officials straightened, adjusted, and straightened the tape measure again. "19 feet! Four! And a half...inches!" the official at the long jump board shouted as they worked their way back to a standing after kneeling at the board to read the tape measure. My parents hooted and hollered from the stands. After not making it to state the year before, I was the new State Champion. I stood atop the podium in my flannel pajamas, bandana, and beanie.

I felt like celebrating. I took my envelope of per diem to team dinner and splurged on ordering an extra entree. My teammates, parents, and coaches congratulated me and talked excitedly about the competition and the day ahead.

The day ahead. *Oh, no,* I thought. I'd have to face Lashauntea Moore in the 100 and the 200. Those were two races I knew I did not stand a chance at winning. The thought of losing all my events the following day settled like a rock in my gut and successfully ruined my appetite for my second entree. Later, in bed, back at the hotel I stared up at the ceiling. *What do I do here?* I asked myself. I held my shiny Ohio-shaped gold medal in my hand; light from the parking lot seeped in through the curtain and reflected off the gold making it twinkle in my hands. *Do I give maximum effort, knowing I'll lose? Or do I just get through it?* I set my medal on the nightstand and turned away from the window. *I'll know what to do in the morning,* I thought, before drifting off into a fitful sleep.

I woke up the following morning a State Champion. I proceeded through the ritual of laying out my briefs, sports bra, and jersey before heading to the shower. The bathroom filled with steam as the hot water showered me into wakefulness. A heaviness brought on by the difficulty of the awaiting competition settled like a weighted barbell across my shoulders. I now knew what it was like to be a champion. I did not want to feel like a loser. I took one final look at myself in the mirror before meeting up with the rest of the team in the lobby to head over to the track.

I was not nervous at all. I warmed up with my team, and from the outside I looked completely normal. What my teammates and coaches didn't know, was that I had withdrawn. Not literally, that would have been a step too far. But mentally and emotionally I withdrew myself from the competition. I no longer had to be nervous because I already knew the outcome of my events. I knew that I was going to just "get through" the day. Apparently, I was too tough to fake an injury and scratch from my events but too scared to actually take my shot at winning. One thing I had failed to realize was that, on any given day, no matter who was lined up next to me, no matter what their previous performances were, anything could happen. Anyone could win, but I had to be willing to try. I was so afraid of the aftermath of putting everything I had into the race and then learning that it wasn't enough. I would ultimately interpret this as ME not being enough.

I took third in the 100-meter dash running 12.10. Second place ran 12.09. At one point during the race, I could have overtaken Tamala for silver and decided in a split second that I was content with the podium. LaShauntea ran 11.68 for the win. Our 4x200-meter relay team also made the podium taking third place. I suspended my "going through the motions" plan for that event because my team needed me to show up as my best self, not my wack-ass, scared shitless self. So, I showed up for them and helped us earn our highest finish. I slipped right back into my lame plan for the 200 taking third in 25.43, losing by almost a second to LaShauntea. I crossed the finish line imagining that I would feel relieved that the day was over, that I would be satisfied with three bronze medals to go with my beautiful gold one. It turned out, I just felt sick. I was disturbed by my approach to the competition. I was disgusted by my inability to "go out on my shield" and embarrassed that, not only did I know I was capable of much more, my dad knew it too, and I had let him down. In the car on the ride back to Elyria from Dayton, my dad caught my eyes in the rearview mirror and shook his head in almost imperceptible bewilderment at my lack of courage. What I had not yet learned was that courage was not the absence of fear, but the ability to do what should be done in the face of it.

NEXT LEVEL

My father's voice floated up to me from beneath my closed door. A man of few words, when he asked to speak to us, we listened.

"So, your mom and I have been talking, and we've decided you have to go away for college."

A statement that seemed obvious. All I wanted to do was leave. I had been counting down the days until my departure since that lasagna dinner with Darryl.

"There's more," he said, sounding like an infomercial. "We're not paying for it. So, you need to figure out how you're going to get to school for free."

He turned to leave. *So it is written, so shall it be done*, I thought as he turned to leave my room.

"Wait!" I had an idea. "If I find a way to earn a full scholarship, I think you and Mom should have to buy me a car. Because just doing the math really quick…" I pretended to solve an equation in the air with my finger, "buying me a car is not even close to the value of four years of room and board and tuition and a meal plan."

My dad raised that eyebrow again, a twinkle in his eye betrayed how impressed he was with my counteroffer.

"Deal," he said as he extended his arm for a handshake.

So it is written, so shall it be done. I was getting a car.

It wasn't the prospect of a scholarship that spurred me into action, but the idea that I'd have a car. I decided, based on my level of talent, that I needed to drop basketball and use that indoor season to run track. That would give me more time to prepare for outdoor and more exposure because of the additional competitive opportunities. Mom and I picked out separates from Walmart as a uniform for me to run unattached in. There were only a few indoor tracks in the area so, as faces became familiar, I befriended two other athletes running unattached on our makeshift circuits. Tiffany Amos and Devin Nolcox were at every meet I was. One day Devin introduced himself to me before I started my warmup ahead of the 60-meter dash, and my soul recognized him instantly. It seemed as though he and I had known each other forever. A track nerd through and through, Devin never hesitated to critique my race, technique, or mindset thoroughly. The three of us called ourselves Team M.A.N., using the first initials of our last names as we leaned on each other to navigate the world of track and field.

The indoor season went really well for me. For the first time we traveled to Landover, Maryland, for the Nike Indoor Classic at the Prince George Complex. I was entered in the 60 and the long jump. I won the long jump, jumping 20' 2" and took third in the 60 at 7.56. But I was most excited about the athlete party. After getting assurances from the Glenville track coach, Ted Ginn, who had also traveled to Maryland from Ohio with his team, that he'd keep an eye on me, I was allowed to tag along to the party. Ted Ginn, Jr., was already one hell of a track star and their whole team oozed with competence and confidence. Happy to be at the party, and with no idea what to do once I was there, I held up the wall as I took in the scene. I had never been happier.

Typically, a person who only needs to learn a lesson once, I approached my outdoor season with a much higher level of intensity. I qualified for state in four events. The 100-meter dash, the 200-meter dash, the long jump, and the 4x100-meter relay. Not interested in feeling the way I felt after the previous year's state championship, I did not care who was in the race, nor what times they ran, or distances they jumped prior. I was prepared to line up and take my shot, period.

I did not come to play. The night before the division one meet was scheduled to start, I stood on the long jump runway prepared to defend my title that I jumped 19 feet to win. I started the following day with a personal best in the 100-meter dash running 12.02 into a headwind. Next, our 4x200-meter relay team, which I wasn't part of, earned a hard-fought point finishing eighth in the final. Our 4x100-meter relay team ran 47.60 to win! Celebrating a victory with your relay team is an unparalleled experience. I celebrated my long jump state title from the year before, alone. Now, we could celebrate together. But before we could do any of that I had to run the 200-meter dash. I lined up for my last event of the day physically exhausted and emotionally drained. But there was a zone I knew I could drop into that would essentially allow me to go into autopilot without overthinking, without emotion. I developed this ability dealing with Darryl in the dark stairwell of the high school. The ability to be there…but not; to observe what's taking place separate from oneself, emotionless and detached. I entered this zone anytime I was afraid in competition; for me it was a place where emotions like fear, nervousness, and doubt have no bearing over what happens. The body, having been trained for this moment for months, in the lead up does what it is trained to do. I battled to the end to win my fourth gold of the meet. Marielle Brinda, whom I beat in an elementary school spelling bee, took fourth in the pole vault for four points. We took six girls to our state meet and finished second overall. We celebrated with the entire city in the square when we returned and promised to deliver them a title the following year.

I was high off my success at the state championship, so we rolled right into summer track. That summer's USATF Junior National Meet was taking place at Stanford, my dream school. I was obsessed with the idea of going to school all the way across the country to an institution as highly regarded as Stanford. I was excited to be able to get my first look at the track and the campus. My father and I were immediately intimidated upon arrival. We had never been at such a high-caliber event with the talent level on display. The track chatter in the lead up to this event was all about the explosive head-to-head awaiting us if Allyson Felix and Sanya Richards lined up to face each other. The long jump field was just as competitive although not as prestigious of an event to be a headliner.

"You belong here," my dad said to me as I stared wide-eyed toward the pit. I nodded my head in agreement, gathered my bag, and joined the competition. Three jumps and three fouls later an official asked me to gather my things so they could escort me back to the warmup stands. I didn't make the final. My heart was broken with disappointment and embarrassment as I looked to the stands for my father. His face was a mirror of mine.

I hadn't yet learned that this was the way of track and field. Amazing accomplishments could be followed by devastating defeats. Every win was probably sandwiched by three or four losses. I hated how being escorted off the track felt, while the rest of the girls continued on. I hated it so much that I thought it was a sign that track and field was over for me—that it was good while it lasted, but this was a new level. And I wasn't on it.

So, I quit. Damn. No new car for me. We were walking out of the stadium with our heads hung in defeat, when we were stopped by a woman who introduced herself to us as Joy Kamani. She talked to my father about an Olympic Development Camp happening that summer and was extending an invitation to us. Unsure of my future in the sport, I stared at my feet while they spoke. My dad shook her hand, and we continued to walk to the car.

"Want to go to Chula Vista?" He asked me as he unlocked the rental car with a beep.

"But I just quit," I said.

"You ain't quit," he said as he laughed at me.

I am dramatic. He has always found it amusing.

"How about we go down, and if you still want to quit after, you can."

There it was. Permission to quit. Oddly enough, neither my sister nor I were forced into anything. We were encouraged to finish what we started, to give good effort; but if we wanted to quit, we were allowed to. I had nothing better to do in the summer with track and field off the table, why not go to an all-expense paid trip to Chula Vista?

OLYMPIC HOPEFUL?

The Olympic Training Center in Chula Vista was almost as magical of a feeling to me as Disney World—almost. The campus sprawled out ahead of us as we drove through the guard gates. Mountains rose from the horizon and accented the desert-like landscape. I was checked in and escorted to the residences where I'd be sharing a suite with three other girls. It made me insanely happy to have the ID card that granted me access to the training center. And even though my thumbnail photo was framed by the words U.S. Olympic Training Center and the Olympic Rings, it still didn't occur to me that the Olympics was something that I could actually pursue. It wasn't that I believed the Olympics was beyond my reach, it was just that I had no idea how anyone in any sport made a team in the first place. I'd never seen any Olympic Trials. I only knew that every four years in the summer, my parents would turn on the television and Team USA would be there competing for medals. Who they were, and how they got there were never questions I thought to ask? Even as I was wandering around the campus, getting acquainted with the quickest routes to the track and the cafeteria, I didn't wonder about the Olympics. After all, I had already quit track...right?

The horizontal jumps camp was up first and led by Richie Mercado. My father and I learned a lot about the penultimate step and the takeoff. We were introduced, for the first time, to the concept of braking at takeoff and force plates. We learned how to bound, and I knew quickly that bounding was one of my favorite things to do. By the end of the camp with Richie Mercado, the bitter taste of being escorted off Stanford track just a couple weeks before because I didn't make the final began to fade.

We had a day off between the conclusion of the horizontal jumps camp and the sprint camp, so we decided to drive to Mexico. None of us had ever crossed the southern border. We regretted that decision as soon as we approached the border by car. Seeing more armed guards than I'd ever seen before in my life, my little sister and I sat up stiff and straight in the back seat. Turned out, U.S. Border Control wasn't all that concerned about us leaving. We visibly relaxed as we drove toward Mexico. We grew more and more tense as we approached Tijuana. Dad parked and locked the car in a paid lot, as the four of us wandered together through an overcrowded marketplace.

"Por favor! Por favor! Mi hija es sick!" A person, with complete disregard for personal space said directly into my face. I jerked my head back, and reflectively stuck my arm out to create some space between us.

"T, you speak Spanish, what are they saying?" My dad asked. He had a grip on my sister's and my shirts, and my mom's arm was interlocked in his as we moved as a unit through the market.

"He said his daughter is sick!" I yelled over mariachi horns. There's a reason why I speak Spanish, and it isn't because I learned it in school. It's because a few years earlier my dad bought a computer for us to use at home but had no clue how to use it and no idea what games to buy. He purchased something that "looked" educational and brought it home. He wasn't wrong. It was educational. But it was in Spanish. I spent countless hours playing and learning Spanish by immersion and most definitely by accident. It became a running joke in our family, especially when Mom took us all along on her work trip to Puerto Rico. Thinking I would be the family translator, my parents were baffled to learn I was afraid to speak in another language. Too insecure and unsure of myself to even try on the last day in the last hour of our stay in Puerto Rico, I purchased a souvenir from a small bodega. "Gracias," I said as I accepted my change.

I heard my dad behind me. "OH, so NOW you know some Spanish," he laughed shaking his head, "Gracias!" he said again in a high-pitched voice mocking me.

I laughed too. It was pretty ridiculous.

I had let our family get destroyed in a Viejo San Juan scavenger hunt because of my refusal to speak Spanish. One of the last things we were meant to find was "Live Agua." All I would have had to do was ask anyone on the street "¿Donde esta la agua viva?" But, nooooooo, I was too scared to. Instead, we wandered inside a cathedral following behind a tourist group. A fountain with water greeted us at the entrance.

"This must be it," my mom said with confidence. "Live Agua! Life-giving water!"

We weren't convinced by her logic, but we were swayed by her confidence.

"You're right this must be it!" Giddily we splashed a bit in the water before realizing we were getting some unchristian like stares from the other patrons.

"Let's go," my dad said.

"Wait, wasn't that holy water?" I asked as the realization of what we'd just done dawned on me slowly.

We were playing in holy water inside the church. Embarrassed, we scurried away from the cathedral, up the side streets of Old San Juan, and right past a food truck with the words "Live Aqua" written in fluorescent paint along the side. Being bilingual was something to be proud of and something that needed to be practiced in order to gain confidence and proficiency. Fast forward to Tijuana, and I was grateful to be able to understand the chaos unfolding around me. From what I could understand there were a lot of sick children, a lot of parents with cancer, and a lot of people needing money. People tugged on our shirts and at our pockets. I took one final terrified glance back at my father as he signaled that our time in Mexico had come to an end. We were in Mexico for less than an hour and couldn't get back soon enough.

The following day, the sprint development camp began which was hosted by Caryl Smith and her mentor, Tony Wells. *Do you believe in love at first sight?* I do. Some people just stop you in your tracks. Caryl was one of these people for me. Before she ever introduced herself, I wanted to know her entire story. Because I was so incredibly taken with her, I wanted to make sure she knew I was a good student, and I wanted to impress her, and by extension Tony Wells. Unlike the horizontal jumps camp, the sprint camp had classroom time. Our first session took place in a sort of field house; plastic chairs were arranged in front of a table and whiteboards. Tony Wells was larger than life, not in size but in charisma. I liked him instantly. He had eyes that twinkled with a hint of mischievousness behind glasses. He was generous with his smile, and his curse words, but it was hard to feel down in the presence of Tony Wells. We all piled into the room and took our seats. Some girls already knew each other, having been running on the summer track circuit for years. I didn't know any girls at the sprint camp, so I chose a seat in the center of the room. I didn't want to appear to be teacher's pet by sitting in the front row, but I also didn't want to send a disinterested signal to Caryl or Tony.

"What's the hardest workout you've ever done?" Tony asked us all in the room. Wanting to impress them both, I shot my hand in the air. They asked me to stand and introduce myself along with the events I competed in. I did, and then I told them what my hardest workout was. Repeat 300s. I was hoping that this would impress the other girls in the group, but they appeared to be unfazed by the prospect of running so many 300s. I, on the other hand, hated workouts like this, but stood proudly as I explained the workout to Tony.

"Why the hell you doing shit like that?" he asked me. I stole a glance at my dad, who was on the other side of the room where most coaches were congregated. It happened quick; my dad's eyebrow raised and dropped just as quickly as Tony's response caught him off guard. I didn't blame my dad for the workout. It was the lovechild of one of the other coaches on the high school team's staff. I had no answer for Tony. Opting instead to listen, there'd be no impressing this group. All week we learned about plyometrics, energy systems, periodization, and testing. We ran fly 30s, a test covering 60 meters where you only time from 30-60. We learned how to take that fly time and plug it into an equation and project anything from your 100 to 400-meter time. I loved this. Back in my room at the end of the day I'd work backwards from 100-meter times I wanted to run one day and calculate what I needed to get down to in the 30-meter fly to make it happen.

We tested for the rest of camp. And our results were shared with Randy Huntington who was heading up the biomechanics side of things. My dad and I met with Randy in his office. "Do you have any piercings?" he asked me.

"Just my ears." I said, confused about the relevance.

"No belly piercings?" he asked again.

"No sir." I answered again.

"Good, don't ever. I'll show you why." He stood and asked me to hold my arm out to the side. I did. "Try to resist me," he said as he attempted to push my arm down.

I worked hard to not let him move my arm.

"Good," he said before asking permission to place his hand on my shirt at belly button level. "Okay, again. Try to resist me."

I lifted my arm again. I couldn't hold it up. Something about his hand being at my belly completely diminished my ability to hold my arm in place.

"You are weaker now, because I've placed my hand at your belly. The energy you could have used to resist me pushing on your arm has been redirected and is distracted by my hand. This is the type of "leak" piercings cause." Randy said, returning to his desk chair.

I found that hard to believe but also hard to disprove because I truly could not hold my arm up the second time; I did not have any other explanation for it other than the one Randy offered. Damn. No belly button piercing for me then.

Randy and my dad chatted further about my testing results, my impressive fly times, and the numbers from the force plate first horizontal jumps camp; I listened from the side. Randy encouraged my dad to keep me in the sport and to integrate what we were learning here into my training. He said he thought I'd be something special one day. Randy didn't know I was just enjoying my free vacation, and as far as I was concerned, I had actually quit track and field.

Randy asked me if I knew how to tie my shoes. I looked down at my tied shoes before looking back up at him.

"Yes, I know how to tie my shoes," I said unamused.

"You sure? Looks to me like you've got an unused hole right there."

I looked down at my shoes. He was right there was an unused hole, but I had no idea what that hole was for, nobody did. I took my shoe off at his request and watched him take the lace out completely. He laced the shoes again and set them on the ground in front of me.

"Okay," he said, "put the shoe back on."

The previously unoccupied hole was still empty and so I began to become irritated at the waste of time this seemed to be, but I put the shoe on.

"Okay, now take the right lace and loop it into the empty hole; don't pull it through, just loop it."

Okay. Done.

"Good, do the other side."

I did. It now looked like I had two bunny ears protruding from either side of my shoe.

"Okay," Randy continued, "take that left string and thread it through the loop on the right. Yep, now do other."

I did. My shoes looked like they had bunny ears, but each bunny ear had a string protruding from the middle.

"Grab the string now and pull tight."

I did. As I pulled the laces the bunny ears got smaller and smaller. I tugged one final time as the shoe seemed to close tightly around my ankle.

"Ooo!" I exclaimed in surprise. "My ankle feels locked in!" Years of basketball left my ankles highly susceptible to sprains. I rolled them often.

"Exactly! Avoid the energy leaks. If your ankles are moving around in your shoes, that's force you aren't able to use for what you need it for."

Amazed, I had had no idea how much there actually was to learn about track and field. Now, for the first time since I arrived in Chula Vista, I questioned my decision to quit. In fact, I wanted nothing more than to put all the new information I had learned to good use. Luckily, although I had fully believed I was quitting track, my dad knew better and left one final meet on my schedule. I was running the 200-meter dash back at Welcome

Stadium in Dayton, Ohio—the site of my four state titles. At junior nationals, earlier that summer I had gotten my ass thoroughly kicked in the 200. I ran 24.60. I was not only one spot out from the nine-person final, but I learned that being number one in Ohio didn't mean shit on the national level. Sanya Richards won that race in 23.31 seconds battling Allyson Felix all the way to the line, who took second in 23.34 seconds into a headwind! I had never broken 24 seconds, and I was ready to see if my new knowledge could translate into faster times. To be sure, I asked Caryl to tell me how to run the race. I remembered earlier in the camp, her lecturing us on the importance of race strategy—that knowing HOW to run a race was just as important as being fast.

I singled Caryl out before the end of camp to ask her about the 200.

"Hey, Mad," she called me, already having found a nickname for me. "You gonna run the 200? You mad you got your head busted, huh?"

She knew I was still licking my wounds and holding on to my poor showing at junior nationals.

"First thing you do, is set your blocks on an angle so you can drive out straight. Run the first 60 meters as fast as you can, like you're running for your life. From 60-80 meters you hold. Hold means HOLD, it does not mean slow down, it also does not mean speed up. Hold means hold. This will give you time to recharge the turbo. Then remember diamonds are a girl's best friend. At the relay diamond, GO."

This race strategy seemed reasonable enough; I was worried about the "hold" though; *wouldn't everyone pass me?* We would find out soon enough.

In another stroke of luck, my father and I got to ride in the van with Caryl to the airport. She would be returning to Alabama where she was an assistant coach. Dad and I were flying to Cleveland, and Mom and my little sister had returned home a few days before. Caryl sat shotgun while my father and I occupied the back row of the cargo van—our luggage stacked in the back. Both of us were engaged in a deep conversation about fall training and how to best prepare me for my senior year. Caryl's phone rang, and the van grew quiet. I took the break in conversation as an opportunity to tell my dad what had been becoming more and more clear to me over the last couple days: I wanted to go to school wherever Caryl was. My dad gave me a look that told me that he was good with that decision too.

"Okay, thank you." Caryl said as she hung up the phone. "I just got the assistant coaching position at the University of Tennessee!"

We shouted our congratulations to her from the back seat.

"I gotta call Greg!" she said as she picked up her cell phone again.

"Guess we're headed to Tennessee too," I said to my father conspiratorially. Now, I just had to earn it.

Shortly after we arrived back in Ohio, I made my mom aware of my decision.

"Mom, I'm going to Tennessee," I said to her proudly.

"Oh?" she questioned, turning to face me slowly, "and what of the other schools you know nothing about and the five official visits you're allowed to go on?"

"Don't need 'em," I said to her, naively sure of myself.

"Okay, T. Well then, it won't matter that you take all five of your visits then," she said, explaining that one of them should be Tennessee.

So that left four visits I could take, not to mention the unofficial ones. I had already started to receive those generic letters sent to me from schools across the country. My homeroom teacher would place the stack of letters on my desk as they took attendance and delivered morning announcements. My classmates looked on curiously, and I, center stage once again, made a show of opening, removing, and unfolding each letter. I developed a system. If the letter said, "Dear Student-Athlete" I threw it away immediately. If a school couldn't be bothered to address the letter to me, I couldn't be bothered to read it. Next, I would skip to the bottom of the letter for the signature. I gave preferential treatment to letters that were actually signed by the coaches; signature stamps I liked half as much, but I wouldn't hold being expeditious against a track coach.

"America's most wanted, over here," one of my classmates said.

I smirked. It felt good to be wanted for something I wanted to be wanted for.

With my heart set on Tennessee, I needed to figure out how to earn a full-ride scholarship into the SEC Conference—a tall order.

My first test was in my last summer track meet which was a week after the Olympic Development camp in Chula Vista. It was time to implement my new 200-meter race strategy. With a confidence I had not had before, I stepped to the line in a new Nike crop top that matched my brief bottoms. For one of the first times, I wore a little gold chain around my neck. I second guessed the decision to wear it when it hit me in the face when I rose into my set position. I had learned a new start too. I now started with both knees down, after being measured and given new settings at camp. My blocks were the only ones set up at an angle. I beat down the insecurity I felt about being the only one doing something different. The starter sent us off with the sound of his pistol.

Hard for 60, I shouted internally as I stormed out of the block. O*kay hold here! Stay...Stay...Stay. GO!* The angled blocks shot me right to the inside line, and I fought to stay there as I came off the turn. I felt amazing. My tank was full and, as I sprinted down the homestretch, I felt like I had more in the tank at that point in the race than I ever had before. I crossed the line, too disoriented by the totally different experience that race was to know how it translated to my time. That unknowing lasted for a split second as the PA system crackled to life.

"And Tianna Madison running unattached out of Elyria, Ohio, takes it in 23.92!"

My mouth dropped open. Oh, hell, yeah! I thought. *I'm definitely going to Tennessee.*

HIGHER LEARNING

I'm going to just say it. Getting recruited was weird. And, although there were a few female coaches recruiting me, the whole process seemed like a strange courtship. I felt like Princess Jasmine, in *Aladdin*, watching suitors parade in and out of the house trying to impress my parents and me. I've hated talking on the phone since the "Richard" fiasco and my attitude toward phone calls didn't change even as division one coaches started to call my phone. I hated it.

And I hated the home visits too. One in particular comes to mind: Darryl Andersen, who was the head coach at Arizona State University at the time, flew to Cleveland, Ohio, drove the twenty-minute drive from the airport to our home, and sat in our bright living room on Oakdale Circle. It was a school night, and my reading for AP European History was piling up. Irritated at the intrusion home visits were, I sat unamused in a chair next to my parents who occupied the couch. Christina joined them on the couch, not because she was particularly interested in the process, but because she was nosey. All three of us stared across the room at the coach who was staring back at us. He was wrapping up his pitch about why we should consider ASU when he turned his attention to me and asked me a direct question.

"What do you want?" he asked. "What do you see for yourself in the near future?"

I sat thoughtfully. "I want to be number one in the world," I said, holding his gaze.

He sat back in his chair, "Now, see. We've gotta be realistic."

Silence settled over the room like fog that settles over the shores of Lake Erie. I looked over to my parents and asked to be excused. I went to my room and did not return. As far as I was concerned that visit was over.

As promised, I took all five of my visits: Purdue, Illinois, Notre Dame, Ohio State, and Tennessee. For my mother's sake, I tried to go into each school with an open mind even though it was already settled in mine. Purdue was a great school and had a decent indoor facility. I enjoyed the campus and what I was able to learn about student life, but I did not like the team. During the down time in my schedule, I spent a lot of time with the men's and women's track teams. I was shocked at how none of them seemed to actually care about winning. They sounded like I did, bragging about the amount of per diem they got when they went to conference.

"How much do you get for nationals?" I asked, taking the bait. I liked cash too.

"Girl, no. We're done after conference. We ain't doing all that."

Oh, ok. I thought. No ambitions for nationals, and after one indoor season, based on the school records they had posted in their fieldhouse, I'd be the new record holder in a few events too. Pass.

Illinois was a much better trip. I meshed well with the coaches and loved Tonja, almost as much as I loved Caryl. The football game was exciting and electrifying. The track girls wanted to go to the after party and meet up with the football team. Not at all interested in hanging with the football team, but not wanting to seem lame, I pretended I was excited to be joining them on this excursion. We stood in the parking lot outside of the club, which seemed to be the thing to do.

"Let's go," one of the girls said as she set off in the direction of the club entrance.

"You have your ID?" someone asked me.

"Yeah, but—" my words were cut short by a shove in the back by another girl on the team pushing me forward. The security guard checked my ID and stiff-armed my chest.

"She's 17," he said to my escorts.

"You're 17!?" the girls said in surprised unison.

"I just turned 17. I was trying to tell you," I said, embarrassed.

"Okay, that's okay. Wait here." I waited outside while the party went on without me inside. Eventually, another teammate arrived and escorted me back to the hotel. I was good on Illinois. I knew what it was like to win as an individual. I loved the feeling of winning as a relay team. I was looking for a good coach, but I also wanted a great team. I wanted a family of friends. They were obviously not that.

My next school visit was Notre Dame. That trip was to satisfy my mom. Academically, Notre Dame was at the top of the list. There were a lot of statues and gargoyles on campus. I was creeped out by the number of graven images on campus. We could not enter or exit a building without stone eyes tracking our movements. But Notre Dame did community well, and I liked the idea of the dorms operating largely like social clubs, and the connection they encouraged among the residents. Making friends was (and still is) hard for me, and I was happy to learn that would be less of an issue at Notre Dame. The football game was fun, and the atmosphere in the student section was fired up and energized. I was feeling really good about my time at Notre

Dame and so decided to spend even more time with the team after the game. It was decided that we would go to the movies together. *The Ring* had just hit the theaters, a horror flick starring Naomi Watts. It was decided that they would just drop me off back at the hotel when it was over. My parents gave me a room key, and I set off for dinner and a movie with what was starting to feel like future teammates. My desire to go to the University of Tennessee had less of a pull the longer I remained in South Bend.

I tried to be a big girl about it, I really did. But the movie scared the shit out of me. Trying to hold it together, I forced myself to laugh at the chatter happening around me as the girls drove me back to my hotel. My skin was crawling…I was so disturbed by the movie. I waved goodbye to the girls and turned to face the automatic sliding doors to enter the hotel. They didn't open. Feeling cold and uneasy, I irrationally started to freak out. I located the call box just as I was about to start pounding on the glass with my fists. *Oh, okay, after a certain hour they lock these doors.* My panic started to subside a bit as the receptionist buzzed me in. I made my way to the elevator. I jumped at the ding it made when it arrived on the ground level. I peeked my head inside before stepping in. I had zero tolerance for any surprises. I plastered my back to the wall of the elevator car. The door opened when I arrived on my floor, and again I poked my head out and looked around before stepping out of the elevator. The hallway seemed to stretch endlessly before me. The repetitive floral pattern seemed to create an infinite carpet of ugly. My room was at the end of the hall. Images from the movie, of the girl climbing unnaturally out of the well, flashed before my eyes, and I began to sprint. Imagining her water-logged hands reaching out to grab my ankle, I tripped and fell in the hall. Like a helpless girl in an opening scene of every bad horror movie, I looked back, half expecting to see my ankle in the grip of a monster. I got up and sprinted the rest of the way to the room. I hit the door with the momentum of a sprinter flying into the crash pads at the end of a 60-meter dash. With shaking hands, I got the key into the slot, the door unlocked, and stumbled inside out of breath.

"Girl! What's wrong with you!" my dad yelled from the other side of the room.

He and my mom were sharing the king bed. My sister and I were sharing the sofa bed. A pony wall divided the two.

"I am so scared right now," I said between panting breaths.

My dad laughed and shook his head. "I told you, Jo," he said, amused, nudging my mom out of her sleep.

I changed into my pajamas and climbed into bed next to my sleeping sister. My dad clicked off the light, and we settled in to sleep.

Ten minutes later I jolted straight up out of bed screaming at the top of my lungs. My scream was so full of terror that both my parents and little sister started yelling too. After my parents and sister understood there was no immediate danger, their screams turned to shouts.

"WHAT IS GOING ON?!" they all seemed to yell at me in unison.

"Something touched my leg!" I shouted back in my defense.

"I'm sorry!" my sister's little voice cut through the noise.

"You're sharing the bed with your sister, T. Come on!"

Oh, yeah. Duh.

I climbed back in bed and fell asleep to images of gargoyles, statues of the Virgin Mary, Touchdown Jesus, and THE GIRL. Yeah, I wouldn't be attending Notre Dame.

I took an official visit to Ohio State out of guilt and obligation. Coach Russ Rogers had been laying it on thick that, as a child of Ohio, it was only right to keep the talent at home—to not even give them a chance would be a slap in the face to the state that raised me. But I wanted to leave Ohio. I wanted to be more than a two-hour drive away from home. I had taken three visits already and an unofficial one to Kent State. I was surprised by how much I liked Kent; the only issue was that it was in Ohio, and my heart was set on leaving.

My official visit to the University of Tennessee exceeded my expectations. Marc Sylvester, the baddest middle distance runner out of Ohio, who was a few years ahead of me, was a Tennessee Volunteer. I begged Caryl to put Marc on my itinerary all but insinuating that, if she could pull this off, it would seal the deal on going to school there. I used to watch Marc run through the holes in the chain-link fences, my mouth open in awe as he destroyed the field, his neck muscles strained against his hemp chokers.

"That's a baaaaaad man," my dad would say when we'd stop everything we were doing to watch Marc's race. He was as giddy as I was when he learned I had demanded Marc be a part of my official visit.

I got to meet with the Forensic Anthropology Department. I was convinced that crime scene investigation was my calling, and I knew that Tennessee's Anthropological Research Facility, aka the Body Farm, was the place for me. On brand, the lead forensic anthropologist's office was in a basement beneath Neyland Stadium. The feeling of descending into catacombs for that meeting just felt...right. We left the stadium, after the meeting, to tour the locker room.

"There's your locker," Caryl said to me as she opened the door.

Compared to the locker room I had become accustomed to at Ely Stadium, that locker room was five-star. The lockers looked more like expensive custom closet fixtures than the rattling metal cages I was used to. A couch sat in the middle of the room in front of a huge, big-screen TV. There was a refrigerator, a microwave, and another set of doors leading to bathroom and shower stalls.

"My locker?" I began to ask until I looked in the direction she was pointing. A placard mounted on the locker door said:

Lady Volunteers

Tianna Madison

Sprints and Jumps

My mouth dropped open.

"Go ahead, open it."

Still gawking over my name plate, I slowly opened the door to the locker, and quickly slammed it shut.

"What!? What's in there?" my parents asked excitedly from somewhere behind me.

"It's, it's full of clothes AND SHOES!" I shouted.

"Want to try them on? They are all your sizes," Caryl said casually. I grabbed up a bunch of items and shuffled to the bathroom, tearing off my clothes, and draping myself in University of Tennessee Lady Vol gear, baby blue, orange, and white. That was it for me. Stick a fork in her folks, she's done.

The following day was "football Saturday" in Knoxville, and I had never seen tailgating that took over an entire city. Everywhere you turned in the sea of orange you could find smiling faces, grills blazing, beers pouring, and music playing. On the corner, a man had set up a speaker and was performing his Rocky Top remix. The energy was contagious, and my whole family joined in as his impromptu backup dancers. To top it off, the Vols won the game!

Even my mother couldn't come up with a reason to veto my decision to attend University of Tennessee. I did not qualify for any financial aid or federal help, but the University of Tennessee ran all of their applicants through a system and automatically submitted them for any available grants. My grades and test scores qualified me for a full-academic scholarship. Caryl had offered me a full scholarship too.

I had done it. My father challenged me to find a way and I did, both in the classroom and on the track. It was time to talk about that car.

ABOVE THE LAW

I signed with the University of Tennessee during the early-signing period, in front of news cameras, with my entire family decked out in orange. UT wasn't far enough south for me to ditch the cold, but they did have indoor facilities, and it was a seven-hour drive from home. I was leaving Ohio! But first, I needed my car.

Two weeks after signing with UT, I drove off the lot in my little Saturn with its suicide door and fancy sound system. There was only one problem; parking at Elyria High School was nearly impossible. Short of arriving at school hours early, odds were that you'd have to park on neighboring streets and walk up to a half mile to the school's entrance. Once, I had to park so far away from the high school we would have gotten their faster had we walked from home. Wanting to avoid that scenario again, I drove my sister, who was a freshman, to school early.

I was in Home Economics, and we were in a cake decorating unit. I wasn't a baker at all until I learned how much I loved it in that class. That day was the day we were getting cake pans. We could either purchase our own, or we could use the teacher's pans at school but on a first come first served basis. I had my eyes and heart set on her SpongeBob SquarePants cake pan, and I did not want anyone else to have it. Perhaps the rest of the senior class had the same idea because parking was even harder than usual to come by. I felt my heart sink as the realization set in that I'd have to roam the side streets, parallel park (which I was horrible at), and walk back to school. By the time I did all that, I'd no longer be early enough to secure my cake pan. Getting pissed in advance, I spotted a parking space on a side street. Christina was in the passenger's, seat singing along to Mariah Carey. I thought back to the tips my driving instructor gave me on parallel parking and remembered I did well parking between the cones in the open parking lot. But I struggled with quickly differentiating my left from my right which made it particularly stressful to park in real-life situations. I didn't have time for that though, I wanted that cake pan. I lined the right mirror up with the driver's side door of the car parked in front of the open space I wanted. I looked over my right shoulder and turned the wheel. The car rocked. One second into my attempt to parallel park, and I already hit the car in front of me. Thinking I was skilled enough to get out of this situation without further damaging the car I turned the wheel again. The high-pitched shriek of metal against metal pierced our ears. A white woman in a dingy house robe and slippers, presumably the owner of the car being scratched to death, kicked open her front door and began screaming at me from her porch. Strings of curses and threats left her mouth only serving to make me more nervous which made me perform even worse in my execution of the job at hand. I finally parked the car. The woman's car was scratched from the front of the driver's side door to the trunk. "I'm calling the PO-LEESE!" she screamed at the top of her lungs. I told my sister to get to school; it would be a while. Dreams of my cake pan faded as I waited for the police.

An officer arrived, and I attempted to explain what happened. The woman continued to scream and shout. The flashing lights on the police car distracted me. I hadn't had a situation with the police since the seventh grade when the D.A.R.E. officer tried to collar me for "gang-related activities." The woman continued to scream, and the officer tried to calm her down.

"I want her arrested! She did this on purpose!" she shouted.

"WHAT?! I'm going to get arrested for not being able to parallel park!? No, I didn't do it on purpose!" I pleaded in the direction of the officer, who did not seem to care in the slightest.

He grabbed my arm.

"I did not do it on purpose," I shouted in the woman's direction as the officer placed a hand on my head and shoved me into the back of his police car. He shut the door and returned to address the woman, who was suddenly as calm as cool water. She was so satisfied to see me in the back of the police car. She smiled, shook the officer's hand, and went back into her house. The police car smelled like old leather and urine. There was a dusty footprint on the seat and another on the roof I tried not to imagine how or why. *I don't deserve this*, I thought to myself as I sat stiff and upright in the backseat of a police car. He wrote me a ticket and dropped me off at the front of the school. I couldn't wait to tell my mom. She's the fixer of the family when it comes to things like this.

We arrived at the courthouse for my court date; the judge greeted my mother familiarly. The clerk was my cousin. We explained what happened and the police officer's actions.

"Wait, he put you in the police car? In the back of the police car?" the judge asked.

"Yes ma'am," I said, embarrassed.

"Did he explain to you why?" she probed.

"No judge, he grabbed my arm and put me in the back, that's it. The lady finally stopped screaming once he did."

I pursed my lips tightly feeling embarrassed, ashamed, and black. Nothing overt happened that made me certain it was racially motivated, but something about the vitriolic spew of the woman and the disregard for me from the cop made me feel like, between my age and my race, I was low on the totem pole.

"Jo Ann, I didn't know it was YOUR daughter who was the track star we keep reading about!"

My mother sat taller, which seemed impossible since she already carried herself with a royal air.

"You're free to go. Keep up the good work, Tianna. Case dismissed."

The gavel dropped. Mom and I drove to Michael's art supplies and craft store to buy my SpongeBob cake pan.

GOOD OL' ROCKY TOP

Later that summer we loaded up the car and drove to Tennessee. My first year there was unremarkable; the best thing I did was avoid the "Freshman 15." Caryl, having put the fear of God in me, threatened to put any sprinter into cross country for the entire season as a weight management tool. We spent many Saturdays on the course, cheering on members of our sprint squad as they shuffled uphill, death in their eyes. Unremarkable as it was, I did qualify for nationals in the 100-meter dash and the long jump, though.

My first NCAA championships meet was being held in Austin, Texas. I didn't make the final of the 100-meter dash, but Caryl was expecting me to score in the jumps. I choked, though. I ran differently on each attempt making it nearly impossible for Caryl to make adjustments to my approach. I'd start my approach with a promising drive phase and a smooth transition to upright, only to start chopping my steps down and stuttering to the board. She was pissed. I was embarrassed. I finished tenth, jumping 6.31 meters (20′ 8½″) —only jumping one inch farther than I had in high school. The winner, Hyleas Fountain, also from Ohio, jumped 6.61 meters.

My breakthrough was off by a week. Still mad as hell at me, Caryl and I went to junior nationals.

"Let's see which version of you is going to show up."

She called wack-ass Tianna by the name of Tina. Tina, using the same letters as my actual name was, according to her, "soft," which was exactly what I was at NCAAs the week before. I didn't disagree. But junior nationals was a new endeavor. Junior nationals was less scary than NCAAs due to the ages of my competitors, but it had a bigger incentive. Top three finishers in this meet would make the junior team that would go to Grosetto, Italy, for worlds! I wanted to make the team and add Italy to my growing list of international trips.

A day before the meet, we went to the track to warm up, get familiar with the runway, and to shake the travel out of our legs. Coach Vince Anderson, the sprints and hurdles coach for the men's team at the University of Tennessee at the time, stopped me.

He said, "Hey listen, you can't be scared out there. Once you're at the top of the runway ready to initiate your jump, there is no turning back. You've got to be like one of those kamikaze fighter pilots knowing that there is no turning back. So, don't hold anything back, and don't be scared. You ever see the Japanese flag, land of the rising sun? I'm gonna get you a bandana. Kamikaze!"

Vince is one of the most gifted communicators I have ever had the pleasure of conversing with. In that moment, on that runway, with a failed performance behind me, and an unknown fate ahead of me, I trusted that what Vince chose to tell me was true. I decided right then, for the second time that I'd go out on my shield. I was fired up and ready to go. Tianna, not Tina, was going to show up.

I jumped 6.60 meters (21' 8") which just the week before would have earned me second at the NCAA championships by just one centimeter. And...I was further encouraged by the fact that the wind reading on my jump was a tailwind of 1.8 meters per second, while Hyleas 6.61-meter jump was done with a tailwind of 2.9 meters per second. Had I found some courage just one week earlier, I would have been named the NCAA champion as a freshman!

I was thrilled. Caryl was pissed. She had known that I was capable of these jumps, but noooo, I just couldn't get out of my own way. When she asked me what clicked, I told her about the conversation I had with Coach Vince. I knew she'd be annoyed that it took someone else communicating the exact same message for it to click for me. But that's the way it goes sometimes. Sometimes you need to hear something 1,000 times before it clicks. And it doesn't matter that I heard it 999 times from you—if that necessary thousandth rep is delivered by someone else, oh well. Although Caryl preferred to act angry with me, I also knew she was proud. I knew her too well to believe that she wasn't elated at my progress in just one year. My suspicions about this were confirmed when she informed the USATF staff that I would not be going to the world junior championships in Grosetto, Italy.

"WHAT!? WHY!?" I finally shouted after we were away from other people.

"Because you're going to the Olympic Trials!" she said.

In the course of a week, I went from choking at NCAAs, to winning junior nationals, to going to the Olympic Trials. I was on a ride.

Back at home in Knoxville, I couldn't wait to tell DeeDee, my college teammate who had become like a big sister to me, what had happened and how I redeemed myself just a bit from the week before. I knocked on her apartment door just down the hill from campus. She opened it, and I began to talk excitedly. I choked on the rest of my sentence because I had finally noticed we weren't alone. DeeDee had company, and he was sitting on her couch. Perhaps the most beautiful boy I had ever seen, creamy beige skin, big brown eyes, plump lips, and a bald head.

"Who's this?" I asked, eyes not leaving the stranger on the couch. Charles Ryan was his name.

"Nice to meet you," I said as I joined DeeDee in her room.

DeeDee was in the middle of an organizing spree. She and I were alike in that way—needing everything in its place and arranged just so. I tried not to ask about him, but she volunteered that he had moved to Knoxville to train with Coach Vince. Having exhausted his eligibility and graduating from the University of South Carolina, it was finally his opportunity to train with the hopes of competing professionally.

Professional track and field was still something I cared very little about. Very much enthralled with my forensic anthropology course load, I saw track as a means to an end, not an end in itself. Besides, all I could tell about being pro so far was this:

1. You went to the Olympics (which I also didn't care either way about)
2. You got cool gear and shoes for free
3. You weren't broke anymore

A good job, in a field I was passionate about, sounded just as good. I left DeeDee to finish organizing her room, and I rejoined Charles, who went by Chucky or Chuck. He invited me to dinner later that evening at P. F. Chang's. I could not believe it. P. F. CHANG'S—that fancy, expensive, place? We were inseparable after that.

We arrived in Sacramento for the Olympic Trials in full Lady Vol gear. We stayed at the DoubleTree, and it took all my discipline to not inquire about the cookies at the front desk when we checked in. It was a different sort of freedom traveling with the coaches post collegiate season. It was much more enjoyable, much more relaxed. They gave you your per diem and sent you on your way. It did not feel to me like something as big as the Olympic Trials was happening in just a of couple days. But they were.

The day of long jump qualifying had arrived. We would have three attempts to jump 6.40 meters or better to get automatic entry into the final, or they took the top 12 jumps overall. Ideally, you want to qualify on your first jump and go home. I did; I jumped 6.44 meters (21' 1½"). Instead of packing my bag and being escorted off the field while everyone continued to compete for the medals, I was packing up my backpack to leave the field while the remaining jumpers tried to punch their tickets. One competitor that I could not believe I had outjumped was lining up to take another attempt, it was Marion Jones. Marion jumped 6.39 meters (20' 11¾") to punch her ticket to the finals. I'd be going into the final ranked number four; the top three make the team. *Was I really doing this?* I thought to myself as I brushed sand from behind my ears.

No turning back, I heard the voice of beloved Vince Anderson in my ear as I headed to the warmup track to cool down.

We returned three days later to contest the final. Marion, who barely pulled it together enough to make the final, opened her series with a 6.80-meter jump (22'). I opened my series with a 6.35-meter leap. It was ungraceful, and I had sort of an albatross landing. My face was covered in sand as I exited the pit. Sitting on a towel near my bag, Marion leaned over to brush sand off my face. I jolted backwards.

"No thank you!" I almost shouted at her.

Surprised, she said, "You have sand *everywhere!*"

"I'm aware!" I said standoffishly.

She turned away to focus on herself.

Who does she think she is! I exclaimed to myself, getting worked up. *I'm sooo not a threat to you in this competition...you'll help me wipe my face!? I'm trying to BEAT YOU!* The imaginary conversation I was having with her in my head was stoking my temper.

Marion was right, I was no threat to her. She won the competition and made the Olympic team, jumping 7.11. I jumped 6.42 for eighth place. And again, had I just jumped what I had at junior nationals, I'd have taken third and made my first Olympic team—replacing Akiba McKinney and joining Marion Jones and Grace Upshaw in representing the USA.

I was so close and yet so far away. But I learned something invaluable about myself. I learned that I was a competitor. A true competitor, one who didn't need to be sure of how I'd measure up before taking my shot. I had a picture of Marion Jones in my bedroom back at home and yet was ready to slap her hand away for touching me as if I were a baby during the competition. I was not afraid of her, although no one would have faulted me for being so.

ROCKY TOP, TENNESSEE

DeeDee turned pro, after making the Olympic team in the 400 and bringing home gold in the 4x400 meter relay at the 2004 Olympic Games in Athens. Her time in the collegiate scene was done. I, however, had performed in such a way over the summer that Caryl expected a lot from me and from our sprint squad. That year's recruiting class was phenomenal. Caryl signed Courtney Champion out of Georgia, Cleo Tyson out of Texas, and LaTonya Loche out of Louisiana. We didn't have enough personnel to give the 4x100-meter relay a legitimate shot my freshman year, but with that squad, we could do it.

We didn't mesh well right away; our personalities mixed like oil and water. One particular day tensions were rising before we began our warmup.

"Don't talk to me like that. You know who you're talking to? I'm a MULTIPLE-TIME STATE CHAMP!" one of my teammates shouted to another.

"AND! I AM TOO," another shouted back.

I looked up from the shoe I was tying like Randy taught me back at Chula Vista.

"Yeah, I am too. Nine times," I said in a soft voice. It fell quiet as we all came to the realization that at this level, everybody is somebody.

Trying to outdo each other, we sharpened each other like iron. Finally, indoor conference championships were upon us. They were to be hosted in Fayetteville, Arkansas, at the University of Arkansas' Tyson Indoor Track. The banked track was incredible, and Caryl explained how you needed to be unafraid to surge up the bank so that you could enjoy the benefit of the downhill with higher velocities. We watched athlete after athlete nearly fly out of their lane coming off the bank uncontrollably. It scared me. Lucky for me, I didn't have to deal with it. I'd be competing in the 60 and the long jump—straight, no chaser.

Tennessee Lady Vols took second through fifth places in the 60-meter dash, scoring 23 points in one event. I also won the long jump on my first jump, stretching the measuring tape out to 6.71 meters (22' ¼"), a new personal best and good for 10 points. I was quite pleased with myself and was preparing to relax and enjoy the rest of the meets screaming for my teammates from the stands when Caryl shot me a look that told me my day was far from over. I skipped down the bleachers expeditiously.

"T-Mad, we need you to run this 4x4 baby," she said, patting me on the back while knowing this was the worst possible news I could receive.

After the women's 5,000-meter run, we were leading Arkansas by just 2.5 points with one event to go. For whatever reason, I was the only remaining person to call on.

With a shaky voice, I spoke, "Okay, how do I run it?"

Pleased with this reply, Caryl pulled me in closer and explained that I'd be running the first leg, and my only job was to get to the break first. The break is the place in the race where all the runners can "break-in" to lane one rather than stay in their lanes the entire way. Indoor tracks are only 200 meters around. So, the 400 is two laps. Runners stay in their lanes for most of the first lap but can "break" into lane one before starting the second. The indoor 400 is a strategic race, how you make your way into lane one can make or break your entire race. It's too difficult to pass a runner, especially on a banked track if you find yourself in a bad position.

"Okay, get to the break first, got it. Then what?"

Caryl turned me to face her, "Then you hold on, we only need to beat Arkansas."

I took a deep breath feeling like an astronaut in an end-of-the-world movie tasked to save the world.

I realized we were in the fast heat, as I set my blocks on the bank—the same bank I was happy not to deal with just days before. My heart rate was increasing exponentially. I slid the left block pedal forward to set it but had to pause because I felt as though I would pass out from the gravity of the situation. If I messed this up, we lost; I didn't want that on my shoulders. I was going to have to give it everything I had. So what, if the 400 meters was over six times longer than my usual distance? I was going to have to figure it out. I slid the right pedal back. I got into the blocks, came to set position, and did a practice start. I could taste vomit in my mouth. I was going to be sick.

"Stand behind your blocks," the starter said from the infield, whistle in his mouth. "To your marks," he said as he raised the starter gun above his head.

This is it, I thought to myself. *Get to the break.*

"Set!"

My vision narrowed, and I stopped breathing.

Bam! The gun went off, and I exploded out of the blocks and surged into the bank.

I like this! I thought as I rode the slingshot off the first bank just in time to approach the second.

You could hear everyone's feet, even with the uproarious crowd. I was flying because I was running scared. The break! I saw it in front of me, a line of mini cones indicating you could ease into lane one. I did it! I got to the break first! Pleased with myself, I begin to surge up the second bank.

Uh-oh! I could feel it. That first lap was a scorcher, and I was about to pay for it on the second.

Just hold on! Caryl's words floated back to my consciousness.

I attempted to pump my arms harder, squeeze the baton tighter, lift my knees higher.

Approaching the second bank, another voice entered my head, *You know you're about to walk, right?* My inner asshole was trolling me.

I will not start walking! I will not start walking! I repeated to myself as I crossed the halfway point of the last bank.

I started walking.

I basically threw the baton at my roommate, Patricia Hall, who was running second leg, and hoped she'd catch it, because I could not run another step. She got the baton, and I rolled off the track and lay on my back staring at the ceiling, yelling, "beat Arkansas!" with as much effort as I could muster. Pain washed over me in waves as lactic acid devoured my entire body. We beat Arkansas by three tenths of a second for fifth place. I didn't see the finish. I was still passed out near the railing in the infield. I came to when a teammate shook me from my stupor proclaiming we had won the title. We had won our first SEC indoor title, beating Arkansas by 15.5 points. Relieved, I rolled back down to the ground still not able to get my legs under me.

Caryl found me before the awards presentation and was beaming from ear to ear.

"You meant to run 50 point, huh? Girl, nobody told you to come through that first 200 sub 23 seconds!" Caryl said teasingly.

"You said get to the break first!" I said in my defense.

"That you did," she said. "I don't know what to call what happened after that, but you did your job, T-Mad. Let's celebrate with the team!"

Booty lock and all, I went to celebrate my individual long jump title and our team title. Lady Vols for life.

Due to the historic nature of our win, and the drama of it coming down to the 4x400 meter relay, ESPN played footage of the race on *SportsCenter*. Back on campus, I was clowned by everyone, from the bus drivers to the football team, for walking that baton home.

"Ha, ha," I'd say, laughing with them. My team needed me, and I stepped up; I was proud of that. We returned to Fayetteville two weeks later for the NCAA Indoor Championships. I was, again, contesting the 60 and the long jump. The long jump was held on the opening night of championships. I was the only one competing that evening, so the entire team was in attendance to cheer me on.

"Who am I talking to right now? Tianna or Tina?" Caryl asked me with a mischievous twinkle in her eye.

Expanding upright to my full height, all 5 feet 6 inches of me, I looked my coach in the eye and said, "Tina? Nah, I killed that bitch."

Smirking, Caryl began one of her curse-ladened, get-hyped speeches. I looked over at her and said, "I don't need that either."

I was dialed in. We had a plan. Win early. If I jumped big in an early round, I'd "tighten their buttholes," as Caryl would say, and weak-minded jumpers would spend the rest of the competition trying to jump a specific distance rather than execute their best jump. It was a successful outing if I could put the competition away within the first two rounds. From there we'd stay warmed up but pass round by round if the lead was secure. I jumped 6.78—nobody else was even close. My high school rival, Marshevet Hooker, jumped 6.56 for second. With my team squealing with delight, I set the tone for us going into the next day.

My 60-meter preliminary round was so stacked I was thrilled I didn't have to take all six jumps. Marshevet and my teammates, Courtney and Cleo, were all lining up in heat one. And, to make the final, you either had to win the heat outright or have one of the next six fastest times. Doable, I thought. I got lit up in my heat, taking fifth place running 7.29 seconds. Fana Ashby took the win in 7.24; Marshevet in 7.25 who tied with my teammate Courtney Champion; Cleo took sixth behind me running 7.31. Only Fana could breathe easily; the rest of us had to wait for the second heat to run to see where our times stacked up to determine the eighth finalist. Toyin, also my teammate, won her heat with 7.24; with both heat winners running the same time, it was safe to say that nobody was safe. The 7.29 time was the second-place finisher in the second heat. That was the time that I ran for fifth place in my heat. That meant that the four of us who finished behind Fana in the first heat were in the final. Sherri-Ann Brookes and Priscilla Lopes rounded out the final. The Lady Vols would occupy three of the eight lanes available in the final. Later that same day, LaTonya, Courtney, and Cleo would make sure that we had three more Lady Vols in the 200-meter final too.

The following day I found myself standing behind my blocks for the

60-meter final. The meet was televised, so we had to wait for the cameraman to go from lane to lane as the broadcasters announced the lineup. Anxious, and downright scared, I rocked side to side. Priscilla, who was in the lane next to me, was emitting a low growl. I eased a little farther away from her. She began to slap her thighs and face preparing for this intense final.

You can be brave for seven seconds, I said to myself as I loaded into the blocks.

"Set!" The announcer raised the starter gun above his head.

I lowered my eyes. BAM! As soon as it started it was over. We slammed into the crash pads at high velocity at the end of the race and immediately strained our necks to see the jumbotron, which would populate the results as they came in. I had no idea where I placed. I was just running scared. Running for my life. Fana Ashby was the victor running 7.18. Toyin let out a controlled squeak when she saw her name at second. It took a minute for the third-place finisher to appear on the board. But when it did, I could not believe it. Tianna Madison had made the podium in the 60-meter dash at the NCAA championships. Marshevet, the rival who gave me so much grief in high school, took fifth.

Because of my experience running the 4x400 meter relay at conference champs two weeks prior, I tried to make myself invisible after my events were done. I avoided eye contact with the coaches so as not to invite their attention, and I avoided eating in case they did actually need me and I'd have to line up. I'd learned that lesson the hard way at Penn Relays the year before. I thought I was finished for the day and was face deep in a funnel cake when Caryl called and told me to warm up with the relay team. Fighting back vomit, I warmed up the best I could and tried to ready myself to run. Fortunately, I was warming up for a "just in case" scenario and my services were not needed, but lesson learned.

Caryl called my name.

Oh, no, not again! I said to myself, this time taking my time making my way down the bleachers.

"T-Mad, if I put you on this 4x4, you gonna run 22 seconds for the first 200 again?" she asked. I searched her face for the joke but there was none.

"Probably," I said as I shrugged. I didn't know a thing about target times or pacing, I had one gear, "bat outta hell." Okay, two gears, "bat outta hell" and "leisurely walk."

"Go sit down," she said with a smile and shaking her head.

She loved to mess with me. I loved it too. Our 4x400-meter relay team took second which delivered us our first NCAA Indoor Championships title with 46 points, 16 of which were mine.

We didn't win the outdoor conference championships title, but I did. I won the long jump with a 6.92-meter effort at the conference meet at Vanderbilt, in a pit placed inconveniently next to a tree with low hanging branches. Our 4x100-meter relay team took second by just two tenths of a second, and the freshmen squad really held their own. We took third overall and began to prepare for the NCAA regional qualifying meet.

The day before we were set to leave for NCAA regionals by bus, I began to feel sick. I made an appointment to see Dr. Morgan who was often frustrated by how frequently I'd arrange to see her. I was paranoid about my health. All of my grandparents had died relatively young of health issues that ranged from diabetes to strokes. My mother had fought and won her battle with uterine cancer. I had a lump in my breast earlier in the year that turned out to be benign but did major harm to my belief that nothing was actually wrong with me. I booked appointments with an attitude of "it's better to be safe than sorry."

"I have a fever," I told her as she directed me, unnecessarily, into her exam room. I was all too familiar with where it was.

"No, you don't," she said gently picking up her thermometer anyway. I always thought I had a fever—still do actually—and I am constantly checking my temperature.

"Well, I'll be…" She said, voice trailing.

I actually did have a fever, and a bad one. Registering at 102 degrees, she asked me to open my mouth which was difficult for me especially because my throat was so sore. It was hard to drink, and as a result my mouth was dry, my lips were dry, and I was dehydrated.

"You still have your tonsils?" she asked without needing an answer.

She was looking right at my oversized tonsils. My tonsils were the bane of my existence, the cause of my snoring and sleep apnea. She drew away from my face.

"I'll need to take a culture but judging from what I can see you have strep throat. I'll write you a prescription for antibiotics and a drip, you're severely dehydrated."

"I told you," I said as I lay back and rolled to my side, relieved I was in good hands.

Caryl came to see about me, "Well, kid, we gotta do this one, no way around it. I've made calls, told them the situation, and you've gotta qualify for nationals like everyone else, doesn't matter that you're NCAA number one or jumped 6.90 or none of that. Bus leaves at 10 a.m. tomorrow. Be on time."

She rested her slender always perfectly manicured hands on my shoulder, flashed me a compassionate smile, and left me with my thoughts and my IV drip. My stomach began to rumble. The antibiotics, ice chips, electrolyte drinks, and the saline drip were wreaking havoc on my digestive tract.

On time to the bus and feeling miserable, I grabbed my seat and slipped to sleep. My fever was gone, my throat less sore, but those discomforts were replaced with diarrhea. I just could not win, and we were on a bus to Bloomington, Indiana—a six-hour trip. I made it. Not wanting to get any of my teammates sick, I was roomed with our team manager, Marquita. She did an incredible job keeping my spirits high in a shitty situation. Literally.

I was attempting to qualify for nationals in the 100-meter dash, the long jump, and to do my part to help the relay do so by running first leg. First up was the long jump, I opened with a 6.02-meter jump—an indication that I was not feeling well at all. Caryl, worried that I'd miss out on NCAAs because of a poorly timed illness, gave me a pep talk that helped me rally. I jumped 6.52 for my second attempt for the lead. I passed round by round. And with just two jumps, won the region and punched my ticket to the NCAA Outdoor Championships. Feeling much better than I had, I once again, decided to go out on my shield. This isn't the first time I've had to compete sick. I flashed back to one of my high school regional meets where I had to somehow qualify for state my junior year, in all four of my events, with bronchitis and a sinus infection. I didn't win my events that day, settling for the "survive and advance" strategy. I collapsed at the finish line of the 200, my day complete and successful, having qualified in all my events. My parents took me to the hospital directly from the track, where I was put on an IV drip, antibiotics, and nursed back to health. At NCAA regionals it would be more difficult to do "just enough." And so, I readied myself for a performance that would require more energy than I believed I had.

"Stand behind your blocks," a starter said. It's a refrain I know so well but it still always sends a jolt of electric anxiety through my body.

"We here now, don't get scared now…" I mouthed the words to one of my prerace playlist favorites, by Cool Breeze, called, *Watch for the Hook*. I turned my focus inward.

Damn, I did not feel well. I imagined my fever had returned with a vengeance.

"On your marks," the starter raised the starter pistol above his head.

BAM! We took off, and already I was behind. At thirty meters, where Caryl had coached us to transition out of our acceleration phases and go short, I forced my knees and thighs to parallel in front of me. I forced that leg down and ripped the other one up; remember that sprinting is an act of force and violence, not passive aggression. I could feel I was running out of real estate to make up ground, and I tried to find a turbo boost from somewhere to help me run myself back into the mix. That was it. That last 1 percent of effort was more than my body was willing to deal with. I lost control of my limbs and my bowels and shit myself from 60 to 80 meters. I was sprinting as it was happening, and each step got slower and slower, each stride shorter and shorter, as I said, *fuck this race*, and started to plot how I'd get from the finish line to the bathroom to a change of clothes without anyone noticing. I came up with nothing. Out of habit I dipped a bit at the finish line and then proceeded to do the worst possible thing I could do—I sat down.

THE CHAMP IS HERE

I survived regionals and advanced to NCAAs in the long jump and the 4x100-meter relay in Sacramento, California. The first day was long jump qualifying and the first round of the relay. I took one jump, jumping 6.71 meters (22' ¼"). Our relay of Courtney, Toyin, Cleo, and me, won our heat and qualified for the final with the second fastest time overall. The following day, I won the long jump to take my first NCAA Outdoor Championship title. Our relay took third in the final, but my long jump victory capped the end of an incredible collegiate season with championship titles from SEC indoor and outdoor championships, and national titles from both the indoor and outdoor seasons too.

All year long I believed that Caryl kept me from competing on the World Junior Team that went to Grosseto, Italy, as punishment for choking at NCAAs two weeks before. Stepping onto the track at The Home Depot Center in Carson, California, for USATF Nationals, I understood. I was unfazed, unbothered, and unafraid of the competition. My "been there done that" attitude allowed me to focus on the things I needed to execute to jump well rather than get caught up in the emotion of the meet and what it represented. Like nationals the year before, this national championship was also a qualifier for Team USA, this time for World Championships in Helsinki, Finland.

I entered the meet with the confidence that being undefeated all year provided me. Grace Upshaw and I battled to the final round. I'd lose the war. We both jumped 6.70 meters (21' 11¾") but when jumpers tie the winner is decided by the longer of the second longest jumps. Grace's second-best jump was 6.60, mine 6.58. Shocked as if I had never experienced losing before I had to be reminded that I'd just made my first senior team. I'd be going to the World Championships! DeeDee made the team too and together we would head to Europe for a tune up, meet in Stockholm, Sweden, training camp, and the World Championships.

I did not want to go in my college uniform. I felt like romping around in my collegiate kit made me an easy mark for the professionals I'd be competing against. I wasn't professional but I wanted to look it. We got permission from the athletic department to suit me in Adidas, our school's sponsor. DeeDee gave me pieces from her closet to wear.

We arrived at Stockholm Arlanda Airport and took the Arlanda express, a rapid train, to the city centre. The Nordic Sea Hotel where we'd be staying was less than 50 meters away from the train station. Coach J.J. Clark, our head coach, had also travelled to Europe with his mid-distance runner, Kameisha Bennett, who had made the world team in the 800-meter run. He gathered us together in the lobby before we went to our rooms.

"Don't go to sleep," he said. "Go upstairs, get settled, but then come back downstairs, get some sun, go for a walk. Do anything but sleep."

We all nodded in agreement. I fully intended to honor his advice, but the pull of sleep was too strong. *I'll just nap for a bit*, I thought as I closed my eyes for a nap. When I opened my eyes, I saw that it was still daylight, so I put on my shoes and headed out to do my walk and have an early dinner—pleased with myself that I had accomplished both things. I did not notice the lobby clocks. Had I, I would have known that it was actually 10 p.m. I spent my first night in Stockholm wide awake and so hungry I ran through my entire stockpile of snacks that I brought with me.

I lost in Stockholm too, and I was beginning to understand that this level was way higher up than the collegiate one. I was worried that I was going to embarrass myself at World Championships. If I couldn't even win a smaller international meet, how the hell was I supposed to win worlds? I decided that in the couple weeks between the Stockholm meet and World Championships, while we were in training camp at a national training center in Boson, just a short drive outside of the city, I'd buckle down, tighten up, and really prepare for the championships.

We weren't the only athletes there. DeeDee and I were joined by Bershawn "Batman" Jackson and his coach, George, and Walter Davis. My curiosity got the better of me, and between training sessions, I explored every square meter of the training center. I followed one long unmarked tunnel to its end and ended up in heaven—an expansive space with a full-sized boxing ring, rows of suspended heavy bags, and speed bags mounted too high for me to reach. Every day I found a new space to explore on my own, after training sessions. I enjoyed being at the training center so much that I had almost forgotten about the championships looming over us.

The moment we arrived at the Athlete's Village in Helsinki, I knew the game had changed. Team USA had booked the entire Hilton, and DeeDee and I were roommates. The cafeteria, where we could eat for free, was located up a hill from the hotel. Too lazy to make the trip, we spent our money ordering from the hotel restaurant. The food there was expensive, but every day they had an entree for ten euros. Every day we ordered whatever was ten euros. One day, after my money had run low, I made the trek to the cafeteria. Mark Jelks and Miles Smith, two runners I knew from the collegiate scene, were seated at a table. I pulled up a seat and sat down. They were making table beats, rapping, and singing together. Miles started to sing an Erykah Badu song from her album *Mama's Gun*.

I jumped in, "Myyyyyyyy eyyyyyeeeeessss are greeeeeeeennnnn, cause I eats a lot of vegetables, it don't have nuthin' to dooooo with your new frieeennnd."

"Oh shit!" Miles said, pressing his fist to his mouth before creating a beat with it on the table. "Keep going!"

I took a deep breath and belted out the rest of the verse. We sat for another hour making beats, rapping, and singing snippets of songs when Mark suggested we go to the athletes' lounge. I had no idea there was one; it was as if a whole new world was up the hill from the hotel. Just like at the training center in Boson, I had found ways to occupy myself without obsessing over the meet. The lounge had loveseats, couches, Xboxes, table tennis, foosball, and snacks. Every day, until the day before competition, I met my group of friends after training for playtime.

Qualification day came, and the weather was absolutely beautiful. The mark to hit was 6.65 for automatic qualification to the final. I wasn't sure my legs had it in them, but I was going to get the mark or die trying. I was worried for nothing. I jumped 6.83 meters, a personal best and the farthest jump by over 20 centimeters. I was going into my first World Championship final ranked first.

I could not sleep. I was scared to death. I was afraid of the Russians. I didn't know anything about doping and I kept imagining my competitors injecting performance enhancing drugs into wherever in order to beat my ass the following day. Eventually I fell asleep, I woke the next morning to the worst possible weather. The weather on the day of qualifying was perfect, 70 degrees and sunny. The weather the day of the final was 40 degrees and rainy. Helsinki was looking a lot like Ohio—a state where it was possible to have all four seasons in the same day.

Oh, well, I thought. I added extra clothes to my bag, and extra gel to my hair. It was just rain; I wasn't going to melt. Warming up is hard to do in the rain, so it's important to have on more layers than you'd like. The officials walked us to the tunnel and into the stadium. I wore a band around my ankle with the bible verse Philippians 4:6-7 embossed in it. "Be anxious for nothing, but in every situation, by prayer and petition with thanksgiving, present your requests to God. And the peace of God, which transcends all understanding, will guard your hearts and minds in Christ Jesus."

I opened the competition with a first-round foul. Some jumpers freak out opening competitions that way. For me, with the speed that I use on the runway, opening with a foul gives my coach a chance to make the necessary adjustments early in the competition. That frees me to go for it on each subsequent round. I had three attempts to make a jump long enough to get me three more attempts. That was the plan. My second-round jump was 6.69 meters. Better, much better. I was losing control of my emotions; I was in the mix. Judging from the body language of my fellow competitors, I could tell that the weather had thrown a lot of them off their game. But me? I was from Ohio; I was used to it. I could feel excitement rising, and on my third jump started *trying* to jump far. That never works. I jumped 6.35 meters Tatyana Kotova of Russia jumped 6.79 meters. Humbled by that wack-ass attempt of a jump, I calmed myself and waited for the official to reorder us. After the first three rounds, the top eight jumpers are ranked in descending order. The leader, Russia's Tatyana Kotova, would jump last. I was sitting in second place going into the fourth round. I fouled again. France's Eunice Barber jumped 6.70 meters to take over second and pushed me into third place. I had nothing to lose and everything to gain out there battling women 10 years older than me. None of them even knew my name. I stood on the runway for my fifth round. I took a deep breath, looked down at my ankle, recited Jeremiah 29:11 to myself, "For I know the plans that I have for you…" and Philippians 4:13 "I can do all things through Christ…" before I started my approach.

There was a yellow plastic marker in the sand that indicated the leading jump, which was Tatyana's last attempt. I told myself that whatever happened I would not drop my legs until I was beyond that marker. I didn't care how I did it or how ugly it was, I was going to use speed, power, and core strength to snatch this title. I jumped 6.89 meters to take the lead by ten centimeters. Tatyana answered with a 6.59-meter jump; Eunice fouled. There was only one round left, and I was leading. Eunice jumped 6.76 meters and into third place. It was my turn. I fouled. Now I had to wait for Tatyana to jump. Although I'd be leaving with no less than a silver medal, waiting for that final jump was one of the most painstaking experiences I had ever had. Time slowed and bent, collapsing in on itself, as I fought off an anxiety attack. Tatyana jumped 6.53m.

I was the new World Champion!

Team USA staffers thought I was such a long shot that they weren't in position to hand me an American flag for my victory lap. I started my lap with both hands in the air waving to fans who had braved the weather and were cheering me on.

"Tianna! Tianna!" I heard a person yell as I jogged closer to the rail to give a couple kids a high five. "Here!" A fan, who had travelled from the US threw me their flag. "Take it; way to go, Champ!"

Moved to tears, I finished my victory lap and the end of an amazing season.

BETWEEN THE EARS, BEHIND THE SCENES

Just 48 hours before earlier, Caryl was visiting my hotel room which I shared with another Lady Vol, DeeDee Trotter. Caryl was brushing DeeDee's hair, and while DeeDee was purring with pleasure, Caryl was speaking to her in gentle motherly tones about how much her life would change after she won the 400-meter title. Sitting across from them and witnessing this exchange, I hesitantly hopped into the conversation, wishing for the same sort of assurance.

"What do you think will happen when I win?" I asked.

Caryl looked up from behind DeeDee's head. "Well, you won't. But you can take out as many bitches as you can."

She went back to brushing DeeDee's hair, and I returned to my books, boiling with anger.

I was angry about everything at this point: angry at my parents for not making the trip to the biggest meet of my life; angry that, as soon as I boarded my flight overseas, the guy I was dating had a new girlfriend (I mean FaceBook profile pic and dating status changed instantly); angry at Caryl for not even bothering to lie to me about the chances I had of winning; angry at J.J. for thinking everybody was always only thinking about sex.

I decided that I was going to win—as an NCAA athlete, and that if I couldn't take home the $60,000 prize money—no one would. I was going to be the spoiler and ruin the experience for everybody. And by everybody, I meant everybody—including Caryl.

Once she got me on the long jump board, (It's my job to run, it's the coach's job to get me on the board—more on that later.) I stopped talking to her completely. She would yell for me to come over and talk to her between jumps—you know, so she could coach. But I hold grudges and since she said to me, "You won't win..." I had nothing to say to her.

Let me "not win" on my own, then.

Obviously, I had other plans. I have always been a student of my sport, have always been competitive, and have literally been fighting to prove myself since I was two-and-a-half years old. I knew these women were worried about the weather, less than 50 degrees and rainy. I'm from Ohio. I'm good.

I knew I was faster than all of the other jumpers, and I had the will and determination to hold my legs up for as long as I needed to, to bypass the leading jump. Back then, they placed a marker in the sand for where the leading jump was. My plan was this: run as fast as possible, takeoff, and don't land until I was past the marker.

I walked calmly back to my Team USA duffle bag and put my clothes on. Caryl could be seen on the jumbotron screaming my name. I ignored her. I waited for the other two jumpers, Tatyana Kotova and Eunice Barber, to make their last attempts. They came up short, and I jogged over to my coach and gave her the obligatory "we did it" hug. I listened to her tell me how she knew I could do it, and I remember my body tensing as the words hit my ears. She was crying; I was furious. She asked if I felt anything, if I needed to cry. I tried to conjure up some tears, but the only feeling I had was anger. A seemingly endless well of anger, about everything. But I knew what I was supposed to do, for the cameras, for the Team, for the other Americans in attendance.

Thank you, to whomever that cameraman was, because that was the first time in days my anger dissipated. I actually enjoyed the lap after that. I enjoyed going to "hair and makeup" to get ready for the podium, and I loved singing the national anthem with the entire stadium looking on. In that moment, no one was better than me. For a short period of time, no one would be able to tell me how I was a disappointment, or that I fell short. In that moment, none of those things were true.

And that feeling is like a drug—one can chase that high for a lifetime. But my coaches successfully blew that high by cutting the celebrations short with their "business" Skype call to my parents.

Coach Clark called my parents on Skype. They had been following the results online but didn't make the trip to Finland themselves. I talked to them briefly, listened to them tell me how proud they were, and then J.J. got back in front of the computer screen with a face that said, "Celebration is over—time to talk business."

He explained to all of us that this victory would open the door to shoe companies who would try to woo me out of the collegiate system with sponsorship deals—we should be ready.

All medalists got a celebration ceremony upon their return to the village. Staff and teammates alike popped champagne and toasted the medalists. Perhaps they would have had sparkling juice for me because I was not of legal drinking age under US law. But I would never find out. Why? Because my coaches didn't allow me to go back to the village after my victory. Instead, Caryl and I stopped at a McDonald's where I ordered french fries (only after I had successfully argued that I had earned them), and then joined Coach J.J.

Clark at his hotel. He was adamant my new World Champion status would make me the target of sexual advances and attention I would not be able to manage. He was more comfortable with my staying with them until things "calmed down."

Hell, calm down! No! I was ready. I was pissed, actually. I dug deep to win a World Championship title and instead of enjoying it, I had to sit in a room and get lectured about not getting pregnant and the pros and cons of entertaining potential future sponsorship opportunities.

In short, J.J. wanted to—needed to—know if I was going to "go pro" now, or if I was going to stay in the college program, to learn more as both a student and an athlete, and graduate. The correct answer was to say, "I'll stay in school and on the team." What I was actually thinking was: *People go to college to give themselves the best opportunity to get a job that pays well. As a professional athlete, I would be taking home the $60,000 prize money—a year's salary for the luckiest graduates—for two days' work. That doesn't even include what a shoe company might offer me. I think my job here is done.*

I think it was my mother who asked when the prize money was actually distributed. The answer was sometime in late December, early January; that meant I could actually return to school as a Lady Vol for the fall semester, and I wouldn't have to give up my eligibility or the money because the money wouldn't have been disbursed yet. We would revisit the question over winter break.

We returned to Knoxville. My family waited in the baggage claim area with my picture airbrushed on white T-shirts and homemade posters. I was shocked, not that they were there, but mostly at the airbrushed tees because, I mean…I thought only family reunion attendees and gang members wore airbrushed T-shirts—and even then, only for their fallen.

Fall semester started shortly after that, and I was B.D.O.C. (Big Dog On Campus). There are certain types of people who would probably flourish in this environment—not me. I had anxiety attacks regularly. On the T, which is the campus transportation network, I would feel claustrophobic and by the time the bus transported me to class I was moments from passing out.

News of my not "going pro" spread quickly throughout the NCAA system, and it wasn't long before *Sports Illustrated - On Campus Edition* came knocking. We were told that the magazine was doing a feature of all the top returning collegiate athletes and that, as reigning World Champion, I was one of them. They arranged a photo shoot, and I put on my one-piece Lady Vol uniform and stood in lane four holding various poses and fake smiles until they "got the shot." I need to confess that, at the time, I thought being a model was my fantasy/dream job. I always want to feel beautiful, and I want pictures of myself feeling and looking beautiful. HOWEVER, I am incredibly uncomfortable when there is actually another person behind the camera. This *Sports Illustrated* photo shoot, sadly, helped me come to terms with the fact that I'd never model. Weeks later, the magazine came out. Instead of it featuring a piece titled, "Top Returning Collegiate Athletes," I flipped open to the main headline that read, "The A-list." The article really was a piece about returning athletes, but with a twist. There, at the bottom half of the page was my picture and the headline: "Female Hottie of the Year."

What?!!

All over the country, people saw that headline—people who didn't know me at all. Their first impression of me was going to be *this?*

It wasn't just the strangers I was worried about; the dynamics on my team changed too. They no longer knew how to treat me. *Was I one of them? Was I more elite than them? Was I going to leave them?* Their solution was to keep me at arm's length or to ask me for money, which I gladly gave. Money can't buy you love, but I damn sure was trying to rent it.

The horrible thing about all this—that no one had any way of knowing—was that publishing my accomplishments in this way inadvertently made me, a prior victim of sexual assault, a sex symbol. The fishbowl that was Knoxville's UT campus became suffocating, my support group unstable, and my future there uncertain.

I won the world title but felt like I had lost everything else.

The intensity of competing and winning an elite international competition is unparalleled, and college athletics completely lost its luster for me. I would sit in team meetings listening to the coach trying to get us jacked up for the upcoming season—for the defense of the Southeastern Conference championship title. I remember sitting in those meetings trying not to die of boredom and registering how unmoved I was by the idea of another college meet. By the time we broke for winter break, I knew my time was over as a Lady Vol.

My decision was met with mixed feelings. My parents were thrilled with the news; my coaches, not so much. Counting the lost points, Coach Clark, in not so many words, accused me of being selfish for putting money before the team. Caryl, who coached me to this situation was proud of herself for taking yet another athlete and coaching them to elite status. But the transition was rocky.

I signed with Nike, but the University of Tennessee was an ADIDAS-sponsored school—issue number one. We had to figure out a way for me to neither violate my contract or the school's rules, in order to train at the facilities. The solution was that I had to buy an entire wardrobe of label-less UT merchandise to train in while I was indoors in the gym or training room.

Issue number two was that my coach now needed a professional coaching contract in order to continue training me. She presented me with a contract for a yearly salary and a bonus schedule of incentives that included designer bags and sunglasses. To say I was taken aback by that whole conversation is an understatement. I had zero guidance concerning the business side of track and field, and DeeDee, who had gone through this process herself two years before, was unavailable to me. Our relationship had become strained to the point where it was more preferable to disengage.

Issue number three was that I was no longer allowed to train with the team; it was said to be an NCAA violation at the time for a professional athlete to train with collegiate athletes. So not only was I isolated emotionally, but I became isolated physically.

FROM RUSSIA, WITH LOVE

We didn't have time for all that bullshit though. I qualified for the USA team that would be headed to the IAAF Indoor World Championships in Moscow, Russia. I was dreading going to Russia. My mom told me an "over-dramatized" version (if that's even possible) of the beat down Rocky took from the Russian in Rocky IV. Tatyana was going to be out for blood, and the emotional roller coaster I had been on for the last few months was not conducive to going to battle with her. But I wasn't going to back down, I never do—not since my sophomore year in high school.

Caryl couldn't travel to Russia with me; she had the team to take care of. So, we made arrangements for my jumps coach Charlie Simpkins to join me. I paid for his passport (which he had let expire years before), Russian visa, plane tickets, and his hotel accommodations at The Cosmos. Everything and anything he needed I was willing to provide for him so that I wouldn't have to travel alone; but at the last possible minute he backed out. I never learned why. I really needed help though. I couldn't do an event as technical as the long jump without an extra pair of eyes. So, I scrambled and arranged for my dad to come be the eyes I needed. We got his visa within 24 hours, and he was on a plane within 72. I met him in the expansive yet dark lobby of The Cosmos Hotel. His smile warmed me and melted some of my anxiety; I gave him a big hug and gave him the rundown.

"Make sure you use an adapter for your electronics, or you'll blow them up, okay?"

He was proud of his portable DVD player that kept him entertained on the flight and would help him pass the time here in Moscow.

"And the US Embassy guy who came and talked to us earlier today said most of the pretty women here are actually prostitutes, so be careful. I've seen them, and he wasn't lying. They are beautiful."

I don't know why I was telling him as if he wasn't happily married, but I did. I asked him what he wanted to do first. He said he was going to go to his room, let Mom know he arrived in one piece and that he saw me, and then take a nap. I gave him another hug and told him I'd see him later. Before we parted, one of my teammates handed me a calling card and their cell phone.

"I got you," I said. "Just give me a few minutes."

"What you got there?" Dad asked.

"It's a calling card with minutes we're loading on to our phones so that we can text or call home without blowing up the phone bill," I answered. My dad's eyebrow raised in curiosity as he was headed upstairs to call my mother straight up, but now thought about doing it with a prepaid card.

"Let me see," he said as he took the calling card in his hand and flipped it over. "T, it's in Russian. How are you…?"

I interrupted him, "I don't know why, and I don't know how, but last night I stared at my own prepaid card for an hour and suddenly I understood it. I didn't believe it either, but here's my phone, and it has minutes. My teammates didn't believe it either until they started bringing me their phones too. I only needed to figure it out the one time as long as the card was from the same company. It was easy."

We both shrugged at the impossibility of it all. Dad took his leave, and I loaded the minutes on my teammate's phone and went back to my own room to watch *Sex and the City*, an HBO television show, on my laptop. Chuck put me on it; it was one of his favorite shows and if we were together on any given evening, we'd watch back-to-back episodes over Papa John's pizza, with him explaining and imploring me to pay attention the entire time. He gave me the nickname "Ms. Bradshaw" because, like it or not, I was very similar to the show's main protagonist, Carrie Bradshaw, a prodigious writer who was very unlucky in love.

Several hours later I wandered back down to the lobby in search of food. Almost immediately, I spotted my dad at the bar surrounded by beautiful women. I smiled to myself; the man was a magnet. He could make a friend anywhere, hold a conversation with anyone, and know at least one person from "way back" anywhere in the world. Not at all worried that he'd solicit one of them, I pulled him away from the bar and to dinner with me—you know, optics. We took our pre-meet meal together. Tomorrow we would begin our campaign to be named indoor world champion.

I desperately wanted to have a good showing there. I won the World Championships just several months before with the shortest distance ever. In fact, the broadcasters called my form ugly and declared it a fluke. I was determined to prove them wrong.

I was well on my way to proving them right. The meet was nearly disastrous. I could not get on the board. My father and I were on two different pages, using two different vocabularies.

At one point, he even said, "Just like high school."

And I remember walking back to my track bag, to grab my sweatpants, thinking, "We're a long freaking way from high school, Pops."

Again, I found myself outside of medal contention with just one jump left.

I was having a complete mental breakdown. The emotions, the frustration, and the anger that I had towards my transition and how tumultuous it was; the disappointment I felt in seeing money become the only glue holding most of my relationships together; all burst to the surface. On my last attempt, I stood on the long jump runway with tears pouring down my face. I was embarrassed, not because of the tears but because I was the *reigning* Outdoor World Champion. There were so many people that had doubts about me. And I was proving them right.

I lined up at my mark. I wiped the last few tears from my face and initiated my approach with all the fury that I was feeling. I went from fifth to second. I took home the silver medal. Tatyana took gold in front of her home crowd.

After returning from Moscow, I called my agent, John Nubani and told him about the experience. I whined about Coach Simpkins pulling out at the last minute, and how hard it was to perform at the meet with none of the coaches who worked with me every day. I thought a change of coach was the solution, and so did Nike. They paid for my move to Los Angeles. I called my parents who helped load a moving truck with my things. I drove my pride and joy GMC Envoy Denali, a mid-sized black on black SUV that I purchased myself with my Nike signing bonus, back to Ohio for a while until I could arrange transport to LA. Nike had arranged for me to join Bobby Kersee and his group. Emotional, disappointed, and frustrated, I boarded a flight to LA with a single duffle bag and a lot of hope.

As a long jumper, this was like a dream scenario. I was thinking that I'd have access to Jackie Joyner Kersee, as well, and she could tell me how to jump even farther. But when I cornered her one evening, while visiting St. Louis, I asked her for her best advice on jumping far and she told me—with a straight face, no less—that the key to jumping far is......drumroll please...... stretching.

Stretching? Was she serious? That was the first and last time I asked her anything about the long jump.

I arrived in Los Angeles just in time to make it to practice. I dropped my duffle bag off at a dumpy motel in Westwood and walked to practice. Bobby told me to warmup, and so he watched me do Caryl's active dynamic warmup.

"Whoa, Tianna, jog a few laps first before you start banging it out like that!"

"Me? Jog. I've never jogged. I don't jog."

"Jog two laps."

"Okay."

I absolutely hate to jog. It is an unbearable limbo between walking and running. I'd rather do one or the other but never settle in the middle. For this reason, my jog is more like a shuffle; it's probably slower than if I'd just stop and walk.

So, I finished the two laps and then did my active dynamic warmup. I saw Allyson Felix, Joanna Hayes, and Michelle Perry stretching (another thing I had never done) so I added a few stretches in myself.

"Okay, you've got six 300s. We'll just ease you into the program for now," Bobby Kersee said.

I looked at Bobby like, "You're joking right?"

At this point in my career, the farthest I ever ran in training was 250 meters. It was a time trial, and I only had to do it once. ONE. TIME. He wasn't joking, though. So, I got on the line and started running. I hated every second of the workout but when I was done, exhausted as I was, I was grateful for the change of scenery and atmosphere. It was obvious I needed a change because just two weeks after arriving in Los Angeles I returned to Indiana for USATF Nationals, and I jumped a season's best. Things were looking up.

SHADE IN THE CITY OF LIGHT

With two medals under my belt, I had quite a few jump meets lined up. There were two meets, in particular, that I was looking forward to: DécaNations in France, which is basically a tag team decathlon, and a meet in Russia where they were going to pay me a handsome appearance fee. Before DécaNations, we had another small Team USA event in England. I was feeling pretty good—hitting full approaches and pop ups with confidence and spring. I was feeling so good that I decided to do one more.

That last jump would turn out to be a mistake.

I popped off the takeoff board, holding my "wonder woman" position in the air, but I landed in the pit on a straight leg, which most jumpers do when they run off of a pop up, except this time my leg didn't cycle forward so that I could run out of the pit. My leg stayed straight, got lodged deeply in the sand, and the force of impact bent my knee backwards.

I knew it was bad.

I had a toddler moment. You know, when they fall down and they look around and gauge the reaction of the people around them in order to determine how they themselves should respond. I locked eyes with Wallace Spearmon.

"Ay, you're good T. Walk it off," he said.

So that's exactly what I did, and exactly what I continued to do for the rest of the season. I ignored the swelling, the fact that it wasn't consistently weight bearing, and that my patella was broken, and my meniscus cartilage was shredded. I took one for the team by jumping in the competition the following day, my knee in a compression wrap, and my body full of ibuprofen.

DécaNations was in Paris, France, that year and my mom decided to come. She had always wanted to visit Paris, and this was a good reason to do so. She booked her own flight and hotel accommodations. Loved ones at international competitions give me anxiety. Not performance anxiety but anxiety about flights, delays, lost luggage, transportation, the language barriers, the who's, what's, when's, where's, and why's. To put it plainly, I worried about them. I'd wait anxiously with cell phone in hand for word that all was well. I decided to walk the streets to distract myself in the City of Light. I was lost in a daydream about Carrie and Mr. Big in Paris when I ran into my mother on the street. "MOM!" I shouted. She turned slowly, like a ballerina executing a slow pirouette; she would never not be a dancer.

"Oh, hey, T!" she said casually.

"Hey," I said back. Before she left the States, I had told her to either meet me at my hotel or send me a message when she arrived, but she hadn't. It turned out that my mother's luggage had been lost, and so she took her rest and waited for word on its ETA at her hotel. There we were as if strangers meeting by chance on the streets of Paris. I waited with her while she purchased her croissant which she ordered in French. Impressed, I allowed myself to be open to the possibility that she and I together in Paris could be a wonderful time.

I suggested we go to Disneyland Paris together. I mean, a lot of our best family memories are from Disney World, so I was really lobbying for this. This felt like a for sure way for us to create good memories together. She reminded me that I had a meet the following day and probably shouldn't do that much walking, so we settled on visiting the Eiffel Tower instead.

In the shadow of the tower, young break dancers battled each other—music blaring on beat up boomboxes. I worked overtime trying to encourage my mother to jump in the circle and bust a move. My mother can dance, like really dance. I argued that, because she was far from home and no one knew her, she could let her hair down and because she could actually dance (unlike me), there was no way the experience would leave her embarrassed. She hit the robot for a few moments but called it quits. We headed to the elevators of the tower. We were going to the top of the tower to look out over the City of Light and Notre Dame and contemplate our mortality. But on the way up one of the passengers farted.

In.

The.

Elevator.

I'm claustrophobic. I was already doing some deep yogic breathing to keep my nerves calm as they packed us into that ancient elevator like cattle. But the stench, the pungent smell of digesting cheeses, croissants, and champagne was just too much for me. I looked around the elevator accusingly.

No one wanted to make eye contact.

My mind was racing.

We've got like 30 more floors to go. There's not enough fresh oxygen. I'm going to die. I'm running out of air. Oh, my God, I can't breathe. I need to get out of this elevator.

"Let me out of this elevator! I need to get off! NOW!" I half shouted towards the ceiling of the elevator car. We got off at the next stop, but my mom still wanted to go to the top. So, we took the stairs, all one million of them (I'm exaggerating), the day before the competition. Disneyland in hindsight, really wouldn't have been such a bad idea.

I invited my mom to be my guest at a team dinner we had the night before the competition began after we shared a cab back to the team hotel with some teammates. We stopped for a red light in front of a dress shop. The storefront looked exactly like one would imagine a French designer's storefront would look. Sparsely populated, well lit, with pieces that were so over the top that they were high fashion. Every item was framed and staged so perfectly that you felt like you had to buy the entire ensemble, including the mannequins and the furniture, in order to pull off the look. The display featured a beautiful white ballroom wedding gown. There may have been other dresses in the display, but my eyes were fixed on this one. Above the chatter of my teammates in the car, I expressed my love for the dress. "When I get married, it will definitely be in a dress like THAT!" and I pointed to the beautiful pearly white work of art through the taxi's window. My teammates grew quiet to admire the couture.

"Then you must be referring to that black one," my mother said.

Immediately everyone's eyes dropped to the floor. Someone muttered "damn" under their breath, and I sat back in my seat, my head resting against the worn leather, wondering why I still had the audacity to hope that these sorts of things would stop happening between us.

THE WAY THINGS WERE

I remember my mom walking me to my first day of Kindergarten. With my little sister in tow, I bounced happily along the paved trail that ran alongside the huge grass field and playground. We stopped at the back of the school building to take the obligatory first-day-of-school picture. I was only going to be gone for half a day. I was registered for Mrs. Brown's afternoon class. I wore a knee-length dress, and my hair was done neatly in a dozen braided ponytails accented with barrettes on each end (I wouldn't come home with any of them). It wasn't going to be my first time in a classroom-like setting, having spent a good amount of time in day care at Abundant Life. I loved to learn, and my capacity for curiosity was limitless.

I stepped into my new classroom and looked around. It was so colorful and bright. There were small chairs, and small tables, and each seat had a name tag. I located my name. My mom shooed me on, and that day I began my lifelong love affair with learning. That is, until Mrs. Brown called for a parent-teacher meeting to discuss my unacceptably bad behavior.

My mother, the head manager of a bank, did not appreciate being called out of work for any reason not life or death. But here she was, black pumps echoing on freshly waxed floors in the now empty hallways of Windsor Elementary.

"Mrs. Brown," my mom said, a greeting that served to acknowledge one's presence, but didn't give any inclination that the meeting would be a pleasant one.

"Please, have a seat, Mrs. Madison." Mrs. Brown gestured toward an adult-sized chair.

They sat.

"Why am I here today?" my mother asked.

Mrs. Brown explained that she thought I should be tested for attention deficit hyperactivity disorder, and perhaps, according to her, be prescribed Ritalin as a solution, if her hunch turned out to be correct.

My mother took in Mrs. Brown's face slowly and solemnly, with the same intent focus of an artist ready to sketch her subject on canvas.

"And why," she began to ask, "or what, I should say, has given you reason to believe that my daughter needs to be medicated?"

Mrs. Brown, finally recognizing the precarious position she was in, began to excitedly explain.

"Every day during the lesson, Tianna gets up out of her seat, and starts to play, either with the toys at the back of the room or in the playhouse."

My mom looked at me. But Mrs. Brown wasn't lying, so I remained seated and quiet.

"It's disruptive to the class," Mrs. Brown continued, "not to mention, she's not paying attention and so she isn't learning. She may need to repeat kindergarten if this continues."

My mom spoke again, "Speaking of learning, may I see what it is they are learning?"

Mrs. Brown happily pushed her seat away as she stood and reached for a book and a pile of worksheets that she then offered to my mother. My mother flipped page after page in silence before looking up and meeting Mrs. Brown's eyes.

"Have you asked Tianna why she keeps getting up?"

A strange look rippled across Mrs. Brown's face, almost as if it had never occurred to her that she could ask a four-year-old about her own behavior.

My mother didn't wait for Mrs. Brown to answer before she spoke again.

"It's highly likely, Mrs. Brown, that my daughter gets up every day because she is bored. You have here alphabet tracing activities. Did you not notice that Tianna can already read?"

I'd once again taken up residence in the playhouse. This specific conversation between adults was much too boring for me, and I also recognized one of the looks my mother gave Mrs. Brown, and it wouldn't be too much longer before someone got in trouble if this kept up—I didn't want it to be me.

"She can read," Mrs. Brown repeated as a statement more than a question.

"Yes," my mother replied, "and count to 100, and to ten in Spanish as well. My daughter is bored in your class and perhaps rather than recommend medication for her, a child whom you've clearly made no effort to understand, I suggest you find a way to challenge her."

She then proceeded to tell Mrs. Brown that their meeting was over and that she'd make the principle aware of the conversation and go from there. She stood and extended her hand to be courteous, wished Mrs. Brown a good evening, and with her hand on my back, she hurried me out the door.

I remained in kindergarten in Mrs. Brown's afternoon class, but whenever the lesson was related to reading or writing, I waited for a hall escort to fetch me and take me to a first grade class. My parents felt that being four years old in Kindergarten was manageable. Being four years old in the first grade, not so much. Being two years behind my six-year-old peers would not be easy on me socially. So, instead of getting up to entertain myself with toys in the playhouse, I got up and skipped down the hall to Mrs. Williams's first grade class.

It would be five years before I got myself in trouble again at Windsor Elementary School. This time for failing my fourth-grade math class.

Mrs. P. gave us a four-question quiz every week. And every week I'd get either one or two of the questions wrong. Ironically, I knew (because I could do the math) missing just one question of four means you got a C, missing two…well, you failed. Week after week after week, this was my reality.

This week was different. This week, Mrs. P. handed out progress reports. And now, what was once a loose mental inventory of all the C's and F's I'd earned over the last several weeks were now documented and staring me right in the face. To make matters worse, if they even could be at that point, in the top right corner was bright red ink that stamped the words "Sign and Return" on my progress report. I knew what this meant. This meant that one of my parents (and trust me I knew just the one) was going to have to look at this report, and then affix their signature to it, and then I'd have to return it to Mrs. P. so that she would know that my parents know that I'm failing her class.

It ruined my day.

I couldn't even eat my bagged lunch.

By the end of the school day, I had come up with a rough plan as to how I would handle this problem of the progress report. My solution was to ask my dad. My dad, Bobby to his friends and family, worked long hours at Nordson Corporation. By the end of his workday he'd typically collapse, slouched on the couch in the den in front of the television, one hand inside his waist band.

That type of exhaustion makes a person agreeable. I know this because my little sister and I became infatuated with the idea of bangs. But we weren't so crazy as to proceed without permission, and so, we approached my slumbering father and asked him if we could cut bangs.

"What?" he said sleepily.

"Can we cut bangs!?" we asked in unison with so much excitement and energy it short-circuited my father.

"Yeah, yeah, go 'head" he said without even opening his eyes. We scrambled out of the den hurrying to act before he came to realize what he'd actually given his permission for.

We cut bangs.

Then wished we hadn't.

But we technically had had permission and therefore were shielded from the full wrath of our mother. The lesson was this, dad agrees to most things when he's sleepy.

So, on this day, my dad was right where I'd thought he'd be.

With my progress report and a pen in hand, I said, "Will you sign this?" Groggily, he asked what it was. "It's a progress report," I said.

"Everyone got one." True.

"But they have to be signed and returned." Misleading.

"Everyone's does." Lie.

Only the students failing the class needed their progress reports to be signed and returned. I know that, but my parents don't because, until now, they've never had to worry about me failing anything.

My dad's eyes opened so suddenly, I jumped back. I wasn't prepared for him to awaken! I pressed on. I all but shoved the progress report and pen in his face.

"Nah…" he said, hesitantly, seeing but not reading the progress report. "This sounds like something for your mom."

Damn. Here I am failing at this too. I made my trek up the stairs from the den with great difficulty.

My mom was at the table doing the household budget. I intuited that this was probably the WORST time to have to ask for anything; she was looking at the money that's going out and the always disappointingly short amount of money coming in, and that funk just cast an air of heaviness over the entire home. But this progress report needed to be returned the next day.

I had to woman up.

I wasn't sure who I was more afraid of, my mother or my teacher. That was, in fact, the issue; I'm not dumb, I am book smart. I can pick up and retain most anything. But my math teacher scared the crap out of me, so if there was something I truly did not understand, I was not at all interested in raising my hand to ask. Hence the poor grades. I decided I was more afraid of my teacher, so I approached my mother as one would a solitary animal foraging around the base of a tree in an otherwise tranquil forest.

No sudden movements.

No loud noises.

Just enough noise from my sweaty feet squeaking on the linoleum kitchen tiles to alert her of my presence. To declare that she need not be alarmed, and to demonstrate that I've arrived in peace.

She turned around slowly. Extremely slowly. Her neck extended, shoulders relaxed, she moved gracefully, a throwback to her past life as a dancer and choreographer. The deliberate slowness of her movements in acknowledgement of my presence was in actuality an admonishment for the interruption. I took a hesitant step forward and whipped the progress report from behind my back and into her face as if it were on fire and I had to get rid of it quickly.

"I need this signed. I have to return it tomorrow."

"Why, what is it?" she asked.

I need to say that her suspicion of me needing her signature was warranted as I had previously attempted and failed to forge her signature on a permission slip that she forgot to sign for a field trip to NASA. I was not going to be the one kid missing out on NASA, I mean come on.

"It's a progress report for math class." True.

"Everybody got one." Also true.

"They all need to be signed and returned." Lie.

"Let me see it," she demanded.

Damn.

I could see the range of emotions **ripple** across her face as she took in the information in front of her. Line after line of pop quizzes, tests, and homework assignments with C's, D's, and F's accompanying them.

Her hand dropped to her lap with the progress report gripped tightly between her long fingers.

"This is completely unacceptable," she said after what felt like an eternity.

"I know."

"How did this happen?"

"I don't understand it," I replied weakly.

"Why didn't you ask your teacher for help?" There. The million-dollar question was finally asked.

At this point, I was staring at my toes, squirming. I hate confrontation, and I've had about enough of this interrogation already. I felt my communication systems overheating- I mean it was only going to be a few more minutes... maybe seconds before I shut down completely.

"Look at me when I'm talking to you," she snapped.

I almost gave myself whiplash I looked up so fast.

"Do I need to repeat myself?" she asked sternly.

"No," I replied, but fell silent. Truth is, I was going to force her to repeat herself to buy myself more time to answer the question, but I wasn't going to admit that.

She repeated herself.

"The teacher scares me."

"Why?"

"She yells at us."

More silence.

"Okay." She takes the pen and begins to sign. The flourished "J" of her first name punctuating her easily recognizable signature. I reached out for the sheet of paper, grateful that the whole thing was over.

I grab the progress report.

She doesn't let go.

"Listen," she says.

I listen, but I don't let go of the report either. I'm taking the damn thing with me and stuffing it into my backpack if it's the last thing I ever do.

"You have two things going against you. One, you're a female and two, you're black. You're not just behind the eight ball—it's like being behind TWO eight balls. You have to be so much better than everybody just to get the same opportunity others will have. Remember that. Work twice as hard and be twice as good. I don't want to see another report like this again."

She didn't.

At the time, the biggest thing I took away from that conversation was that I got my signed progress report and didn't get a spanking or any other punishment. The actual lesson in her words wouldn't make sense to me for several more years, but for now I was happy I could head back to Windsor Elementary with my head held high, that is, until the next quiz.

Unbeknownst to me at the time, my mother went to the school the following day and had me transferred from that math class to the only other math class with an opening, "Advanced Geometry." I was happy to be away from Mrs. P., but was really apprehensive about the "advanced" level class, especially since as I was barely understanding the "basic" material. However, my new teacher was so warm and so kind that I flourished in her class. She would finish teaching us a lesson and say, "Capisce?" Italian for, "understand?" And for the first time I raised my hand and nervously said, "No."

She smiled and explained it again. The rest is history. I became an honors student from that moment forward.

Now, in the back seat of a taxi in Paris, I wondered what I had done to lose my champion, and what else I could possibly do to win her back. We said good bye to each other the following morning, and my mother returned to the States, I was headed to Moscow.

FROM RUSSIA, WITH LOVE
PART TWO

I got to the Moscow meet, I had been looking forward to, an entire week before any other athletes would arrive. The meet director arranged my hotel, and I had a nice apartment-like suite adjacent to the sports stadium. It was late August. My birthday was the following day, and I was preparing myself to be depressed about spending yet another birthday alone, in a foreign country, when I got this message: "Tianna, a dear friend of mine will be by to pick you up tomorrow. She will show you Moscow and bring you your birthday gift." I was elated. This is before every birthday was accompanied by hundreds of tweets and Facebook posts from strangers sending you birthday wishes. This was back when you'd be happy with just one non-family member sending a text or calling to wish you a good one. I felt special again.

Knowing I would spend my birthday abroad, I had the foresight to pack a dress (for when I took myself out to dinner or to a museum). It was a sort of safari cargo, khaki-looking dress with a lot of zippers, pockets, and strings. It was from Banana Republic, if you catch my drift. So, I was tying the final set of strings when I got the knock I had been waiting for. A petite young woman was standing at the door with a gift bag which I was more than happy to relieve her of. My gift turned out to be a giant nesting doll. Nothing says Russia like nesting dolls. We headed out together and as we made our way through the city, I was all too aware of the stares from other people.

I said, "There must not be too many black people in Russia, huh?"

"There are some," she said, and by her tone I couldn't tell if this was part of a larger issue—like how Americans feel about illegal immigration, or if this was just the directness I've found typical of a lot of Russians. She continued, "they are most likely thinking you are a famous sports person or a model because why else come to Russia?" Made sense to me. Why else come to Russia? A little while later as we strolled through a botanical garden, she was proved right. I ended up taking several pictures with people who assumed I was a model. I obliged them. I wasn't about to start pissing off Russians. I was flattered though too, and the day just kept getting better. We went to a huge mall, had a couple slices of Sbarro's pizza, (yes, really!) and met up with her best friend. Her best friend was…BLACK.

I just stared at her as the two of them spoke rapid Russian. She looked like we could be cousins, her complexion just a tad lighter, and her hair done up in micro-braids (where can you even get your hair braided in Russia? They sell weave too?) I was in awe of her. I learned that her father was actually from Ghana but had a professorship at one of the universities in Moscow. I decided I liked Russia and would be back for vacation. I've been to Russia four times; it is a beautiful country. Although our two countries may still have some residual bad feelings and general distrust left over from the Cold War and most recently the 2016 election cycle, the architecture, the culture, and the people are worth exploring and experiencing for yourself. We all should make up our own minds about the way things are.

Eventually the week passed, and it was time for the meet. The meet went horribly as I was on borrowed time with my knee. But as promised, the meet director handed me my envelope with my appearance fee in it, $10,000 cash. I happily counted my money as I packed. I maybe even pretended to be in my own music video throwing $100 bills in the air and rolling around in them as they fluttered down to the bed.

My car was scheduled to pick me up at 3 a.m. to deliver me to the airport. So, I stayed up all night after the meet. My driver was the brother, cousin, or nephew of someone who ran the meet. He picked me up in a car that could have been featured on Fast & Furious, neon interior lighting and all. Between the Russian rap music, the lighting, and the smoke, I thought I was in a night club on wheels. We did eventually get to the airport, after having to do a few reroutes due to illegal street races taking place. It was a crazy thing to witness. They were not only trying to out race each other, but they also had to outrun the police, and in the type of car we were in it would have been easy to "mistake" us for one of the racers.

I imagine jail is not a pleasant experience. Jail in Russia is what nightmares are made of. I was never so happy to get to an airport three hours early in my life.

THE FULL SCOPE

When switching coaches, you can't and shouldn't hire off reputation alone; you have to take a good look at the training. Then you need to decide if those are the types of things that work well for you based on what you know about how your body responds to different training scenarios. Despite the fact that things weren't exactly going well in my training, Bobby and I became friends. After practice, I knew he would be at his "office" which was the neighborhood bar. I had very few friends, so I would join Bobby at the bar. I didn't drink with him, but I did avail myself of the bar menu (which eventually made me fat and exacerbated my performance struggles). The time spent at his office was enlightening. Sometimes his friend Dave would join us, and we covered every topic imaginable. Mostly we caught up on the Lakers or baseball games. Other times we debated who was better: Pavarotti or Boccelli? Bobby was the talkative father I didn't have. I remember one lecture about his annoyance with the way athletes behaved on the European circuit—specifically women. This is what he said, "The more times I see an athlete in the lobby, the more confident I am that they won't perform well." Because if you're in the lobby, your focus is what? Being seen? Being social? He wants his athletes to be invisible, off their legs, focused on the task at hand.

The "lobby rat" theory, which is what I came to call it, morphed into the circuit husband/wife lecture. This is a phenomenon that certain athletes maintain a relationship overseas although back on US soil they have another relationship, entire families even. They operate with the understanding that what happens on the circuit stays on the circuit. Bobby said that he wanted me to be like the "Soup Nazi" from Seinfeld (which I had never seen). He explained that as stingy as the Soup Nazi was with the soup is how stingy I needed to be with myself.

I was looking forward to getting back to those conversations at the office and the perfect LA weather. After the long flight from Moscow to LAX, I could no longer stand. I sat on the ground near the baggage carousel with both my legs stretched out in front of me, my damaged knee was the size of an elephant's knee.

One afternoon, while walking down the street in Santa Monica, my knee gave out on me; I hit the pavement. Onlookers and passersby flowed around me like water flowing against a boulder in a stream. It was over, my knee was done being tortured. I called Bobby, he arranged for me to see a therapist. A week later I was in St. Louis getting prepped for knee surgery.

People who train with Bobby also spend a lot of time in St. Louis, Missouri. Jackie, never a fan of Los Angeles, maintains their residence in St. Louis, and they have training and treatment facilities the group can utilize while in town. The MRI on my knee showed that I would just need an Arthroscopic surgery. They would go in with small tools, stitch up my cartilage, shave my patella, and send me on my way.

I asked if they could use local anesthesia so that I could observe the procedure, but one of the nurses convinced me that I wouldn't want that. I assured her I wasn't squeamish about blood or gore in general, and she impressed on me the fact that it's not the blood, that would be the problem, but the way he twisted the leg around or pulled on the patella that would turn my stomach. She was adamant that surgeons can be quite rough on body parts. I recalled my reaction from years ago when I watched a caesarean section performed. Needless to say, I gave the go ahead for general anesthesia.

When I got discharged from the clinic, Bobby was waiting for me. I was just figuring out how to navigate my way on crutches when he took them away from me.

"Walk," he said.

I took one limping step.

"No, walk. Without limping," he said again.

I looked up at him for a long second, decided it would be pointless to argue, and walked to the car. Hours out of knee surgery I walked out of the hospital on my own without limping. I trusted Bobby, so when he suggested I fly to St. Louis for knee surgery and my rehabilitation, I didn't question it. What I didn't know was that shortly after my knee surgery, Bobby would get the same procedure done on his. Both of them. At the same damn time.

For a while, Jackie (as in THE Jackie Joyner Kersee) was taking really good care of us, making sure our knees were packed in ice and elevated. We struggled to make our way down the stairs where they had a home theater and a full bar. We watched *March of the Penguins* with his godson Remeggio, and all of us sat quietly in tears as Morgan Freeman explained to us how the males are able to identify their returning mate by their unique songs when the females returned. Another time I had to sit through *Scent of a Woman* and listen to Bobby recite the entire movie. Every single word. And let me tell you, that movie is HEAVY on dialogue.

What I was most grateful for, was that he chose to be there for me, in the most outlandish way possible; he went through that situation with me. From injury, rehabilitation, to full recovery.

The body will heal, but if you're not careful your mind may not. Each day I was not on the track or in the field was another day I was not working towards defending my title at the 2007 World Championships in Osaka, Japan. Fortunately, as the reigning World Champion, I had an automatic bye which granted me a little extra time to prepare. US national championships meets are our qualifiers to make international teams. It's the hardest meet on the planet, and so a lot of our training programs are built with a target to peak for nationals. If you're smart enough, you can time another peak for the global championships a month later, but those typically require a lesser performance than our national championships do. I returned to practice three months after my surgery, itching to run. I still remember the workout: six 200s. I was supposed to take it easy; I was so excited to be running that I pushed it. Even my more accomplished training partners asked me if I maybe wanted to slow down a bit. I was running well, but when it came time to jump, I was hesitant...afraid even. I'd replay the incident that caused the injury before jump practice and only half commit to the takeoff or the landing. I was going through the motions. I was at the point where I could run repeat 400s but couldn't jump 20 feet. High school T would kick so-called professional T's ass coming and going and twice on Fridays.

I was growing increasingly embarrassed by the struggle. My mental health deteriorated fast. You see, this was Los Angeles. I could not walk down the street without meeting someone who presented themselves as one thing but wanted to be another. Every waitress was actually an actress. Every bag boy was a screenwriter.

My homeless friend, Gray, was a tall, slender black man, who wore a burgundy beanie slouched sideways on a salt and pepper head. He had a beautiful smile, when he showed it, and the signature rough leathery hands were due to a lifetime of manual labor. I used to walk by him quickly, trying not to make eye contact. I couldn't afford to give him any money. I was hardly keeping up with my own expenses. With my knee and my confidence shaky, my ability to earn income from racing and jumping was in jeopardy. If I didn't pull it together, I'd lose everything including my condo, which was 450-square-feet of prime real estate on the corner of Roebling Avenue across from the In and Out Burger. By the way, I did not go there even once in my three years living there. But it also felt wrong to dehumanize a person by refusing to look at them. And so, one day I stopped.

"Hey, how are you?" I asked him.

He started a bit, not expecting to be engaged in conversation.

"Can't complain," he said.

"I'm sorry I don't have any money, but I see you all the time and I thought I'd stop," I said to him apologetically.

"Baby girl, it's all good. Gray's the name," he reached out a hand.

"Tianna," I said, and I shook his hand.

Before that moment I realized that I often recoiled from touching homeless people. This made me feel so ashamed. We smiled at each other, as I leaned back against the wall he was seated against. He looked at me with the same expression my father would, one eyebrow cocked up, struggling to make sense of this strange situation. I rested my head against the wall, silently watching other people try to avoid eye contact with us. Watching people watch us. After several minutes had passed, I took my leave but not before asking if he'd be around the next day. He looked to the sky as if to check some calendar written there.

"Should be," he said.

"Cool, see you tomorrow then."

The next day I located Gray not too far from the spot I found him in the day before.

"Yo, Gray!" I yelled to him from across the street. "You like arcades?!"

His body language said he wouldn't mind being in the air conditioning, and he scurried up to his feet and joined me across the street. I bought us cheap snacks, and, with the twenty dollars I budgeted for the outing, we played arcade games--neither of us particularly good at them. Both of us were happy to have something to laugh about and happy to have company.

Los Angeles was the loneliest time of my life. So, it wasn't a completely unselfish act to befriend Gray. We needed each other; when I ate out in the village and I could find him, he ate too. When I was out wandering the streets of Westwood because I needed to get out of my condo and out of my head, I'd find him, and we'd sit together. But Gray disappeared after a few weeks. I looked for him every day.

None of the women in my training group made much of an effort to befriend me, although I tried to befriend them. Superstars that they were Michelle Perry, JoAnna Hayes, Allyson Felix, Dawn Harper, all were well entrenched in their lives there and with their peer groups. Cordial enough of an atmosphere at practice, I knew that once practice ended, I'd be on my own. My phone never rang; I was not invited to anything, and to make matters worse my friend Gray had disappeared.

TRIGGER WARNING

I had started to have nightmares, and night after night I'd wake up sweating, crying, and screaming. It was a night terror that forced my hand and led me to buy the plane ticket back to Ohio. In that particular dream, I had been traveling overseas. Our plane had crashed in what seemed to be the desert at first but morphed into jungle terrain at some point. I was standing on my knees with my hands tied behind my back, a gag in my mouth, and a bag over my head. If I opened my eyes, I could see the light filtering through the black cloth. If I stayed calm, I could take deep inhales through my nose and exhale gently through my mouth without ingesting the cloth. There was a person to my right. I intuited that he was in the same position as I was. I heard voices, in no language that actually existed on this planet, a language exclusive to dreams, just foreign enough for the subconscious to communicate to me that I was far from home. A light pressure was applied to the back of my head as a faceless person pulled the sack off. I blinked my eyes open to take in my surroundings. A concrete slab, beautiful, lush green plants, and people without faces held guns without safeties. I made a choking sound as a scream, caught in my throat, was blocked by the gag and transformed into a groan. I looked at the person to my right, his head was still covered. One of the faceless people ambled over to him, placed their gun to his right temple and pulled the trigger. I was covered in warm splatter. The previously faceless person now had a smile as they approached me. I began to squirm making more noises against my gag, drooling saliva from the corners of my mouth. They raised the gun, pressing it so hard into my temple it twisted my neck. Tears streamed down my face as this nameless, faceless, person pulled the trigger.

I woke up screaming at the top of my lungs, opened my MacBook, logged on to delta.com, and booked a reward ticket using every mile I had to get back to Cleveland. I really needed to be around the familiar and away from a city that placed so much value on the superficial. Nothing was as it seemed. All I had was my condo and a Honda Accord (a symbol of the first blow to my fragile ego. I learned quickly that commuting from Culver City to UCLA every day in an SUV on the 405 in LA traffic was not only unsustainable but unaffordable). And even though I was making my own money, Los Angeles made me feel like a loser.

Back in Ohio, I did my best to fight off the depressive state I was in. The trip was good at first; back in my old bedroom I was lulled into the circadian rhythms of home. My little sister was home from college for a medical procedure to remove screws from her femur. She had broken it the year before at take off during a long jump competition. *Cool*, I thought, *glad I'd be home for that.* It seemed like a big deal. She'd have to have general anesthesia for the procedure, and it was an unspoken expectation in our family that if somebody had to be put under, we would all be there if we could. We all drove to the hospital together. Christina was wheeled off to her room, where they did pre-op tests. My parents and I waited together in the lounge. No more than half an hour had passed before we were greeted by the doctor again.

Is there something wrong?" one of my parents asked.

"No, but we cannot do the procedure today. We can't safely put her under. She's pregnant," the doctor replied.

My mouth, my dad's mouth, my mom's mouth all dropped open in surprise. Immediately, I was angry—not at Christina but at the doctor who had just violated HIPAA laws and my sister's right to privacy. And he did so to my very Christian parents; I knew and I'm sure Christina, who was still back in her private room, knew that this day would not end well.

Eventually, after a family conversation in the hospital, we returned home. Quiet and tearful, the screws in her leg that caused her so much discomfort—that she was willing to go under the knife again to remove— were making her miserable. I sat musing about how it just so happened that I had a nightmare that would make me book a last-minute red-eye flight that got me here just in time for this fuckery. My parents scowled in silence and shared disappointment. Christina took up residence on the couch extending her leg out for more comfort and clicked on the television. One of Christina's superpowers is her ability to "sit in the shit." She has always had this uncanny ability to just process bad situations in real time, and when it was over it was over. Whereas me, I just may carry it with me for years. I carried the events of the day up the stairs and to my old room. I heard my mother's voice calling to me. My parents had retired to their bedroom, likely needing space and time to talk privately. I walked down the hall, past Christina's bedroom door, past the spare room that doubled as an office, and stood in the doorway of their bedroom.

"This is your fault," my mom said to me.

I lost my balance a bit.

"Had you been a better role model, this would have never happened."

I stumbled backward a step.

"What?" I said in a whisper, not accepting the words I was hearing.

How could she believe this? I took school seriously. I was a successful student, a successful athlete, was financially independent, owned my own home, and had never ever been pregnant or even worried that I might be pregnant. How am I the failure here? I stared up at my mother with broken-hearted eyes. My father remained at rest, his head on my mom's shoulder, quiet.

"You should have been a better big sister," my mom said.

I collapsed in slow motion to my knees as if I had been shot. The dream. Just like in my dream. Tears began to stream down my face, but it was my mom who pulled the trigger.

FULL-TIME JOB

Sometime later, after returning to LA, I got over my devastation and called home.

"Hi Mom," I said when she answered the phone.

"Hi, T! " My mom said in her usual sing song way. "Let me get dad."

If I called one parent, even if I called their cell phone and my other parent was home, they always got the other and placed the call on speaker phone. Unless I explicitly stated I needed to talk to just one parent, I was always prepared for a three-way conversation.

"Hey, T," my dad said from somewhere deeper in the room.

"Oh cool, you're both there. I'll need both of your views on this," I said.

I could hear my father say "uh-oh" under his breath as he moved closer to the phone.

"It's about the book of Job," I said jumping right in.

"Oh, Lord," my dad said, steeling himself for one of our often lengthy and frustrating philosophical discussions.

I had all but left the church I grew up in.

✴ ✴ ✴ ✴ ✴

The church I grew up in was just a group of adults, no pastor, but a group of elders (usually all the men). They sang, prayed, took communion, and held open discussions. Everyone in attendance was on equal ground. I could literally (and did almost every week) request to sing a song, and they would sing it. We were an a cappella group. Every now and then, a few brave women would try to harmonize with the "brothers" to jazz it up a bit; every now and then, someone wanted to do an encore and so would go solo for a verse until everyone else caught up. It was usually the tone-deaf person that would do that—yes, Bill, I am talking about you.

On occasion, someone would feel like free-styling or ad-libbing an entire song with customized personal lyrics that no one could follow. Again, a shout out to Bill.

Other times, a person would call out a hymn to sing and add specific instructions like, "Sing only verses 1, 3, 7, and then finish with 4."

You were allowed to do all of this.

You could even stand and say, "I'd like to sing a song I wrote earlier this week. I made copies for everyone," and then pass around your copies—and teach everyone a new song.

The only general rule was that before communion you'd select songs from one half of the hymnal and after communion you'd request songs from the other half. When someone would violate this unspoken rule, there'd be a moment of hesitancy, and if the song-caller didn't correct his or her error, we'd just sing the song.

Oh, well, "make a joyful noise unto the Lord" the good book says.

We would have guests (usually other members' family members visiting from out of town) and sometimes they had a guitar; and, my goodness, we would feel like we were rocking out.

I always asked what the church was called. It was in a nondescript three-story building, with a dungeon for a basement and a banquet hall for an attic; the second floor was a three-bedroom apartment; the ground floor was where the meetings were held.

"It's called The Church in Elyria," they would say.

I remember thinking that the "The" in the title was a little arrogant. There clearly was more than one church in Elyria.

"Is there a 'THE Church in Detroit'?" I asked.

"Yes."

"Is there a 'THE Church in Columbus'?"

"Yes."

"Is there a—"

"Tianna, there is a church in every city. We are the local church; there are local churches in every city."

"How do you know?"

This follow up question wasn't a challenge it was rooted in intrigue. I couldn't believe it. There were people all over the country sitting in rooms like this doing the same thing?

It was true. My dad pulled out a directory. Listed by state, and country for international locations, were the names of all the cities where there were local churches including the phone numbers and email addresses of the contacting Elder. There were a lot of them.

This amazed me…this sense of connection. In line with this spirit of connectedness, The Church in Elyria was a fully enveloping presence in the lives of its members. There was a term for it—it was called the "church life." The local church was supposed to be a lifestyle.

Sunday: Morning: Sister's Meeting aka bake the communion wafer. 10am: Lord's Table Meeting. 11am: Prophesying Meeting, which I refer to sometimes as Open Discussion. There was also a Sunday evening meeting, but I really can't remember for sure now; it was a school night.

Monday: Brothers/Elders Meeting

Tuesday: Prayer Meeting. I only attended one prayer meeting voluntarily. September 11th, 2001. I think you can understand why.

Wednesday: Off. No meetings that I was aware of.

Thursday: Administrative Meetings at the Church office on the second floor.

Friday: Home meetings, aka in-home Bible studies. I loved these, people came over and there was food. Also, Pizza. Enough said.

Saturday: Service Meeting aka clean the church, cut the grass, set up chairs.

"You know you're in a cult, right?" my older sister would say to me teasingly in our still rare phone calls.

"Shut up!" I'd yell in a screeching whiny voice. "It's not a cult!" I'd say defensively.

"Oh, Lord Jeeeeeesssssuuuuuusss!" Adrianne would shout mockingly.

"Ughhhh…STOP IT!" I'd scream back at her while also trying not to laugh at her perfect imitation of the "sisters'" voices.

At least four times a year there was a huge "Training." The conference was hosted by "The Church in Anaheim" but if you couldn't make it all the way to California, they recorded the conference on VHS and shipped them to each local church. The "Trainings" were such a big deal that it required a new seating configuration at our church, the television would be rolled in, a table set out with name tags (so unnecessary for ten folks), and a table with coffee and snacks. My parents didn't even attempt to try to make me sit for these videos but if they had, on my seat I would have found a stack of literature that would have stated Fall, Winter, Spring, or Summer Training, the year in which it was taking place, and the theme.

Before pressing play on the tape, prayers of gratitude and requests for an openness of spirit, souls, and hearts were offered up. The image would flicker and and what looked like a blue screen filled the display. I soon learned that this blue screen was a blue chalkboard as an elderly frail looking Chinese gentleman took his place in a chair at a table in front of the board. He reminded me of Yoda, he was quite old, had a distinct voice, and although his eyes were fully open, they did indeed always look closed.

His name was Witness Lee.

I'd seen that name before. He was the author of nearly every piece of literature in the church and in my father's personal library at home. From what I could tell, these local churches hung on his every word. There was a book titled, *The Holy Word for Morning Revival*, known to its partakers unofficially as, "The Morning Watch." You were to read it every morning, preferably with a partner, pray over it, and be ready to discuss it in the open discussion (prophesying) portion of the Sunday Meeting. My parents were faithful participants in this practice. Any attempts to participate consistently myself fell off after a week every time. Whenever I did feel compelled to share some personal testimony or revelation that occurred to me after reading the assigned portions on Sunday, the other members of the church made me feel like I had just had the deepest revelation of all times, like I was Moses coming down from the mountain with the ten commandments on two stone tablets. One could get addicted to such affirmation.

But there were two things that bothered me. First, already an avid reader by that time in my life, I was greatly disturbed that the church read only the works of one person: Witness Lee. No other author was taken into consideration nor, I daresay, permitted in the church. Growing up I read anything and everything I could get my hands on, I had firsthand knowledge about how reading different things by different people could be beneficial to your development. If I were limited to one author, I'd be stunted. This worried me, and I'd often look at the countless bindings of the books on my father's bookshelf checking for, at the very least, a co-author who wasn't named Lee.

No such luck.

Second, every now and then the "Training" video would pan out and show the audience. You could see that there were hundreds upon hundreds of people in attendance. But they looked homogeneous. Like clones of each other.

"Who are those people?" I asked my dad during a break once.

"Those are the full-timers."

"Full-timers?"

"Yes, the people who go to Anaheim to be trained full-time in the Lord's Recovery."

"The Lord's Recovery?"

"Yes, this is the Lord's Recovery, we are working to recover the church back to oneness."

"And the 'full-timers?'"

"They feel called to give their lives full-time to this goal."

Well, alrighty then.

Just so you're in the know, full-time trainees went to the Church in Anaheim's campus or compound (I don't know for sure; I've never been) where they lived in group homes under the careful eye of a married couple if it were the "sisters'" house, or a single "leading brother" if it were a "brothers'" house. They would spend all day, and most of their evenings diving into the various works and teachings of Witness Lee. To graduate would be to become a "co-worker" in "God's Economy." God's Economy was what Witness Lee called God's plan to "dispense Himself into His chosen and redeemed people as their life, their life supply, and their everything." These so called "co-workers" would then disperse across the globe and become "serving ones" in other localities.

In the "Lord's Recovery" there was no room for secular or so-called pagan holidays. We did not celebrate Christmas, we had no tree, and exchanged no gifts.

I asked about this once, and the reply was: "We celebrate the birth of Jesus EVERYDAY."

Got it.

We were strongly discouraged from uttering the name Santa Claus. Why? Because with a little manipulation of the letter "n" the word "Santa" could become "Satan." So, can you imagine my little face trying to get around this during my elementary school Christmas Concert?

"Up on the house top reindeer pause. Out jumps good old hmmm hmmm Claus!!!"

Clever parents that they were, they pulled what I like to think of as a good old-fashioned bait and switch around Christmastime. We may not have celebrated the holiday like everyone else, but we would spend Christmas vacation at Disney World in Orlando, Florida, almost every single year. So, it forces a child to contemplate two conflicting options. One, question not celebrating Christmas? Or two, don't mention it and go to Disney World for two weeks? Disney wins. Always.

Obviously, Halloween was out. Growing up I literally thought that demons roamed the earth on this night; that to be outside was to put yourself at risk of demonic possession; that to even open the door for trick or treaters who had the misfortune of accidentally stopping at our place was to open a portal that allowed legions of dark spirits into our home. My parents were so adamant about not participating or having anything to do with October 31st that we sat deep into our darkened house as if we were hiding from overseers and bounty hunters until trick or treating was over. In fact, my parents (usually my mom because she worked in town) pulled us out of school before the class Halloween party started. So, yes, I had to be THAT kid. I finally trick or treated as an adult with my older sister and her son who was dressed as a Backyardigan and I had a great time. So there.

Thanksgiving was inbounds. Countless scriptures indirectly advocated for this holiday anyway. Like 1 Thessalonians 5:16 "Always rejoice, unceasingly pray, in everything give thanks, for this is the will of God in Christ Jesus, for you." I wouldn't say my parents were cooks. My mom could "fix" dinner, and my dad specialized in omelets, grits, cornbread, and barbecue sauce. So we mostly made a pilgrimage either down south to Birmingham, Alabama, or northwest to Detroit to let the extended family do the heavy lifting. My parents were often the ones to request the holding of hands and go around the circle with each person saying what we are thankful for. I actually do not besmirch this practice at all—but it was always ill-timed.

New Year's Eve was a church event. Everyone came over to our house, but instead of doing the ten second countdown to the new year everyone would repeat, "Oh, Lord Jesus!" until the ball dropped. Dick Clark's broadcast was on mute, naturally. I used to yell, "Oh, Lord Jesus" too, but I was usually competing to be the loudest. If I got loud then someone else would get louder and someone else louder still.

Valentine's Day was an approved holiday too. Because "God is love," obviously. As long as it wasn't some little boy declaring his love for us directly, love was something to celebrate.

Easter was an interesting one for us. Because, like Jesus' birth, "we celebrated Jesus' resurrection EVERYDAY," but we ate a special meal and often visited Christ Temple's special Easter Sunday service. So, the jury is still out on whether or not we "observed" Easter Sunday.

So, I lived that "church life" full-time for 15 years. Until Joo Joo, my friend from church in Los Angeles, put the final nail in that coffin, when, over lunch she took a call. She told whoever was on the other end, another coworker, I'm sure (that's what they called each other in the Lord's Recovery remember?), that she'd get back to them in about an hour when she was done with this appointment. *Appointment?* I thought to myself. I thought we were just two friends hanging out. I asked her about this. She told me that she was assigned to me—I don't know by whom—to bring me back into the fold. I was so disappointed that all the time we spent together playing in arcades, watching movies together in comfortable silence, splitting dessert I should not have ordered, was all a means to an end—the end being to save me, the backslider, apparently. I abruptly ended our lunch and that was the last time we saw each other. Joo Joo left shortly after that lunch date to visit family in Korea, but when it was time for her to return to the States, she was not able to. She was blocked, by either our government or hers, from coming home.

"What about the book of Job, T?" my mom asked carefully, snapping me back into our conversation.

I'm sure she almost did not want to know. They knew I was growing more and more skeptical of religion and that I jumped on every chance I could get to challenge the teachings I had been indoctrinated with.

I took a deep breath. "Well, it starts out with Job, minding his own business taking care of his 10 kids and his wife, his 7,000 sheep, etc., etc., right?"

"Uh-huh," my dad said. I could see his raised eyebrow in my mind's eye.

"Let me get my Bible, T," my mom said shuffling away from the phone.

"And…" my dad prompted me on. He was right to be wary of the direction of this conversation. Once, several years before, after watching our family favorite, The Ten Commandments (my favorite because of Yul Brynner, my mom's favorite for Charlton Heston), I sat quietly, a perturbed look on my face.

"What is it?" My dad asked.

"Dad, which one of us would die?" I asked him, tears welling in my eyes.

"What?" he asked, growing concerned.

"If the first born of each family died, which one of us would die? Me? Or Adrianne? Adrianne is your first born, but I'm Mom's firstborn! Do we BOTH die!?" Gravity jerked a tear from the little pool forming in my eyes. He sat staring at me, silent. We stared at each other.

And finally, he sat up a little taller and said, "Nobody, we're covered in the Blood of the Lamb." Relieved he had an answer for me, he visibly relaxed. I gave him one last look. I did not find the answer satisfying, but he wasn't wrong. The question was irrelevant if he slaughtered a lamb and spread its blood over the door so that the death angel would pass over our home. I did wonder if God had an answer for me in the event that we did not wish to slaughter little animals, but I left it.

"It says in Job 1:6 that Satan came to visit the Lord. And that Satan told the Lord that he had been people-watching on planet earth," I continued.

"That's right," both of my parents said in unison. I was being careful with the conversation. I wanted to be just respectful enough to them so they'd be open to having it and dramatic enough to build the tension. I was pacing myself, and they were growing impatient.

"What about it?" my mom asked with a hint of annoyance in her tone. I decided to speed it up as I was at risk of losing my audience.

"It was THE LORD who said, 'You see my boy, Job? He's amazing, is blameless, and he fears God.' And then Satan was all like, 'That's real easy to do when you're super rich and literally nothing has gone wrong for you in your life. Take it from him and see what happens.'" I had major problems with this: "And then, the Lord says okay…bet. Do your worst, Satan.' And the rest of the story describes just how thoroughly Job was fucked with—"

"Language!" my mom shouted, interrupting me.

"Watch your mouth!" my dad said in agreement.

"Alright, alright. My point is, it is messed up that the Lord granting Satan permission to fu— mess with Job like that. It was literally a side bet. And the only reason Job was targeted is because he was a child of God, living exactly as his God commanded," I railed.

"That's right, he was tested and, even through all that, he did not sin against Him," my dad said, happy we got to the main point of my grievance.

"Because he was a child of God, he was a target for Satan. Is that right?" I asked again, just to be clear.

"Yes, that's right," both my parents said.

"Cool. How and where do I opt out of my 'child of God' status?" I asked. My parents gasped.

"What?" my mom asked in a tone I had never heard before.

"I have not slept in two months, Mom, not once! My Lunesta prescription ran out, and the doctor won't prescribe me more. I'm headed to Osaka for World Championships and the ONLY reason I'm even going is because I have a bye. It's going to be the wackiest title defense. I'm lonely. My boyfriend broke up with me via text. LA is too damn expensive. I have spent more than I have earned trying to survive here. I can't do this anymore." Silently I began to cry.

"Your faith is too small, T. The Lord doesn't give you more than you can handle." my mom said, meaning well, but absolutely saying the wrong thing.

"So, this is my fault then? My faith is too small? That's why I'm struggling? What about Job's faith? Huh? Clearly it does not matter how much faith you have. Doesn't this same Bible also say having faith the size of a mustard seed is enough? Which is it? No. I am not handling this. I'm not handling this at all."

I grew silent.

My parents were unaware of the suicidal ideations that had intensified. It was becoming too much for me…watching everyone else in my training group collect accolades, contracts; just recently one of them swerved into the parking lot with a brand-new Mercedes SL 500 convertible as I was deciding which was more important to spend my last few dollars on, the internet bill or Whole Foods. I paid my internet bill and satisfied my appetite with fast food which was only exacerbating my problems.

"So, I'm not going to be a child of God anymore. If it's damned if you do, damned if you don't, I'd rather just go it alone, it already feels that way. I'm gonna go now, thanks for listening."

"We'll keep you in our prayers," they said.

"Good luck with that," I said.

"The Lord be with your spirit," they said.

"Grace be with you," I said out of habit. I hung up the phone and laid back in bed staring at my untextured white ceiling wondering what Satan and the Lord our God had to say about that.

NOBLE TRUTHS

We had been based in St. Louis for a final training camp, rehab, and treatment before heading to Osaka, Japan, for the Outdoor World Championships when Bobby informed me to expect Ginnie Powell later that day. *Huh?* I thought. Ginnie was on fire and had a full schedule of top-tier meets lined up. She had made the World Championship team and would be representing the USA along with Michelle Perry and Lolo Jones. But now she was back in St. Louis because she and fellow competitor and trainer partner Michelle Perry clashed in a hurdle race; as a result Ginnie hit hurdles, the track, and did damage to her knee.

I was pissed for her. New to our group, she was welcomed to the inner circle of the existing training squad but wasn't nearly as standoffish with me as the others were. I gravitated toward her, and I was about to learn why.

She arrived at Jackie Joyner Kersee's house where we were staying. I know, right! I've spent summers at JJK's house! Me! Anyway, I knocked on the door to her room to see if she needed anything. It wasn't so long ago that I was needing to be waited on hand and foot with knee problems, in this same house.

She was chanting. I didn't hear that until after I'd knocked. Grateful that she didn't stop, I went back to my room with the intent to check on her later. More time passed, and I knocked on her door again.

"Girl, come in! I was just doing my prayers," Ginnie said as she sat up in bed and readjusted the pillow that was keeping her knee elevated.

"I heard; what language was that?" I asked her. I had an idea, but I didn't want to be wrong.

"Japanese," she replied.

"Thought so," I said, puzzled. "Why do you pray in Japanese?" I asked.

Patient as ever, Ginnie explained she was Buddhist, born and raised. This shocked me, I didn't know there were black Buddhists. At that time in the world, I had not yet seen *What's Love Got to Do with It*, the movie about Ike and Tina Turner in which Tina chants, "Nam-myoho-renge-kyo," the same words Ginnie was chanting. Intrigued, I asked if I could sit on the edge of the bed and if she wouldn't mind sharing more about it with me? She told me her family practiced Nichiren Buddhism, a Japanese branch of Mahayana Buddhism. It was a lot to take in, and she gave me a magazine to read and a website to look at.

Before I took my leave to bring her a new ice pack and start my internet tour of Nichiren Buddhism, I asked her if she was pissed at Michelle—if she thought she did it on purpose, and what she was going to do about it? Ginnie sighed. It seemed to me that Ginnie did think Michelle had purposely tried to take her out, and yet she stopped short of expressing anger toward her.

"How can you not be angry?" I asked her.

"How does anger fix my damn knee?" she asked back.

She had every right to be angry, and yet she chose not to be because it didn't serve her and her goals to return back to health so she could race at the World Championships in Japan. I now understood that would mean much more to her and her family than simply attending another big meet. Impressed, I left to bring her a new ice pack.

"Thanks, girl," she said as she cracked open a book looking completely at ease and at peace.

If this is Buddhism, I thought, *count me in.*

I scrolled through the website, following the rabbit of curiosity down through countless holes. I knew I hadn't learned everything there was to learn about Nichiren Buddhism, but I had learned enough to know that I was not going to keep up with morning and evening prayers, chanting, and sacred texts and symbols. But something about Buddhism overall was calling me. So, I did what I always do when I'm curious about something. I went to the bookstore and found several books on the subject.

I made myself comfortable on the floor and cracked open the first book. I got a crash course in who Buddha actually was—a man named Siddhārtha Gautama. The story goes that 12 or so years before his birth, it was prophesied that he'd become a sage which was a very low paying gig. Therefore, his father, a wealthy chief, kept Siddhārtha in a very wealthy bubble where he was never exposed to anything that would make him long for something else. But as with most humans, he longed for what was out beyond his palace's walls. So, he snuck out, like Princess Jasmine did in Aladdin, and was shocked by the suffering he saw. He then learned that sickness, old age, and death await us all—whether you're occupying a palace or not. Unsettled, he dedicated the rest of his life to finding the way out of suffering.

Fast forward a bit and, after a lot of studying, listening, and meditating, he awakened enlightened. A little while after that he shared with the world The Four Noble Truths.

The first Noble Truth: there is suffering.

Whoa! I exhaled for the first time in a long time. Finally! Validation for my experience that is not blaming my faith or lack thereof. It was simple, there is suffering.

The second Noble Truth: there is a cause to your suffering.

To this one I said, "no shit" and kept reading.

The third Noble Truth: there is an end to suffering.

This was what I was here for, the end of the suffering I was going through. Where was the answer to that question? I read on hungrily.

The fourth Noble Truth: the end to suffering is contained in the Eightfold Path.

Wait, what! I thought to myself as I closed the book.

I was not expecting such a cliff hanger. Appetite whetted; I searched the indexes of my short pile of books for the Eightfold Path. I flipped to the indicated page.

THE EIGHTFOLD PATH

Right View
Right Intention
Right Speech
Right Action
Right Livelihood
Right Effort
Right Mindfulness
Right Concentration

All eight practices seemed completely reasonable and practical to me. It was not asking me to suspend belief or settle into the cognitive dissonance that often arose when marrying science and religion together. And my favorite thing about Buddhism that I learned there on the floor in the bookstore was that Buddha, who was not a god and did not claim to be, said this:

Don't blindly believe what I say. Don't believe me because others convince you of my words. Don't believe anything you see, read, or hear from others, whether of authority, religious teachers or texts. Don't rely on logic alone, nor speculation. Don't infer or be deceived by appearances. Do not give up your authority and follow blindly the will of others. This way will lead to only delusion. Find out for yourself what is truth, what is real.

Permission to question, permission to seek, was all I needed. I left the bookstore with the book, *Buddhism for Beginners* by Jack Kornfield and began my practice of Buddhism. I slept that night, for the first time in months. I finally had some hope. I started my self-study of Buddhism by devouring every book I had on the subject and trying to meditate. I sucked at that. Frustrated, I went back to the bookstore where a new book, Against the Stream by Noah Levine, caught my attention and changed everything about my practice.

Head out of the clouds and armed with a more practical guide for my day-to-day, I turned my attention to Japan—excited by the idea of visiting temples I now had a slightly stronger connection to. I was also looking forward to entering a competition with a new mindset, from a place of non-clinging and non-attachment to the outcome. My entire career revolved around winning and medals, and it was causing me to suffer. I still hadn't worked out how to be *unattached* enough to make myself not suffer. Armed with hope, books, and resolve I landed in Japan ready to give my best to defend my World Championship title.

LAND OF THE RISING SUN

I had read *Way of the Peaceful Warrior* by Dan Millman and The Alchemist by Paolo Coehlo before touching down in Japan, convinced the Universe was conspiring for and with me, I passed the days in the lead-up seeing signs in everything. It wasn't lost on me that I was now in the same country Coach Vince referenced ahead of my long jump breakthrough. This had to mean something. I was sure of it. Something big was going to happen.

I was so starved for signs that all would be well that I interpreted absolutely everything as a good omen. The walk signal turns just as I approach the crosswalk...OH, MY GOD, the Universe is telling me to WALK! To keep moving forward! Oh, my God! When I got my bib number, I gasped. The number 980 was imprinted on the front. *OH, MY GOD*, I thought. I have the same three numbers from the 2005 champs in Helsinki WHICH I WON! The Universe is giving me a sign! I'll be World Champion again, never mind that my bib number in Helsinki was 809. Same three digits, sure. Symbolic? Nah.

I should have stretched before doing as much reaching as I did as a purveyor in the signs of the Universe. My parents made the trip to Japan too; they had already made the mistake once of staying home for meets they didn't think I would win; they wouldn't be caught home twice. I too, took this as a sign. OH, MY GOD the Universe is setting the stage for me to win in front of my parents! The Universe knows how bad I want this; how bad I need to do this IN FRONT of my parents! My mom!

Giddy. I smiled wider and more often than I ever had before. In my own room, because medalist in individual events don't have to have roommates on Team USA, I made playlists on my iPod classic, and binge watched the television show, 24. Some people brought their gaming consoles overseas. I brought DVDs and books. I settled in with snacks from TEAM USA's athlete's lounge and passed the time until evening when I'd have a pre-meet dinner with my parents. OH, MY GOD! The last time I had a pre-meet dinner with a parent I won a medal!

I met my parents in the lobby of their hotel. My mother was upset. My father looked unbothered. I turned to face my mother.

"What happened?" I asked her, not looking forward to breaking my streak of good omens and positive signs.

"Nothing! I was just enjoying myself!" he said defensively. Wondering how the hell my father managed to upset my mother because he was "enjoying" himself, I asked them to tell me the whole story from the top over dinner.

Turns out they had spent the day together at the spa or had planned to. Things were going swimmingly when they decided to avail themselves of the hot baths. My mom was ushered by the spa attendant to the ladies' locker room, my father, ushered to the men's.

She changed into her bathing suit and followed the signs that directed one toward the baths; the door was attended by another spa employee who directed my mother back toward the lockers and informed her with broken English and sign language that, to use *these* particular hot baths, you had to do so in the nude.

"Oh no," my mother said to the attendant, "no, we didn't know. Please can you let me inside so I can let my husband know?"

The spa attendant obliged.

What my mother saw next would be seared in her memory forever. My dad, in the nude, in the bath with a bunch of strangers. His head was tossed back as he enjoyed the steaming hot water.

"Bob!" she whisper-shouted in his direction, opening one eye and then the other.

He turned his attention to his wife.

"Get dressed! We're leaving!" she said.

"But I just got in. I'm not even in the water good, Jo!" he said back.

"Now!" she said again.

Begrudgingly my father climbed out of the bath, water dripping off his naked body and headed into the locker room to get dressed.

I choked back a laugh. My mother was so upset that it felt rude to laugh at the comedy of this situation. My dad had no such qualms, and I was giggling to myself, feigning innocence.

"What?" he said defensively. "I'm in Japan. Those people don't know me. I was enjoying myself."

The man had a point.

"All these years of marriage and I'm still getting surprised," she said exasperated. "I just knew he wouldn't go for it. I just knew it. Only to step out, and this man is enjoying himself butt naked! Butt naked, T!"

I lost my composure at that point and descended into a fit of giggles so contagious the three of us laughed about it all the way through dinner.

"You know I'm telling this story at the team meeting, right?" I said.

"T, don't," my mom begged.

Dad shrugged, "I was just enjoying myself."

The following day was long jump qualifying. I had placed fifth at our national meet jumping 6.57 meters (21′ 6¾″), but it didn't matter because I had the automatic bye. When a country has a reigning World Champion with a bye in an event, they still get to qualify their top three athletes. So, we had a total of four jumpers representing the US in Japan. Grace Upshaw, Brittany Reese, Rose Richmond, and me. To punch our tickets to the long jump final, we had three attempts to jump 6.70 or pray we were among the top 12 performers. I opened with a 6.28-meter jump. "Fuck!" I said to myself, hand on my head, embarrassed as I walked back to my gear to slide my pants on. Brittany and Grace fouled their first attempts and Rose jumped 6.13. I was leading the Americans in a pathetic showing.

The second round went better for me; I jumped 6.59 meters (21′ 8″); Grace jumped 6.44 (21′ 2″); Rose leaped 6.45 (21′ 2″). Somehow, I was still leading this sad delegation of jumpers. Brittany was up. She jumped 6.83 meters, well over the automatic mark of 6.70. She was free to pack up, leave, and prepare for the final—a position I envied. I was preparing for my third and final attempt when Brittany walked past me on the way back to her track bag.

"Oh, you still jumping?" she said to me. "I thought you'd qualified."

I shot daggers with my eyes in her direction. Through clenched teeth, I told her I hadn't qualified yet. Pissed and a little flustered, I took my last jump. FOUL. Now I had to wait.

I qualified in the twelfth position, out of 12—as the reigning World Champion. Bobby patted me on the back when I eventually made it to the warmup track.

"You got the job done. You'll live to see another day."

OH, MY GOD! I thought. *How glorious my victory will be tomorrow having just barely made it into the final by the skin of my teeth. The Universe is setting me up to be a testimony for never counting yourself out!*

I put my headphones in and boarded the bus back to the hotel—walking on delusional clouds. I was brought back to Earth when my parents told me they were in the lobby. I ran down to greet them.

Before I could get a word in, my mother said, "Was that you *trying* to jump far?"

In a single moment, I dropped all pretense that my struggles were a setup for a comeback here at the World Championships.

The truth was that *was* me *trying* to jump far. And I wasn't jumping far at all. The top qualifier of the day jumped 6.96 meters—a distance I only dreamed of jumping. I finally had allowed myself to accept that there was no chance I'd walk out of here retaining my title, no chance that I'd even medal. My bubble of delusion burst, and I went into the final three rounds deflated. I fouled the first jump, jumped 21-feet on my second jump, and improved by four more centimeters on my third jump. Top eight get three more attempts to battle it out for the medals. I was tenth.

Ashamed, I walked through the mixed zone ignored by the journalists who didn't care about losers. I would have preferred to stand there with any of them in the hot seat explaining why, as World Champion, I was leaving in tenth place, but I was so irrelevant to them, no one even saw it as a shocking loss. Back in the warmup area, Bobby consoled me the best way he knew how. He told me it just wasn't my year, that my time would come, that this road required patience.

*But all the signs...*I thought to myself, descending into a pity party.

I was right that I was seeing signs. But I was dead wrong about what they meant.

REDUCE, REUSE, RECYCLE

I got my reduction letter from Nike in the mail. It's correspondence that explains why they will no longer pay the same salary moving forward. In summary my letter said, "This isn't personal, but we need to pay you a salary that reflects the exposure you give to our brand. We have reviewed your performances and your world rankings and have decided to reduce your salary by 25 percent effective January 1, 2008."

Now *that's* a sign.

I took the letter to practice. Bobby said he'd handle it. My reduction was retracted. Lewellyn Stark told me I was never meant to get a reduction because I was with a new coach, one of their Nike-sponsored coaches, and it would take a little time for me to adjust to a different program. He told me that it was oversight because he had a stack of reduction letters to get through and didn't take the time to read them.

I noted how fucked up that was but held my tongue opting instead to thank him and Nike for correcting it. I'm sure I ended the call making grand promises of what was to come the following season. I always felt like I had to do that, in hospitality rooms, in emails, and on phone calls I never ended an interaction without promising the world. It made me feel like shit.

I flew back to Ohio after Osaka, Japan, to reevaluate my entire life. I moved to Los Angeles on an $80,000 salary before taxes. I now lived in and owned a half million-dollar 450-square-foot condo in Westwood. My mortgage was $3,500 a month; the math comes out to $42,000 a year. That left me with $38,000 before taxes to cover the car note, insurance, utilities, groceries, treatment, and incidentals. I was starting to feel like I could not afford my life. Two years prior was the last time I earned any substantial income above my salary.

I decided I would not return to Bobby's training group. I didn't know where I would go next, but I knew I couldn't stay in LA for much longer. I called Bobby to break the news.

"Just wait, T.I." That's what he called me; I had no idea why, but I loved that he did. As if every time he went to say my name, he decided the "Anna" wasn't necessary to enunciate. And so, he didn't.

"Wait?" I asked, puzzled at his response. This was a hard call for me to make. I loved Bobby; he was my friend, but I couldn't afford to stay if I wasn't going to jump well. And I wasn't sure my body was translating the repeat

300s and 500s I was running in my daily track sessions, to feet and inches in the long jump pit.

A couple days later Bobby showed up at my parents' home. He had literally meant "Wait." We sat down and spoke open and honestly about what was going well and what wasn't. He changed his training plan for me. Touched by his concern, his willingness to meet me where I was, metaphorically, I literally wanted to give it another shot. All would be different after I made the Olympic Team. I was going back to Cali.

With another year of training under my belt, I headed back to another Olympic Trials. I qualified ninth out of the 12 spots jumping 6.45 meters, just over 21 feet. Back in the warmup area, a familiar scene unfolded.

"You got the job done; you live to fight another day." Bobby said to me.

OH, MY GOD! I thought. *The Universe is sending me a sign.* No longer illiterate, I knew that this sign was preparing me for an ass whooping. The following day I jumped 6.58 with the help of a too strong tailwind to finish fifth. Two spots out and 22 centimeters away from making the Olympic team. Brittany Reese won with a jump of 6.95 (22' 9¾"). Grace Upshaw, the epitome of solid, made her second Olympic team.

The ramifications of this loss were huge. I was going to have to leave Bobby and Los Angeles; leave Ruth and her kids behind, the only real friend I made since moving to Los Angeles; and sell my condo, which I had turned into an incredible bachelorette pad. The thought of it made me incredibly sad, but I could not survive there. I just couldn't. I was a long way from home, with no real support. I needed to call it quits before I ended up sleeping in my car. Wracking my brain about what I could do, I swallowed my pride and picked up the phone.

THE PRODIGAL DAUGHTER

A few days after the long jump final at the 2008 Olympic Trials, I sat down with Caryl, her husband Greg, and their son Osiris at the Pancake House. I was preparing to swallow my pride and ask if we could work together again. She was no longer a coach at the University of Tennessee. She had gotten the head coaching job at the University of Central Florida in Orlando.

The conversation was uncomfortable to say the least. She recounted how hurt she was that I left, and how I hurt her family as well. She said she needed an apology before she could move on and consider coaching me again.

So, there I sat, over a plate of pancakes hearing myself say, "Coach Caryl, Greg, Osiris, I am really sorry for the pain and hurt I caused all of you by my leaving. I hope you forgive me and that we can work together again."

Like magic, as soon as my apology was said, she accepted, and breakfast became an enjoyable reunion.

I moved to Orlando, and although I still struggled to overcome my fears of jumping, Caryl did an excellent job developing my speed. She took my 100-meter time from 11.20 to 11.05 in one season. So, although I was still mostly a jumper—getting into races every now and then helped me make ends meet.

At this time, I also initiated "PLAN B." I enrolled as a full-time student at the University of Central Florida as a molecular and microbiology major (now referred to as the less cool sounding biomedical sciences). I had a growing sense that it was only a matter of time before I walked away from track and field. It was only going to take me two years to finish the degree, at which time I would enroll in medical school. This was attractive to me because of the prestige and the challenge. I also figured that it was the best way to avert a conversation like this:

"Wow, you were a World Champion once?"

"Yes."

"Wow! What happened? Why'd you quit?"

I could say, "Well…I lost my sponsor because I started to suck year after year after year, so I had to get a job, one thing led to another…"

Or I could say, "Medical school happened."

Medical school it is. And because of the shortage of minority females in STEM fields, I was not at all concerned with my ability to finance medical school. With my almost complete social work degree, and this new major, plus my adventures in the world of professional athletics, my application would be pretty interesting reading to the application review board. I was confident that between my GPA and my extracurricular activities, I would get there.

Running at this point was serving to pay my tuition, pay for books, groceries, and rent. So, training and competing was a priority in as much as it provided me with the means to do those things and implement my "PLAN B."

That would be my downfall.

Excuse me, *another* one of my downfalls.

It was the beginning of finals week, and I sensed the tension and pressure the whole campus felt. Caryl called a practice that conflicted with my academic schedule. As a college athlete there is no question that you must go to class. As a professional athlete, Caryl expected me to come to practice.

I chose class.

She chose to call a meeting.

She asked me to consider retiring because it was obvious to her that I had other priorities. She convinced me that there would be no shame in me leaving the sport now. She said I'd won two medals which was more than most track and field athletes could say. Retirement was the next logical step if my heart wasn't in it anymore.

I agreed.

I retired.

For all of three months.

There would be just one caveat for my return, I couldn't allow Caryl to coach me anymore. Something was unfixable between us and had been since I signed my first pro contract. As I was writing my honors thesis at home, in my barely affordable apartment and somewhat enjoying the break from being bossed around or in constant pain from training, I was able to get the distance needed to see my circumstances clearly.

My oldest friend "anger" reared its ugly head and had a full dialogue with my innermost self.

Wait a minute. I should retire on my own terms not because someone convinced me it was ok to.

If I want to go to class because I'm the one paying for my education, then I should be able to go to class. I'm a grown-ass woman.

I'm paying you to coach me, to work with me, not boss me around, and tell me to quit when you don't get your way.

No. She couldn't coach me anymore; it was obvious to me that her priority wasn't me. So, I called another meeting with the goal to end our coach-athlete relationship in a professional manner so that I could once again move on. She presented me with what I felt was an invoice of astronomical proportions.

"Wait, what? I haven't even trained this quarter, how are you owed money?"

"Because I still spent a lot of time building your training program."

"You spent time building a training program for an athlete you told to retire?"

"Yes, just in case."

"No. No. That's not how this works. This is a service industry. No services equal no pay."

"I disagree"

"You can disagree. Doesn't change the facts."

Our meeting ended without resolution. Later that day I got an email from her husband Greg asking if I was going to blow up the friendship over money.

My response—absolutely.

Because a month before that my Los Angeles condo was sold at auction, and I got a bill from the mortgage lender for $128,000. And a week after that, I had to declare bankruptcy. And weeks after that, I sat eye-to-eye with the judge as I, in front of a room full of strangers, recounted the hardships that befell me and brought me to this lowest of points. I felt judged. I felt like the entire world saw me as a statistic—another black pro athlete who blew through her money.

"Sounds like a typical case of letting debt get away from you," he said in a failed effort to make me feel better.

I took a sideways glance at my attorney as if to ask whether it would be a good idea to share with him why I was really in that seat, taking responsibility for things I didn't do just to stop drowning in debt that I didn't get into on my own. But the attorney touched my hand; I remained quiet, and the judge discharged me and most of my debt. I left the room full of anxious clients hoping to also hear those same words to get some relief from their own struggles.

A week after that I watched through the window as Honda Financial came to repossess my car. I gave it up as part of the bankruptcy.

I was back in my Saturn, the one from high school. So, would I blow up a friendship over money? *Why not?* I'd lost everything else.

WORK FOR IT

I had been struggling. After my bankruptcy, I set out to rebuild my life. I worked three part-time jobs, hopped in my Saturn, and drove to Disney's Wide World of Sports to train. I was grateful for my sponsorship with Saucony. A far cry from what my salary had been with Nike, Saucony's offer of $20,000 a year was a lot better than no dollars. But my rent was $1000 a month. That left $8,000 with which to eat, get gas, pay coaches, and travel to open meets, and nationals (which weren't paid for by event planners or meet directors).

I had to put my ego aside and get a job. With no college degree my best options were in the world of retail. I started my search close to home so that I could eliminate the desire to eat out and cut down on my commute time and gas expenditure. The only place hiring in the area at that time was the Family Christian Bookstore. I kept the fact that I was a practicing Buddhist under wraps and got the job. My resume, filled with track and field accomplishments, was reframed in terms of transferable skills to the workplace. I threw in my high school jobs at Kids "Я" Us and Marc's Grocery store as proof I could work a cash register and play well with others. I love books. So, working at a bookstore was actually a dream of sorts. I didn't enjoy the monotonous musical track that played in the stores, but after a while even that faded into the background. I stocked books, bought books, rearranged shelves, talked to customers, and waited longingly for my shift to end.

Mike, the manager, was a good guy. He's what I would call a "lifer" having been the manager at that specific location since, I don't know, Old Testament times. I was shocked to learn about the importance of performance at the store. I figured if Jesus was involved when we made a sale that was great, when we didn't it wasn't God's will. Nope, occasionally Mike would saunter to the front of the bookstore from his office with a binder in hand.

"We aren't anywhere close to meeting our revenue goal today, one of you will have to go home," he said to a coworker and me.

As I stood on my aching feet behind the register, I shot my hand up.

"I'll go." I didn't want to sound too eager about not wanting to work, so I continued, "I know we all need to work, but I need it just a little bit less right now."

Acting as if I were taking one for the team, I signed off my register slowly, each key stroked with the dramatic heaviness of someone being forced to type against their will. I gathered up my water bottle and handful of sugar-free Werther's Originals hard candies I had stashed beneath the counter and shuffled back to the break room to get my things—smiling slyly to myself on the way.

At some point, as an observer of Buddhism working at a Christian bookstore, things were going to come to a head. In fact, my "staying power" surprised my entire family and my boyfriend, who was a Jewish atheist. Still new in my spiritual journey, we got into plenty of arguments about religion, heaven, and hell. But my final straw at the Christian bookstore had nothing to do with doctrine and everything to do with commercialism. First, there was a program called World Vision; we had to ask each customer if they wanted to sponsor a kid in a far-off land. I hated asking. When Mike gave me the run down on World Vision, I asked how we knew the money went directly to the children being sponsored. He said we trusted God for that.

I said, "In God we may trust, but Man...not so much."

He shrugged and reiterated the importance of asking each customer, and he found it helpful to invoke Jesus by reminding the customers of His words about how we treat "the least among us." I was on thin ice already by not asking every single customer if they wanted to sponsor a child in Africa. I had also gotten so used to hearing "no" that the one time a customer said "yes" I couldn't complete the transaction because I couldn't remember how to sign them up! Thankfully, being bad at upselling Christians using subtle guilt trips isn't a sin. But greed is.

My final week of work at the Family Christian Bookstore was during Easter. Eastertime at a Christian bookstore is like Black Friday. We were killing it. Our Jim Shores and Willow Tree collections of figurines were flying off the shelves. Study guides, Bibles, music, children's books about the resurrection, Veggie Tales stuffed animals, you name it, were impossible to keep stocked. But there was one thing that just wouldn't sell: a replica crown of thorns. I was stocking the shelves when I stumbled across it. Picking up the box I looked inside. I thought maybe it would be more like a sculpture, you know something made to look like a crown of thorns. But, no, it was an actual crown of thorns. The box even featured a disclaimer that this specific crown wasn't the one worn by Jesus on the cross. I checked the price. It was almost $100! *No wonder it hadn't sold.* I thought to myself as I continued stocking and organizing the shelves around it. One day, while on register duty, I noticed a woman who had walked past the crown twice, and was about to make a third pass when Mike stepped in.

"Amazing innit?" he asked her.

"Yes," she said, not looking up, but staring into the cellophane window at the crown.

"Can you imagine?" Mike asked.

"No," the woman said to him. "This is incredible," she continued "it's just more than I can afford, but wow." She bent down to return the crown to its place on the shelf.

Mike stood taller and rested his hands on his belly, "Well, yeah, maybe." Both she and I perked up at this strange response to a customer saying they couldn't afford something.

"But consider the price Jesus paid FOR YOU." Mike said as he meandered away. My mouth dropped open as I watched the guilt wash over that poor woman like a rogue wave. She picked up the box; she bought the crown; and I quit.

Down to two jobs now, I requested more hours at the Apple Store and The Body Shop. Two very different jobs but both 100 percent me. I had never worked so hard for a job as I did for Apple. The three-day training that took place at the Gaylord Palms Hotel was like attending a Herbalife Convention.

"We're changing lives!" our team leaders would yell into their microphones.

"No, we're selling computers!" I'd scream back in my head.

I learned long ago never to drink the entire vat of Kool-aid. Drink, sure. But leave a drop. And this is coming from a woman who does not own a single non-Apple device. I was the top-selling freshman in my store, largely because I spent most of my time explaining to customers that they did not need what they came in for. For example, an elderly woman entered the store and flagged me down.

"How can I help you today?" I asked her.

"My grandson says I need a 15" MacBook Pro," she said shrugging one shoulder.

"Is that so? What did you tell him you'd be using it for?" I asked her.

"Well, I'm into scrapbooking and photos these days, so I think I just want something to make nice photo-books on."

She smiled just thinking of the projects she could do on her new computer. I smiled back.

"Those will be the sweetest gifts," I said, "all those memories you can keep and make beautiful books using iPhoto."

She nodded her head, "Yes, iPhoto."

"Well did you know iPhoto comes on all of our computers? You can make the same beautiful photo books on a MacBook as you can on a MacBook Pro, and it will cost you $1,000 less!"

Her eyes grew large. Encouraged, I continued explaining why the MacBook was a better option for her. After a few minutes, she agreed.

"You've been so helpful!" she said to me.

Then leaning in, she asked, as if it were between just us girls, what else she could get that I thought she'd like? She may have spent less on her computer, but she splurged on accessories, and that was how almost all my transactions went. First, I listened, then I provided a solution. Too many of my colleagues tried to present solutions before understanding the need. When training on the track got too intense for me to stand all day during my shift in the store, my managers at Apple put me on the phones. In the underbelly of the mall, from a workstation in the stock room, I answered AppleCare and customer service questions between scrolling timelines on Twitter and Facebook. I gave my two weeks' notice when it was time to travel to Europe. They said they couldn't hold my job for me but that when I returned in the fall I should send an email to the manager and he'd help me reapply on a fast track.

The Body Shop was two doors down from the Apple Store. On days when I had to work both jobs, I'd peel off my Apple T-shirt and change into my skin-tight black on black outfit. I'd freshen my makeup and darken my eyeliner. I'd finish preparing for my shift by moisturizing my lips and hands—after all we were selling beauty and skin care products. My manager was Andrea, a makeup artist, who was also one of the first people I befriended while church hopping when I first moved to Orlando. You see, for all of my Buddhist practices, I still enjoyed the fellowship that church offered. She was a great friend to me, taking me with her on modeling gigs, inviting me to her home, and giving me a job. "Always, always preach the gospel and only when necessary, use words." Andrea totally embodied my mom's favorite quote. I didn't even have to give a two weeks' notice, when it was time to go to Europe, she simply said she'd see me when I returned. I never did.

THE HAPPIEST PLACE ON EARTH

During that time, I ended up at Disney's Wide World of Sports training with Brooks Johnson.

I knew Brooks prior to training with him; when our family went to Disney World for Christmas vacation, it was Brooks who provided us access to the track so that I could continue to train over the break. My father and Brooks' wife knew each other growing up in Ohio. I know, "It's a small world after all."

Brooks is probably the most interesting coach I have ever worked with. Before every practice we would gather together in the stands and have a debriefing. We'd go around and report what our heart rates were when we awoke that morning. I hadn't yet learned about all the information a resting heart rate could tell you, but I dutifully reported mine. David Oliver, Justin Gatlin, Delloreen Ennis, Joel Brown, Novlene Mills, and Aubrey Herring all had crazy low heart rates, in the forties and fifties. I was in the seventies! They would all just laugh and shake their heads when it was my turn to share.

Brooks nodded after each person reported their rates and would always say, "Damn, girl," after I reported mine. Next, Brooks would say something like, "Why wouldn't one say, 'revert back'?" And we'd collectively answer that, because revert by definition means "back," ergo, it's actually redundant to say, "revert back." And he would say, "Very good." Then he'd tell us what each of us was going to do that day.

I loved my training group. We laughed so much. In hindsight, that shouldn't be the thing you like best about your group. But I had more stress in my life than I cared for, and it felt really good to enjoy driving through the Disney gates to get to practice and enjoy the people I was training with.

Brooks is an old-school coach and probably has more forgotten and irrelevant knowledge than most people ever acquire. He was the first coach of mine to appeal to my nerd side. Yes, Caryl Smith Gilbert and Tony Wells taught me the formulas behind 30-meter projections and how to calculate speed using stride length and stride frequency, but Brooks taught me the practical application of physics. With sidewalk chalk on the track just in front of the long jump board, he had me write in giant letters:

$$F=MxA$$

Force equals mass times acceleration. This was the first time the light bulb turned on for me concerning the actual processes involved in the long jump take off. Our jumps practices were interesting. I was still afraid to jump—still struggling to mentally recover from my injury. Brooks doesn't do well with cowards.

My nickname in that group was "bird" short for "thunder bird" mostly on account of having what's called "thunder thighs" and flying bird-like through the air as a long jumper.

"Bird, put your foot down on the damn board—flat-footed like you are smashing cockroaches. Nobody likes damn roaches. Hit the board like you hate roaches."

That was another light bulb moment for me. Up until this point, I hadn't actually thought about how one went about converting horizontal velocity to vertical lift, terms Brooks taught me actually. I still wasn't jumping far but I did begin to learn what it would take to jump far. There was one major obstacle to my pursuit of overcoming gravity: my weight.

Brooks introduced me to what he liked to call, "The Rainbow Diet" meaning eat any food that has color and avoid white foods. Truly solid advice. I didn't follow it though. White foods were less expensive than colorful foods, and at this point I was getting paid in a year what I used to get paid each quarter. Although I was getting multiple paychecks from my part-time jobs, I couldn't afford to save a cent. My one attempt to overhaul my refrigerator and pantry by shopping at the Fresh Market left me almost sick to my stomach as I swiped my debit card to pay nearly $60 bucks for less than twelve items in the express lane. Needless to say, for my income, "The Rainbow Diet" wasn't sustainable.

Between the types of workouts I was doing and the diet I couldn't afford to be on, I didn't really stand a chance of breaking through again. I did two sorts of workouts with Brooks: jumps practice and race modeling. He'd set up what he called "gates" at certain intervals along the straightaway, and I was supposed to run through these gates either accelerating, holding, or reaccelerating. Caryl used a lot of race modeling in her training as well, using phrases such as "go short" from 30-60, or "diamonds are a girl's best friend" to cue 400-meter runners on where to start their build up to the finish using the relay "diamonds" as markers. The difference between what Caryl did and what Brooks taught was that Brooks' gates were in smaller more manageable chunks. So, I was able to learn to be aware of what I was doing for 10 meters, and then 20, and so on. This helped me place third in the 100-meter dash one year when USATF Outdoor Nationals was in Iowa. I was happy about placing third but not overly so because it was an off year and no one of note bothered to show up. But it made my sponsors happy to see me on a podium, and it earned me a bonus, and a couple lanes at meets I wouldn't have otherwise gotten.

I wasn't running fast, but somehow I was willing my way to podium finishes. That's another thing I'll give Brooks a little credit for. He helped me to further develop, my "f—k it, let's do it" attitude. After workouts, or at least when we *thought* we were finished, Brooks would add on a "tag." This meant that in his infinite wisdom he decided that he wanted to tag a run on to the end of the workout just to see how we would respond. For the short sprinters and jumpers, they were tagged 200s. There was one condition: the tag also came with a time that you absolutely had to beat. I pity the athlete who didn't beat the time. Rumor had it, you didn't want to be that person. One day Brooks told me I had a tag 200, and that I needed to run faster than 24 seconds.

"In practice? After all that?"

"Get on the line," he said.

I walked to the line like I was an inmate walking the "green mile." My training partners were shouting encouragements and some of the professional NFL players training in the infield started shouting too. This was obviously "must-see-tv" for several reasons:

1. I hadn't run a 200 in a long time.

2. I was tired.

3. I had only run 23-mids before, and that was *in* competition!

4. I wasn't in the best shape for sprinting fast, aka I was video vixen thick.

I got on the line, but something within me clicked into place.

I was either going to find a way to beat the clock, or I was going to suffer the consequences.

I was not about to suffer the consequences.

I tapped into my abyss of anger and disappointments again and surged off the line like it was life or death.

Because in a way it was.

To a certain extent one could say tags weren't about what you could or could not do. They were about what you thought you could do, and you'd either validate or debunk those thoughts.

Tags are akin to asking deep philosophical questions like:

What are you made of?

What's in you?

What do you have left to give?

Will you give it?

I gave it.

I ran 23.88, and my training group and the guys in the infield erupted with cheers, shouts, and whistles. I felt like I had won a major meet.

It was a shadowy bittersweet reminder of the athlete I had once been.

Under Brooks coaching and with my sponsor Saucony's support, I traveled to Des Moines, Iowa, for US nationals. It was an off year, which means nationals is just another meet. It does not serve as a qualifier for a World Championship team or an Olympic Team. In off years, many athletes decide to skip the national meet altogether opting out of footing the bill for a meet that offered less money than staying in Europe and competing on the circuit. I knew that this was a greatly diminished version of USATF nationals, but it was an opportunity for me. I was able to save money by staying with my then boyfriend and his family at their home in Ames, Iowa.

The meet was held at Drake Stadium; their signature blue oval hosted the always spectacular and well-attended Drake Relays. A lot of our usual fans stayed home, opting out of making the trip to Des Moines, preferring their living rooms over the humid Midwest summers. I made the 100-meter final. I took third behind Allyson Felix and LaShauntea Moore.

"BIRD! If there was a team to make, you would have made it, girl!" Brooks shouted at me when I returned to the warmup area where he sat cross-legged and shaded under his signature straw hat.

I made a noise to acknowledge his comment without voicing my disagreement. I ran 11.43 for third. If there was a team to make, 11.43 would not have made the final. I knew it, he knew it. But I appreciated the reframe he was offering me, and although my tenure with Brooks did not produce breakthrough performances, it did shine a light on some of the dark places.

DARK PLACES

Meet directors the world over watch the results of the USA Nationals closely. How we perform here in the US goes a long way in opening doors to the critical international meets that take place between the national championships and the global champs. Each competitive opportunity is like iron sharpening iron—helping us polish and prepare to win medals later in the summer.

My third-place finish opened the door for my agent, John Nubani, to put together a nice summer circuit for me. Most of a professional track and field athlete's competitive opportunities are in Europe, Asia, and Africa. Flying back and forth is costly, and so most agents or coaches with large training groups set up base camps overseas to eliminate the number of times we travel across the Atlantic Ocean. My first stop would be Morocco, and because I was too broke to afford a hotel, Nubani arranged for me to stay at one of their training centers. My cell phone only worked on Wi-Fi, so once I touched down in Tangiers my phone became a very expensive paperweight. I waited for my driver for a few moments, after clearing customs, and we drove for about an hour to a compound in the middle of nowhere. Dusty from desert sand, I wheeled my luggage to the front desk.

"Hi, my name is Tianna Madison, and I'll be staying here with you for the next few days until the meet hotel opens," I said to the receptionist.

"Who?" they eyed me, confused.

Oh, no, not again, I thought as panic began to set in. *Were they not expecting me?*

Just the summer before I had an incident where I flew from Crete to London and somehow in the air along the way the rest of my itinerary was canceled, leaving me stranded in London's Heathrow airport with no way to get to my next competition. Without a working phone and too broke to enter my debit card information into the airport's splash page to pay for WI-FI, I swallowed my frustration in a dramatic gulp, flipped open my phone, toggled the roaming settings to on and called my agent. Eight hours, a stiff back, and a bad attitude later, I arrived at my destination. Now, in Morocco, I stood face-to-face with a confused receptionist. I could hear voices in the background, and as I turned to look, I saw the Moroccan Men's National Basketball Team was gathering in the lobby for a team meeting. Out of place, they all stopped to stare at this strange black girl with luggage and the confused receptionist. Once again, I flipped open my cell phone toggled the roaming setting to "on" and called my agent; I handed the phone to the receptionist because Nubani could speak Arabic. Tangier was an interesting place, you could hear Arabic, French, and Spanish all within the same block of the market; however, here in the outskirts of the city, at the Training Center, Arabic was the language.

After several long minutes of feeling like a caged animal at a zoo, I was escorted to my room—a small dorm with a single bed and tiny bathroom. *This will do*, I thought, *this will do just fine.*

I rolled my bag into a far corner of the room and unpacked. It's a quirk of mine; I always unpack. No matter the length of the trip, I always unpack my luggage. My bag was heavy. I had packed books from the library to accompany me on the trip, knowing that I would be spending very little time in English-speaking countries. I had bought books to entertain myself, knowing I wouldn't be able to enjoy television. The book I was reading was titled, *Chant* and *Be Happy*. I had fully leaned into my exploration of Buddhism and had been flirting with giving chanting mantra a try. I decided that a foreign country, all by myself, would be the place to start my chanting practice. Fluffing the pillows up for support, I scooted back against the wall crossed my legs, closed my eyes, and began to chant "Om." I didn't set a timer. I figured I'd stop when I felt like it. When I blinked my eyes open, it was dark outside and my bladder was ready to explode. But I felt strangely at ease, wonderfully calm. The vibrations of "Om" still reverberating among my cells, I went to the bathroom to pee; a stomach cramp told me I needed to do more than that. Settling in, I rested in the residue of calm. Finished, I reached for a non-existent roll of toilet paper.

"FUCK!" I shouted, the word echoing back to me off the walls, bursting my Zen bubble. *Think, think, think,* I said to myself as I contemplated this fix I was in. *Just shower! You were going to anyway! I* smiled to myself for coming up with a somewhat gross but clever solution to my cleanliness problem.

Post flight showers are so satisfying, and I could not have been more grateful for hot water and good water pressure. I turned off the water pulled back the dingy shower curtain and reached for a non-existent towel. *Damn it, no toilet paper, no towels.* I stepped carefully out of the shower dripping water across the tiled floor. I dug around for a washcloth. After my first year overseas, I learned how rare it was to get a face cloth, so I never set off for a trip without heading to Walmart and buying an entire pack of face cloths; they are so cheap that I have no problem leaving them behind. I dried off with the little towels and flipped open my phone to call my agent again. I wasn't sure how he would pull off getting me toilet paper and towels but that was his job. He told me to hang tight; someone would be by for me. I dressed, grabbed another book, and went downstairs to hang out on the grounds, kick my feet up, and wait.

An hour or so later, Rashid Ramzy, Moroccan by birth but representing Bahrain in the 800- and 1500-meter races pulled up to the front of the training center in his Volkswagon Touareg. He told me John sent him. He and two of his friends were going to take me to the store so I could grab what I needed to be comfortable in my room for the next couple days. I knew of Ramzi from the circuit; I didn't know who his two friends were, but my options were few: stay in my room with no water, no toilet paper, and no towels, or go with them. I chose to go with them. I would not return to my room for two days.

Unfortunately for me, it wasn't the first time I'd gotten into a car in a foreign country and the driver refused to take me to my desired destination. The first time this happened to me was at Pan Am juniors in Barbados. Carol Rodriguez and I were in the marketplace, and after strolling around for the afternoon, we hailed a cab. The cab, nothing more than a minivan, hardly seemed drivable, but there weren't any other available cars, and we needed to be back on campus in time for the mandatory team meeting. So, we got in. The driver asked us a million questions. Notoriously tight-lipped about my private life, even then, I kept quiet. Carol babbled on. The conversation was turning as the man shifted his questions toward our plans for the night, and the minivan was taking corners on two wheels, on a route we had never travelled to and from campus.

"Sir, we need to get back to campus or we'll get in trouble," I said.

"No, we won't," said Carol. I whipped my neck in her direction wishing she'd just shut up. I was 16 years old and still saw every adult as an authority figure.

"Sir," I said again.

"Yes, soon, soon," he reassured me.

The minivan slowed and eventually stopped. I looked out of the window; it appeared we were at some kind of repair garage or old gas station. Men loitered in the dirt parking lot with rum and beer. I was afraid. Carol seemed unbothered as the driver chatted with the others and pointed toward the cars. *I'm going to be raped today* was my last thought before the driver along with one of his friends returned to the car and began to drive again. Two more stops later, we were dropped off at the campus. Grateful to have not been violated but still frightened at the possibility and annoyed with what I thought was Carol's complete obliviousness to the danger we were in, I slid the minivan door shut and walked to my room in silence. I called home despite the roaming charges. I'd have to give up my allowance for a long time to cover that charge.

Having made it out of the Barbados joy ride unscathed, I sized up my current situation in Morocco. I decided that if anything were to happen to me, John Nubani would know exactly who to call and where to look, plus he spoke the language. My phone, practically useless, was still up in my room. I climbed into the back seat as I watched the men's basketball team watch me drive off. Our first stop was for toilet paper, water, and snacks, and my anxiety dimmed a bit since we were actually doing what my stated mission was. The hunt for bath towels was a little more difficult, impossible for some reason; and Ramzi suggested in his broken English that I borrow one of his from his house, but that it was time to eat dinner. The skies had darkened more. *I could eat*, I thought, and the four of us began the search for dinner. Ramzi chose a spot near the water that had no sign on the door. The doorman gave Ramzi a knowing nod as he walked by, and he shot me a wink when I did. It looked like a night club. I had no idea at the time what hookah was but if I had, I would have known this was a hookah lounge. We sat at a table away from the designated smoking area and looked over the menu. I already knew what I wanted: lamb. A server came by and asked for our drink orders. Ramzi ordered water, and I ordered a Smirnoff ice. Eyebrows raised in surprise, and smiles crept across their faces as I placed my order.

The music was like chanting. The restaurant was so dark, we could hardly see the food on the plates in front of us when it arrived; but the smell, I still remember the smell of my lamb. Like a bloodhound, I sniffed out the location of the lamb in front of me, needlessly stabbed it with my fork, and took a bite. My anxiety melted like the tender meat did on my tongue. Half a dozen Smirnoff Ices, and another entree later, we were still kicked back in the lounge, faces flushed with satisfaction, the music lulling us to sleep. Ramzi and his two friends were speaking lazily in their native language, while I—one hand resting on the top of my head and the other rested on my well-fed midsection—chuckled as if I understood what was being said. I may not have understood the words they were speaking, but I understood the vibe, and it felt a lot like how I felt after chanting. Ramzi signaled that it was time to move on, and so we thanked the server. Ramzi had paid for everyone's food—something I had forgotten to be concerned about in the moment. We piled into his car and drove in the direction of his house for my towel.

Lights flashed up ahead. "Shurta! Police!" said the still unnamed friend in the passenger's seat. Ramzi slowed for a moment, before slamming his foot on the gas. We shot by the officers so fast I could hardly hear their shouts.

Screaming at the top of my lungs in the back seat, all I could think about was *Locked Up Abroad*, that series on *National Geographic Channel* about tourists doing stupid things and going to jail in crappy conditions in foreign countries.

"OH MY GOD! WHY!?"

Ramzi eyeballed me through the rearview mirror, "Is OKAY. They want money. I say no," he shrugged.

He would know, I thought. The police did not give chase, and we made it safely to Ramzi's apartment. Where my dorm room was scant, Ramzi's place was luxurious, boasting air conditioning, satellite TV, internet, and a PlayStation. This is what it must be like, the rewards of being from a country so small that any success of yours is also theirs.

Is this what I have to look forward to? I wondered to myself. Already the owner of two medals, I knew all too well how quickly that light faded and how short-lived that financial windfall really is.

"The towels?" I asked after taking in the room.

"Yes, yes, sit." I sat.

Ramzi's two friends took up controllers to the PlayStation while he settled in an armchair and fell asleep. Then I fell asleep. I was awoken the next morning by Ramzi gently nudging my shoulder and telling me it was time for breakfast.

We walked to breakfast together, the four of us, and posted up at a table outside in the bright sun. The server brought us fresh mint tea and pastries, and as much as I wasn't where I was supposed to be (*what if the drug testers came?*), I decided there was no place I'd rather be. I had a boyfriend back home who had just moved in with me who would probably have a problem hearing that I spent the night with three guys I didn't know. But I knew I'd never tell him. I'd learned early the power of secrets. Whatever happened in Morocco was going to stay in Morocco. I sat back into my metal chair sipping my mint tea, heart open to adventure and possibility.

I still didn't have a towel. Unprepared for a sleepover, I was still in yesterday's clothes. I could smell my armpits, but at that point there was no way to tell which of us was the musty one, so I decided not to care. We stopped by the beach and then another spot for a midday snack. We went to dinner earlier the second night at a different spot but with the same vibe. I ordered lamb again as spices mixed with sweet smelling smoke and the music lulled me into a different frequency. So entranced was I with the atmosphere and the music, I lost all track and concept of time. We sat for dinner at 8 p.m.

in the evening. It was 8 a.m. when we left. Skipping "home" altogether, we grabbed the same table at the same cafe and enjoyed mint tea and pastries for the second morning together.

"The meet is soon," I said to everyone and no one in particular.

Ramzi nodded his head. There was one thing he took seriously, and that was competition. Back at his apartment, we grabbed a bath towel and he drove me, my snacks, and my toilet paper back to my dorm room. I closed the door to the car.

"Shukran!" I yelled to him, "Thank you!"

I placed third in the 100-meter dash at the meet, behind Sheronne Simpson and Carmelita Jeter.

It wasn't my first or last trip to Morocco. And for the first time, for my last competition of the season, I'd get to visit another African country, Ghana. I almost never knew who would be at a meet before I arrived, and I hoped I would know some people well enough to hang with while we were there. On the plane I was happily surprised to see people I knew on the flight. I didn't know them well enough to call them friends, but their faces were familiar which eased the discomfort I always feel flying to a new destination. One of those faces belonged to Nichole Denby who was a hurdler for the US. We landed in Accra and parked on the tarmac a long way from the airport and jet bridges, as far as I could tell. A flight attendant spoke over the PA system. "We will be deplaning by stairway, mind your step." Having been upgraded to first class because of my frequent flier status, I was one of the first people off the plane. I was startled at the sight. There was a welcome party of at least two dozen people at the foot of the stairs.

"WELCOME HOME MY SISTER!" one man near the front of the crowd shouted showing every single one of his white teeth in a huge smile. His arms were outstretched as if he wanted me to jump into his arms from the top of the staircase.

I descended the stairs carefully and hesitantly. The welcome party equally tugged, hugged, and dragged me deeper into the crowd. They did this greeting for every athlete deplaning who they recognized. It was much more fun to be part of the crowd. I watched amused at Nichole descended the stairs fully embracing her royal welcome.

We cleared customs and then the meet organizers took our passports. I panicked. One of the first things I learned on one of my first trips overseas was to never part with your passport. Yet there I was, less than an hour into my first trip to Ghana, and my passport was in the possession of God knows who, headed to who knows where. Still without my passport, we were loaded onto a minibus and told we had "a bit of a drive" to the meet hotel. This wasn't unusual at all. And so, we loaded onto the bus, and settled in. I readjusted my headphones and neck pillow and prepared for an hour to an hour and a half drive to wherever we were headed. Somebody was smart enough to ask how long the drive would be, and we all gasped at the answer. The drive would be 4.5 hours long. None of us were prepared for that. No passports in our possession and a 4.5-hour drive through the tropical forests of Ghana. Two hours in, someone asked if we'd be able to stop for a bathroom break. I was scared. I kept envisioning scenes from the movie *Blood Diamond*, staring Leonardo DiCaprio and Djimon Hounsou, and child soldiers ambushing our party—such a narrow, ignorant, and naive view I had of Africa.

"Of course," our driver said cheerfully, "just ahead there is a place."

We gathered our things and secured our bags in preparation to hop off the bus, stretch our legs, use the bathroom, and buy water and snacks. The stop was just in time; my stomach cramped as it was finally reacting to the less-than-ideal foods available to athletes while traveling. But there was no place to do any of those things.

"Where's the bathroom?" someone in the group asked.

"Here," the driver said handing a roll of toilet paper to that same person. "That ditch there behind that little wall is where you may relieve yourself." My eyes grew big in horror. We were going to have to straddle a ditch and pee. No, I was going to have to straddle a ditch and take a dump. I doubled over both in pain at the intensified cramps and embarrassment in advance as the group shuffled together to the ditch. Mindful of our shoes we did our best to straddle, squat, and reduce splash as we passed the roll of toilet paper up and down the row. Ashamed, I boarded the bus again, put on my noise-canceling headphones and wished for sleep.

A couple of hours later we emerged from the forest as the Golden Tulip Resort revealed itself in the darkness like a flower greeting the sun when winter turns to spring. Happy to have finally made it to our destination in one piece, we poured into the lobby, waiting for check-in. Somehow our passports arrived before we did. I was roomed with Nichole. We were a perfect match. She loved to talk, I loved to listen. And she told me all about her coach, Rana Reider, and how he was returning to Florida, and that she could not wait.

Hmmm, I thought. *Is this something I should look into?*

THE GOING PRICE

I won that meet in Ghana, the last of the season, but I couldn't help but feel that my time in the sport was also over. It had been six years. I hadn't made an Olympic Team, but I had been to three World Championships and had won two of them. That was more than most of my colleagues could hope for in a career. And yet, I was largely disappointed with my time in the sport. It's one thing to retire on your own terms, in a manner you can be proud of, it's another to just suck so badly you'd rather just fade into the annals of sport history. A World Champion at 19; the "next Jackie Joyner Kersee," they'd said. But there I was, fresh out of bankruptcy court, with three part-time jobs, a $20,000 Saucony contract, a tax bill that would be impossible to repay, and performances that gave me no indication things would turn around anytime soon. It was time to seriously consider implementing PLAN B.

When I had returned to Caryl, who was coaching at UCF in Orlando, Florida, I reenrolled in school to finish the social work degree. I had started it but hadn't completed it when I attended the University of Tennessee. My heart wasn't in social work, it was in science, and once it occurred to me that, because I was paying my own tuition, I could study whatever I wanted. I switched my degree program to molecular and microbiology. My plans to attend Stanford were back on, but this time it would be for medical school.

I decided to visit Chuck before the fall semester began. He was the one person who I could have those types of candid conversations with. He was the head coach at the Academy of Art University in San Francisco but had made arrangements for me to attend a Stanford football game and tour the campus, almost like an official visit. He assured me that there was no wrong answer, no wrong choice, that I was brilliant enough to be successful at whatever I decided, and that if I wanted to go to school at Stanford, together we could make it work. If there was anyone on the planet who knew how to thrive while broke, it was Chuck. I took his words to heart but wasn't too keen on returning to California to live. When we said goodbye to each other at the end of the weekend, I knew I wasn't ready to call it quits on track and field. I reached out to Rana to find out where in Florida he would be relocating to and if he would be willing to coach me.

I was exhausted and lonely though. It had been six years since I'd done anything of value in an outdoor track season. My financial woes, although alleviated by bankruptcy, weren't completely eradicated; my romantic relationships had all crashed and burned, and I was tired of fighting. I was tired of living in my little sister's dirty apartment, tired of working three jobs, tired of being defensive about why I even bothered to continue in the sport, tired of going to bed alone, and feeling misunderstood and uncared for.

And then I met John.

We met at a restaurant called Timpano's in an Orlando neighborhood called Doctor Phillips. He was driving an Audi A8, I was still in my three-door Saturn with four bald tires, but nobody saw me get out of the car. I parked a hilariously far distance from the restaurant's entrance. The patrons didn't need to know that the meal I planned to order was just about the last thing I could afford.

Anyway, my soul was tired, and so I was open to the possibility of falling in love and therefore I did not try to manipulate the who, what, when, where, or why of it all. That would have required more energy than I had.

John had dimples.

Not only did he have dimples that made me melt when he graced me with his mega-watt smile and perfect teeth, he had a ruggedly handsome face and kind eyes. He exuded the sort of confidence that came from staring down some of life's hardest pitches, swinging for the fences, and knocking it out of the park.

He wasn't without his losses, but he was used to winning.

Our first conversation didn't follow the typical small talk and superficial conversation you'd expect when getting to know someone. For me, our first conversation was akin to someone slapping me in the face with a "reality check." Basically, in that first conversation he made it clear that I was both responsible for where I was in my life and my discontent with it, and that if I wanted to, I could turn it all around.

I don't know why, with my notorious distrust of people, and my tendency to play my cards very close to the chest, I swallowed his "lecture" hook, line, and sinker. Ultimately, I came to the conclusion that this man, who was successful on his own, had no reason whatsoever in the world to lie to me. None at all. So, I believed him, and I took the confidence he exuded and repurposed it for myself.

The one thing he said to me that stood out that evening was that until I decided to do all the right things 100 percent of the time, I would never actually know how good I could be. He told me that it sounded like I had never once fully committed to both a diet *and* proper training at the same time. He told me that maybe, if I could do that, commit to not taking shortcuts, I could surprise myself.

The logic made sense. Everything he said was true, even as we sat at a booth in the bar lounge, I had one foot out of the door preparing to leave the sport entirely. Perhaps, with a new coach and a new man I could begin again.

And this is the part where I tell you that everything you've read up to this point was a lie. Well, not a lie but a highly selective story the two of us narrated together for public consumption. Here's the truth, he found me on Match.com, his profile featured no photo and all the answers to the form questions said, "ask me." Contrarily, my match profile was my entire life story complete with a gallery of photos. John spammed my inbox with messages that ranged in subject matter from his telling me about his house, name dropping famous neighbors, and begging for "a shot." I finally agreed to meet him after he sent me a message explaining that even if nothing came of our meeting romantically, he would have been happy just to have met me at all. So, I agreed to meet him at Timpano's, a restaurant in the upscale neighborhood of Dr. Phillips in Orlando. For some reason, he did not want people to know that he used dating apps, but I was quite proud of joining Match.com! I was so tired of being single that my broke ass actually paid for my membership, which was a big deal for a girl as broke as I was. He contacted me on just my second day of being on the site. After several dates, he asked me to cancel my account, and my immediate reaction was "BUT I JUST PAID FOR IT!"

Anyway...

Rana Reider didn't quite have all his ducks in a row about his move back to Florida. It was loosely understood that Daytona Beach was going to be the place, and Emory Riddle was the university's facilities we'd use. But he was still somewhat open to other places if the facilities and the price was right. So, I asked John if he could look into training facilities for Rana too, because either half of the local population were associates of his or the other half had done business with him. John met Rana in person before I did.

I'd only talked to Rana, mostly by email, up until that point. He had to send me an introductory strength program since under Brooks' tutelage our weight room experience was limited to bench press and bicep curls. I lifted at Gold's Gym in Altamonte Springs with the occasional help of a friend named Sam. His only job was to make sure I didn't pin myself under the bar trying to build a foundation of strength after years of little to no strength training at all.

This "lifting 101" program lasted about four weeks. In the meantime, Rana locked down Daytona Beach as the location we would train. I lived in Sanford at the time, which was about 30 to 45 minutes away, depending on the traffic. John lived in Tampa which was about two hours from Sanford. I'd go to practice in the morning, then classes and sometimes on dates with him in the evening, and down to Tampa on Saturdays after practice.

He and I had some memorable dates; we laughed constantly, but he also was extremely busy running two companies. One, a tech startup that focuses on bringing people together through events, and the other a boutique wealth management firm he started when he was in his twenties. Because he was so busy and I hoped that maybe he'd look up from his work and realize he had some free time for me, I started to drive to Lakeland, Florida. Lakeland is less than 40 minutes away from his office but an hour from where I lived. I would sit in Lakeland at the Starbucks doing homework in the hopes that he would call and say he had some free time just so I could then say, "Funny you should say that, I just so happened to be down the street from you right now," but that rarely happened.

Rana's Daytona Beach training group was called DBTC which we jokingly said also stood for the Dead Broke Track Club. Rana's fee was $1,000 a month due on the first of each month. After paying Rana $12,000 for the year, that would leave me with $8,000 before taxes. I was paid quarterly, so that left me $2,000 to live on for three months after paying Rana; not to mention, I was paying my own tuition and had a full schedule of classes. With training and a full course load, getting a job would be difficult. John Nubani was able to talk Saucony into including a coaching stipend in my $20K a year contract, but the stipend did not go into effect until the new year. I started training with Rana in September. That left $4,000, which I didn't have, that needed to be paid before my sponsor took over. John covered it for me, no questions asked, and with no mention of payback.

But John knew nothing at all about track and field or what training looked like or how competitions were structured. After dating for a couple months, I started to drive to Tampa on Fridays after practice. We'd get up early and drive to practice together on Saturday; on our way back to Tampa we'd stop at the AMF Bowling Center and bowl a few games. I'd drive back to Sanford on Sunday morning to prepare for my week of training and classes.

Those weekends in Tampa were like a window into another world. The neighborhood was exclusive and quiet, the house something straight out of a magazine I'd pinned to my vision board. Born into an Italian family, John had learned how to cook from his parents. He cooked for me all the time.

His cooking for me ended up being the turning point in my diet. My dinners were steaks, sautéed mushrooms, spinach, and if it was a particularly tough training week, I enjoyed a large steaming bowl of garlic pasta. You knew it was Sunday because Boccelli played through the Bose sound system that was integrated into every room in the house, and the smell of Applewood bacon wafted through the air. He'd pack all of these meals up for me in Tupperware, and I'd drive home to Sanford with a week's worth of food. I started to drop weight for the first time in a long time. Once, as I got ready to head back to Sanford, he told me he had something for me; he reached out his hand and placed a wad of cash in mine.

"I can't accept this!"

"Why not? You're driving back and forth on the highway. The car needs gas, and a person should always have cash."

"But this is YOUR cash."

"I'm giving it TO YOU."

My dilemma was this: When the man you're dating has way more money than you, do you dive in and enjoy the spoils? Or do you make it clear that you're there for his company—not his money? I wanted to make it clear I was in the latter group. He assured me he got the picture but forced me to keep the money.

I drove away floored. I hadn't had that much cash in my possession in years. It was the first time I felt, *safe*. I breathed a sigh of relief; I didn't have to wonder how I was going to fill the gas tank or if I could buy groceries. I was taken care of. That was the most freeing feeling of all. No, money can't buy you love, and it can't buy you happiness, but it can buy you gas and groceries and sometimes that's all a person needs. Five hundred bucks. The going price for my soul.

THE FIRST TIME

Thankfully, I finished the semester. With training more difficult than anything I had ever done before, plus a demanding class schedule, and all of the driving I was doing to spend my free time with John, I could not be happier for the break. It was New Year's Eve, and he and I were hanging out on the couch in front of the television watching a *RedBull* stunt involving a snow mobile and a motor bike. It was after the snow mobile flew, what appeared to be an impossible distance, John turned to look at me.

"You know, 2012 is an Olympic year. What do you say we go for it? Together, me and you, and see what happens?"

I remained quiet which is my initial reaction when it feels like the ground is about to shift beneath my feet. The Olympics was not really a goal of mine. I tried twice and failed twice. The second time nearly broke my spirits because it broke me financially. But this was another moment like our "first date" moment where I could find no reason not to dive in headfirst.

So, I did.

I chose not to register for classes in the spring semester. *School will be waiting for me when I'm done*, I assured myself. Plus, I struggled to maintain my grades in my evening classes and labs that were held after training. I was just too damn tired. John asked me to move in with him, so I did—although most of my possessions remained at my sister's apartment in Sanford. And thus, we started our journey to the Olympic Games together.

John was surrounded by a lot of people who went out of their way to thanklessly take care of him, and once I moved in, I was thrust into this makeshift family of people who would do most anything he asked of them. There was somebody to check the weather, someone to check the traffic, someone available to travel with me if he couldn't make it, someone to purchase tickets, someone to invoice my sponsor, someone to wash and detail my car, someone else to do the laundry, someone to clean the house; the list went on and on.

He truly seemed all in. He started a training program of his own, and by the time the championship season came around he was down over 50 pounds. He would ask me later how I could "fall in love" with a fat guy, and I told him that between how I felt about myself when I was around him and what I saw when I looked into his eyes, I hardly noticed. And that was true until he punched me—the first time.

We were driving back to Tampa from practice in Daytona Beach, a 2½ hour drive I made the other five days of the week. We were having a conversation about branding. You see, he had had a whole plan for my "coming out party" that included how to dress, how to handle the media, and how to act at practice. I don't remember the exact question he asked me, but I do remember that it required thought. Apparently, I took too long to answer because the next thing I remembered was my head rebounding off the passenger window. The right side of my face left an oily smudge on the glass.

If thinking slowly was what got me into that predicament, my mind was now moving at the speed of light. I began to talk to myself, question myself.

Did what just happened really happen? So, the relationship is over right? I've always said I would leave the moment a man puts his hands on me. But we're on a highway going 80 miles an hour. I'm in this car with him for another hour. What the hell do I do?

I sat taller in the passenger seat and stared at the cars in front of us on the highway.

And then I answered the original question, whatever it was.

"See," he said, "all you had to do was say that in the first place."

And then I apologized.

And because I apologized, he apologized.

And I hated myself a little from that moment forward.

But once we pulled into the driveway at home he was back to his charming self, and slowly, albeit apprehensively, I returned to "normal" too.

And although I never forgot "the incident," I did allow myself to believe it was an isolated one. It wouldn't be.

INDOORS

February ushers in the indoor season. My first meet was in Boston. We arrived at the meet hotel and were met by a flustered John Nubani, my agent. Apparently, the meet director tagged me as expendable and gave my lane in the 60-meter dash to someone else. They paid me $1,000 for the inconvenience. Disappointed, I took the elevator to my room. At the same time, unbeknownst to me, and without my permission, John fired my agent in a shouting match in the hotel lobby.

My next meet was already on my schedule and confirmed to take place in Fayetteville, Arkansas, for the 2012 USA Track and Field Classic Indoor Meet. I was entered in both the 60-meter dash and the long jump. The start list was stacked; everyone except me were bona fide sprinters: Allyson Felix, Veronica Campbell Brown, Gloria Asumnu, Murielle Ahouré, and Jeneba Tarmoh.

There was a preliminary round and a final. Sandwiched between those two rounds of the 60 was the long jump. I was in the outside lane for the first round. I got out of the blocks faster than I ever have and stormed my way to the finish line. I looked up at the results board to see my time.

Holy shit.

The board said: 7.05.

It was a new world lead.

My personal best before that moment was 7.18.

John was pumped; I was in shock, and Rana had this goofy grin on his face as I walked to the long jump area to change into my long jump spikes. Rana was hanging over the spectator rails trying to get my attention. I saw him and jogged over.

"I'm pulling you out of the jumps."

"You sure?"

"Yeah, I'm sure. I want you to win this fucking final. Go scratch and then get over here and get your legs up."

"Okay."

So that's what I did. John paced nervously nearby.

It was time for the final.

Now, because I had won my heat, I was in one of the middle lanes. But according to Ato Boldon, a commentator for NBC, the story was really about the battle between longtime rivals Allyson Felix and Veronica Campbell Brown. No one was paying attention to me when the gun went off.

But somewhere around 30 meters...

I hit my turbo button.

Which is another way of saying...

I tapped into my anger.

And I decided I wasn't losing that race, and the Universe could take all my old relationship sagas, financial problems, coaching issues, family drama, and shove it up its you-know-what.

I won that race in 7.02—a new World lead.

Channeling that kind of anger helped me compete at a different level, but it had side effects. That race in Arkansas was the first event I'd won of any real consequence in seven years, and I did not know how to handle it. I couldn't process it. The only thing I could do was sit, and I wanted to sit in silence because I needed a minute to get through my fog of fury and to see myself and my life clearly.

I wasn't sure how to feel. I had learned from experience that being victorious and its implications for your future aren't always things worth celebrating. I let past baggage taint how I processed the present.

John was FURIOUS about my post-race reaction, and he didn't care who knew it. My father, who was also in attendance, tried to explain I just needed a minute.

I said, "It's been seven years since I won something. Seven years."

I kept repeating the words, "seven years," over and over as I sat alone in the warmup area. I was later escorted to drug testing and afterward John, my father, and I went out for a celebratory drink. When we returned to our hotel room at the Embassy Suites, he wasted no time telling me how disappointed he was in my reaction. He told me that since I didn't feel the need to give him credit for my return to the top, that our relationship was over—that if I was really in love with him I would have jumped into his arms after the race, not stopped for an interview, not even needed a minute to myself for myself.

It was clear to me that I would need to modify my behavior if I was going to continue traveling to and competing well in those indoor meets.

My experience at Tyson turned me into a nervous wreck at competitions. I was constantly worried that the next time a colleague tried to greet me with a hug they'd get stiff armed by him, or worse he'd accuse me of having some previous sexual relationship with them.

"Why do they all think they can touch you?" he asked me once.

"It's been a long time. It's the first couple meets of the year. Everyone's just saying hello to each other again," I tried to explain.

"You can hug people if you want, but it doesn't make a lot of sense for a girl who was molested in high school to have no problem hugging people." This comment, I knew, was a dig. So, I changed my behavior, again. I went from a girl who loved hugs, to a hands-off person.

I made sure I took on the most standoffish persona possible to keep people away from me. I'm sure people noticed. But if anyone said anything it was to each other, never to me. By March, there wasn't any way for people not in my immediate circle to reach me.

One night, as John was making us dinner, he asked me about some old tweets of mine.

The tweet in question was about the movie Green Lantern and in addition to being a fan of comic books I mentioned that Ryan Reynolds starring in the movie was an added bonus.

"I just want to know if you think Ryan Reynolds is attractive," he asked me while seasoning thick cuts of ribeye steaks.

I sat on a barstool, knowing I was in a tricky situation. The tweet was out there, sent well before I met him. In fact, I sent it from the theater while on a date with another guy. I figured the truth would be harmless to tell.

"Yes, I do think he's attractive."

The silence between us stretched on.

"How could you sit there and tell me that you find another man attractive?" he demanded to know breaking the building tension.

I sat on the barstool dumbfounded.

It wasn't the first time he'd spent his free time scrolling through old tweets. Something told me it wouldn't be the last. Once during a Saturday practice, he spent the entire time in the men's restroom scrolling through the email inbox on my phone. After practice he asked me about every email exchange that he could find that included a member of the opposite sex. Rana gave me a pat on the back and mumbled under his breath that he was impressed. I got through the workout thinking that what was going on in the bathroom was behind us.

I thought it was me.

I thought that there was something about my behavior that made him feel like I didn't love him enough. So, I kept modifying my behavior thinking that if I changed myself, it would change him. That was a familiar space for me to occupy; I have always felt I had to prove myself and my worth. But just because something is familiar doesn't mean it's normal, and just because it's normal doesn't mean it's healthy. I managed to win the rest of my indoor meets, including Birmingham, England, and USATF Indoor Nationals. John invited my parents to our hotel room to brag about how he was able to turn me and my career around. Look at her, look at her body. My parents grew uncomfortable and flashed awkward smiles as they nodded their heads in agreement and praise. "Show them your abs. Go ahead, lift up your shirt," John prodded.

"We know she looks good," my mom said, trying to spare me the exhibition. I raised my shirt. John beamed with pride. I shrank with embarrassment, as did my parents as they made an excuse to leave.

I stood naked for him often. Reminiscent of old slave auctions, I stood at attention as his eyes wandered up and down my body. He'd pinch a fold of skin near my armpit or lower back and either praise or admonish me for my size. The only thing missing was a rudimentary check of my teeth. Sometimes he'd take a picture for reference, which he stored in his photo vault app full of pictures of who knows what and God knows who.

In the two weeks between indoor nationals and the IAAF Indoor World Championships taking place in March, all of my social media accounts were shut down. My blog was shut down, and my phone number and email addresses were changed. I went along with this because I did not want to find out what would happen if I didn't. These changes happened quickly and caught my mother's attention. My mother sent an email asking him to explain what his motivation and plans were with taking me offline and shutting down my blog. Her questioning him enraged him, and it was from that moment on that he decided it was better that they weren't in our lives at all. He used stories that I shared with him about my relationship with my parents (my mother specifically) to persuade me that it was the best thing for me too.

And I'll be honest, I was grateful at the idea of getting a break from trying to impress my mother. In a twisted way, all the issues I wish I could have raised with my parents he raised for me. And he told me he would handle it. Except he didn't.

He wrote a script for me, and I called my parents and told them how "I was an adult, and I didn't need them hovering over my every decision. I would take it from here, and he and I would be married soon. Then I asked them not to come to the upcoming championships in Istanbul, Turkey.

After that phone call, John was the only person left in my life.

I didn't handle my new reality well going into IAAF world indoor championships. My appetite was gone. I was losing too much weight and as a result was losing strength. I wasn't sleeping. Emotionally, I was all over the place. I packed my bag for this trip to Istanbul in a haze. I forgot my makeup bag. I forgot my hair products. I even forgot my fresh wig. I rolled up to the World Championships looking like I had been dragged in from off the street.

I hadn't fully understood the terms and conditions of my estrangement from my parents until I arrived in Turkey. Upon my arrival in Istanbul, I texted my parents that I had arrived safely—mostly out of habit. They thanked me for the heads up, told me to be safe, and that was that. I thought nothing else of the exchange.

Until I ran into them in the hotel lobby—in Turkey.

After I told them not to come, and they said they weren't coming, we ended up choosing the same hotel to stay in. What were the odds?! John was with me in the lobby. Had I been down there alone and saw them, I'd have an entirely different story to tell you now.

Instead, a quick risk calculation in my head determined I needed to stay quiet. So, I didn't say anything. My parents and I wordlessly locked eyes as John grabbed my arm and pulled me through the lobby, to the elevator, and up to the room.

"You told me they said they weren't coming," he shouted.

"That's what they told me!" I shouted back. I was scared. We were about to have one of our "loud" arguments in a foreign country. In Turkey where I strongly doubted I'd get a lot of sympathy for running my mouth off at a man.

"Give me your phone," he demanded. I handed it to him. He read me the last text message I sent to my parents about arriving safely.

"Why would you do this to me?" he asked.

"Do what?" I asked, legitimately confused.

"Why would you contact them?" he asked again. I didn't have an answer. And I knew from experience that not having an answer was a dangerous position to be in.

He approached me where I was sitting on the bed, and I jumped.

"Why are you jumping? You think I'm going to hit you? You're afraid of me now?" John was stocky but he wasn't tall. He puffed up his chest and stood over me. Part of me was disconnectedly amused by the whole ordeal. I found it absurd that he would question why I would think he was about to hit me.

Like why wouldn't I, at this point?

But we were often each other's mirror. Seeing me jump as he approached me was a reflection he wasn't yet ready to reconcile with the man he wanted to believe he was.

But there was another part of me that was thinking, *fuck, what happens if we get into a fight here…*

I stood up to create some distance between us. I backed away from him and into the wall of the room. He followed, not even an inch from my face, ranting about choosing between him or them—the first of many times I'd be given this ultimatum.

In that moment, I knew what the right answer was. But my lips felt almost glued shut. Adrenaline began to flood my system as I tried to shrink myself as if somehow the wall would be able to absorb me if I wished it hard enough.

Spittle.

I think that did it. Spittle hit my face.

I saw red instantly. I was convinced he didn't spit on me on purpose, but I was aware of his very intentional posturing to intimidate me. I was trapped in a corner. His body was blocking my access to the rest of the room.

The room was a split-level suite. When you entered the room from the hallway you were actually on the second level. There was a small office space and kitchenette on that level. From there, one could descend the cedar staircase to the bedroom and bathroom.

I was pinned to the corner where the bathroom met the bedroom. To my left was the king size bed, to my right the bathroom door, and just beyond that the staircase. It made no sense for me to lock myself in the bathroom. But John's body was blocking me from getting to the stairs. Still shouting at me and already uncomfortably close to my face, he stepped forward again, bumping his chest against mine in an attempt to pin me to the wall.

In a movement so fast, I hardly registered it myself, I shot my right hand forward causing him to stumble backwards a step. That surprise move gave me the time and space to make a break for the stairs. If I could just get out of this room, I could make it to the front desk, locate my parents and be rescued from this situation. But I didn't make it, John grabbed me again and I could feel hope fading from my body as I reached for the door being pulled deeper into the room. "You ungrateful cunt." We'd been together for six months, and I already was unfazed by being called such an ugly word. He spun me around to face him, my back once again against the wall. Spit, vitriol, racial slurs spilled from his lips. And even that wasn't enough, he bumped his chest against mine shrinking the space between our faces completely.

I panicked; my claustrophobia was mixed with terror and created the perfect haze of desperation. I no longer knew what my end goal was. I could only think of rescuing myself from that specific moment. "You got something to say? Where you going?" Each move I made was met with a counter move by him. He pushed and shoved me repeatedly into the wall. "Huh? Nothing? Nothing to say about your shit parents? Tell me again how good they were to you? Tell me again about how shit your life was before me. Where you going?"

That was it. One tease, one taunt, one shove too many. I pivoted away from the wall. With a strength foreign to myself, I struck John's neck with my left hand, pinning him against the wall. I could feel his pulse under my thumb, and how it sped up. I saw the look of surprise mixed with the tiniest hint of concern. I leaned in. I had his neck in a death grip. I squeezed his neck tighter and tighter as his face turned red and then purple.

Oh, shit! I'm killing him.

Almost as if in shock, I released his neck, stumbled backward toward the bed, and sat down like I weighed a 1,000 pounds. I buried my face in my hands and cried large pain-filled tears of sorrow.

I didn't recognize myself. I lost myself so completely, I nearly killed a man in a hotel room in Turkey. A frequent binge-watcher of *Locked Up Abroad* on *Nat Geo*, I was terrified all over again about how close I was to guaranteeing that two lives would have been lost that day. John approached me carefully and began to speak. My face was still buried in my hands but something about his voice captured my attention, so I looked up to look at him. The left side of his face seemed to be melting as it sagged and drooped down. His speech slurred horribly. Both of us frightened, it was my instinct to call for a doctor. John stopped me. He looked as though he had Bell's Palsy. I knew enough from my incomplete molecular and microbiology studies in college to know that that was my fault and that I had cut off a lot of his supply of oxygen to his brain. I was feeling horrible before. Now, I just felt guilty.

Later that same night, we lay side by side in bed talking about the 60-meter rounds that were happening the next day. And the lie we would tell, about what was happening with his face. Heart heavy with guilt and shame, I turned toward him and told him that I didn't want him to die, apologized for choking him, and promised I would never do it again. We kissed each other goodnight and rolled away from each other to sleep. I stared at the wall wondering about my parents, if they'd be in the stadium, and if I'd be able to forget all about the events of the day enough to win a medal the next.

I woke up the following morning with diarrhea, no appetite, and what I did try to eat I couldn't keep down. John didn't have any credentials to get into the warmup track which is the only place he wanted to be. I was more stressed about how this would work out than for the race itself. At championships like these, TEAM USA has a national coaching staff. They don't actually coach us, but they serve as liaisons, remind us of check in times, check our uniforms, collect our bib numbers, hold our electronics if we need to get rid of them before entering the call room. Additionally, most of us have personal coaches. But if we allowed everybody and their personal coaches into the warmup area, there'd be no room to warm up! Besides, Rana was my coach. The one personal coach credential I had I reserved for my actual coach. We boarded the bus without incident. We arrived at the stadium at the athletes' and coaches' entrance. I told John to stay close to me. I approached a Turkish man with kind eyes who searched my backpack and my credentials. He waved me through and then waved John forward.

"Teüşekkur ederim" I said, Turkish for thank you. "Shukraan," I said again all but shouting the Arabic word for "thank you" as I grabbed John's hand and pulled him forward. "He's my husband." He wasn't. But it worked in my favor in this country to be a woman with a husband.

"You're a fucking genius," John said beaming from ear to ear, pleasantly surprised at the lack of pushback I received for getting a non-credentialed person into a highly secured area. With that potential problem behind me, I turned my attention towards Rana and my upcoming race.

I was the weakest I had ever felt. I was stressed more than I had ever been before—the most distracted I had ever been before a race, dehydrated, and jittery from my pre-race magic elixir Neuron by Optimum EFX. How I pulled off a bronze medal I couldn't tell you.

PAYCHECKS AND PRICE TAGS

Indoor season is merely a pit stop on the way to the outdoor season. I got two days of rest before jumping back into training full time. It was a 2½-hour drive from Tampa to Daytona Beach for training. I made this drive six days a week, without complaint, for 25 weeks. I wanted to demonstrate my commitment to training and to John.

My discipline had side effects.

As soon as I rolled out of my car after that long drive, I was ready to train. I was completely uninterested in wasting a practice session.

I remember one time when I was getting ready for the training session— always one of the first people to arrive, it was just Rana and me for a few moments. I asked him what he had planned for me that day and he said: grass strides.

I laughed at what I thought was a joke because why would he let me drive 2½ hours to do grass strides?

I said, "No, for real Rana, what are we doing today?"

He paused for a moment and I could see that it had only just then dawned on him the absurdity of me driving all that way to run barefoot on grass when I could have easily done the same minus the drive.

From that moment forward, we agreed to communicate with each other before I left Tampa each morning, that way I could be absolutely sure that once I made that drive it would be worth it.

Rana tried to convince John to get me an apartment. I could live in Daytona Beach, but he quickly realized this was a waste of time and energy. Sure, driving that much was NOT a good idea, not good for my legs, or my body, and was often dangerous as I would struggle to stay awake when driving home after tough training sessions.

At the same time, being in the car was the ONLY "me time" I had available to me. I was able to listen to NPR (National Public Radio) without judgment or someone reaching over and changing the station. I consumed dozens of audiobooks. By the time I reached the track in the mornings I was ready for the day. And by the time I reached Tampa, I was unwound from the session.

I was exhausted by it though.

I'd sometimes drag myself into the house and back towards the bedroom. John would help me strip out of my training gear, hop into the shower with me and scrub me down, often while I attempted to not fall asleep standing in the shower.

Every day was the same schedule with no deviations. Wake up, get dressed, hop in the car, eat on the way to Daytona Beach, train, hop in the car, eat on the way home, shower, eat, sleep—repeat.

That level of discipline showed both on the track and off. The only activities I did that weren't related to keeping John happy or my own training were watching movies at night through half open eyes and bowling on Saturday afternoons after training.

Because John shut my blog down that was housed at tiannamadison. com, I wasn't even writing anymore.

My social media accounts were all shut down, so my entertainment and company were books. I amassed dozens upon dozens of them. This approach to training was extreme, but it worked.

I just let a little of myself die in order to do it; I believed that the Olympic Games were worth it, because winning would be the pinnacle of a career. We had heard tales about Olympic medalists signing instant endorsements, how their value as medalists increased exponentially as they became commodities; and so, we dreamt of the glitter and gold that would await us post Olympics as a medalist.

It would be three months until I learned that was a lie.

But until then, the regular outdoor season was upon us, and it was time to compete. The first meet on my schedule was in Ponce, Puerto Rico.

Rana wasn't going to make it. Our training group was large, and the coach couldn't just leave the group behind to go be with one person because they were competing.

Well, they shouldn't, but they do—for the right person, for the right price.

As for me, I was broke, so Rana wasn't traveling anywhere with me. I couldn't afford it. And this is how John as "coach" was born. At first, he was a significant other accompanying me to meets. But it became clear after our Fayetteville, Arkansas, fiasco, in which I didn't credit him sufficiently with that 60-meter victory, that he wanted a larger role than that, even if he was grossly underqualified.

I discussed this shift in dynamic with Rana, and we agreed that it would be better for all of us if we let John monitor the warmup. He became the time and pacekeeper for my warmups. This wasn't an unimportant job. It allowed Rana to tend to other people and allowed me to warm up without checking the clock as often, or losing track of time, and missing the call room.

If you've ever been in a warmup area with John and me, you've seen it. He reprinted the warmup and created pocket-sized cards that he laminated. I'd often be wearing over-the-ear noise-cancelling headphones, so you'd see him using what appeared to be sign language to tell me the time either to speed up the warmup or to slow it down.

It turns out he WAS the best man for this job, and he did it with pride.

He stepped into that roll for the first time at Penn Relays. I had been invited to join Carmelita Jeter, Bianca Knight, and Allyson Felix to run the 4x100-meter relay under Jon Drummond's direction. After an hour of practice, we had our order down, and the following day we beat Jamaica handily. With Team USA's history of botching the 4x100-meter relays, our quartet was a breath of fresh air and a shot of hope going into the Olympic Games.

So that was the deal when we descended on Ponce, Puerto Rico. John covered the warmup, I competed. It was John and me against the world.

My opening meet.

I was in the long jump and in the 100-meter dash. I had given up on competing in the long jump in the indoor season, but I loved the event too much to walk away from it for the outdoor season, especially in an Olympic year. I just felt like we had unfinished business.

So, I jumped, and it was a modest showing. I think I jumped 21 feet that day. The long jump ran over time, as it tends to do (especially if it's before the 100 on the timetable). So, I walked from the pit to the starting line.

I set my blocks, took a deep inhale, and a slow exhale.

It was island muggy, and I was feeling a little taxed from the jumps. I was trying to muscle my way to big jumps (FYI - THAT never works) and I was killing my shins and quads at takeoff.

"On your marks!"

I loaded into my blocks.

"Set"

I raised up.

The starter shot the gun.

I ran like hell.

I crossed the finish line first.

I looked at the clock, 11.01 it said.

The fans in the stands were cheering with mouths open, and I had another "holy shit" moment at the finish line.

I stood there looking as surprised as a Miss America finalist on stage.

But I remembered quickly how to act post victories and I ran to find John, basically jumping into his arms, and yelled, "We did it!"

I was done for the day.

But John sensed blood in the water.

He asked me about the 200.

I was good, done, totally uninterested in pushing my luck—incredibly unprepared for the deuce.

The meet director, pleased as punch for how I overperformed in the 100, didn't hesitate to put me in an open lane of the 200.

There were only two problems:

1. I didn't know how to run a 200

2. I was already exhausted.

John convinced me that sitting down would be the death of me. So, for the half hour remaining before the race I stood, alternating between pacing back and forth and leaning on the fence.

I called Rana.

"So…I'm in the 200 now. How do I run it?" I asked without saying hello.

"You can basically run it as a sprint-float-sprint. Sprint most of the turn, float off the turn, and then bring it home," he answered.

"That's it?" I asked, confused by the simplicity of the explanation.

That was it.

I walked to the line, scared, tired, but determined. If I placed high enough in this 200, I'd make almost the equivalent of my entire year's salary in this one meet because of prize money and bonuses.

"On your marks!"

I loaded into my blocks.

"Set"

I raised up.

The starter shot the gun.

I ran like hell.

I got to the end of the turn and floated like a butterfly.

The entire field passed me.

I decided that I'd floated enough and reactivated my turbo.

I ran as hard as I could with everything I had.

I abandoned any pretense of form about 30 meters out from the finish and nearly threw myself across the line.

I won.

In 22.37, it was a lifetime best by over one second.

I made $17,000 that day.

Before leaving the track John, had managed to call almost everyone he knew to tell anyone who would listen about how I competed that day and how much money I had made.

I could hear the pride in his voice, and in turn, it made me proud too.

The meet shuttle dropped us back at the hotel, and we made a beeline to the bar. It was now our tradition to have a post competition drink.

I always ordered double Baileys and Kahlúa on the rocks. John always ordered an old fashioned. At the bar waiting for his own drink was a former Tennessee Volunteer, Gary Kikaya, a 400-meter runner from the Congo. I hadn't seen him in ages. I didn't even know he was still running, and with my busy schedule that day, I didn't notice him at the track. We gave each other a big hug and quickly asked about how things were going. I introduced Gary to John. Gary shook John's hand, then took his drink and left.

"What's up with that guy?" John asked.

"What do you mean?" I asked, nursing my drink.

"That hug. Were you fucking him?"

I looked up shocked. "God, no." I said, not ready to believe this was a conversation that needed serious attention, but noting the storm brewing in John's eyes.

"You don't hug a person like that who you aren't fucking or haven't fucked."

"Well, you're wrong because we have not. I did not."

"What were you, a whore in college?" he asked as I slid my unfinished drink back towards the bartender.

"I'm so tired. Room?" I asked, ignoring the question.

We were quiet on the way up. But for the next couple hours, until John fell asleep, I was regaled with completely fabricated tales of my so-called whorish collegiate days.

By morning he was proud of my accomplishments again and back on the phone with people he hadn't gotten a hold of the night before, to tell the story of how "Tianna made her entire year's salary in one night in Puerto Rico."

The rest of the regular season went pretty much the same. I didn't run the 200 again, but I ran more 100s than I ever had in my life—none of them slower than 11.00 seconds.

For my first year of sprinting seriously, that was a wild ride.

People started to pay attention to the "second coming" of Tianna, and the new older man she reappeared on the scene with.

We had already been telling everybody we were married (we weren't actually, but I'll tell you about that later). So, when we registered for the Olympic Trials, it made sense that I registered as Tianna Bartoletta.

This was a mistake.

It seemed as if I had become the target of investigative journalists. Inquiries for interviews started to pour in for me and were fielded by my agent. Most of them wanted to know what they could attribute my sudden emergence as a sprinter to.

Was it the new coach? The new man?

Is it because you're "Bartoletta" now?

But John had a "plan" for my brand, and that was not to say anything at all—let my performances speak for themselves. It makes sense on the surface. But I must warn you, if you don't take charge of your own story, you are essentially granting other people permission to fill that void with their own takes. And almost always they will be wrong, because without your voice, it's incomplete.

THE MIDAS TOUCH

Rana was the best coach I had ever had. He seemed to see me as a puzzle that he needed to solve. For our first couple weeks together, I ran strides for him without him giving any feedback or input. When he had decided he'd seen enough he gave me drills, cues, and exercises to fix and address every issue he had observed. He dismantled me with surgical precision and rebuilt me with the same. But Rana also had the type of personality that a person either loved or hated. There were very few people who fell in the middle. Straightforward and filter-less; I appreciated finally dealing with a person who was exactly as he appeared. He was rough around the edges and sometimes those edges rubbed people the wrong way. But not me; I absolutely loved him. I went to practice knowing I was not going to be coddled or talked down to. Rana broke me down like a classic car enthusiast who spent time in the garage on the weekends. From the ankle up, we addressed my strength levels and my mechanics.

We identified four areas where I needed improvement:

The first one was obvious. My diet needed work. I wasn't fat by any means, but there's the healthy body you need for general life and the body you need for elite performance. There's the body you have and the body you need to commit to creating temporarily for specific physical goals. I had not made the connection before then. I was the athlete who would sit in a drive-thru at a fast-food restaurant and rationalize my purchase by its affordability and then convince myself that I'd simply burn off the excess calories when I went to the track. I also ate my emotions, and cheese was the most soothing of companions.

The second area flagged for improvement was my power. This may come to a shock to some, but jumping and sprinting do not come naturally to me. I have to think my way through training and cue my way to proper execution so many times that I think about it less in a competition. I'm rarely ever in the position where I can *not think*. I'm in a flow state in competition when execution is the *only* thing I'm thinking about. I returned to the gym and began to build my base of power and hang cleans, squats, snatches, and the occasional bench press. I loved the gym. Embry Riddle's gym was grimy in the best way. It was poorly lit, with old machines, and rusted plates—I felt like Rocky in training.

The third area: my mechanics were the biggest obstacle to improving. After watching me run for a while in training, Rana told me I was no longer to do anything that wasn't a B-run. A B-run is a high-knee sprint where you pull your knees and thighs up to parallel, while driving them back down by clawing the foot out and back under your center of mass. It didn't matter if we were doing the warmup or W.F.O (wide fuckin' open) sprints. It didn't matter if he gave everyone else different instructions. We had to overhaul my wiring and overwrite my bad habit of backside mechanics. Between Ralph Mann and Rana, I dorsiflexed and B-ran all day, every day. Even walking on campus I'd do the walking drills Ralph showed me during my biomechanics review sessions.

With my mechanics issues addressed, Rana focused his attention on the fourth area that needed work: my acceleration pattern and block start. Rep after rep of block clearance, drilling pulling the heel through low without dragging the toe, drilling driving the foot down, and back landing up on the spike plate, so the heel remained high on touch down.

We'd be on the track for hours doing all of the small things that supported our end goals. Hurdle mobility, medicine ball throws, barefoot walks, and plyometrics bookended our training session for the day—six days a week.

TRACKTOWN, USA

I told John that it was Paul Doyle, my agent, who registered me as "Tianna Bartoletta" for the Trials. But I had done it. I thought, because he—we—had been telling everyone we were married, it made sense to me that in order to continue perpetuating this lie I needed to register under my "married" name.

John was flattered, at first, but then a call from Dennis, John's close friend and accountant, burst his bubble. We were in a connecting airport, en route to Portland, Oregon, from Tampa, Florida. John excused himself to take his call, but not before I heard Dennis' voice on the other side. I sat flipping through *Scientific American Mind*, a magazine I always and only buy in airports, for some reason. A lot of time passed before John returned. He looked sick.

"What's wrong, is there a fire?" I asked him. I did not mean a literal fire. John referred to issues at the office as fires. When his mood turned sour, it was almost always a result of one of two things: me or something bad happening at the office. I knew I was in the clear. I had been on my best behavior. I wanted NO problems going into the Olympic Trials. I did not want my ability to showcase my hard work weakened because we had an "incident." Although I had become callused to the incidents, I noticed it was taking me longer to "recover" from them—not physically, but emotionally.

"No, it's Shauna," he said shoulders slumping forward as he sat down next to me. I knew who Shauna was, his ex-wife. They'd had a beautiful fairytale-like wedding in Italy. Shamefully, when I moved in with John I "explored" my new home and opened every door and every drawer. In the bottom middle drawer of the library/smoking room, I found cards, photos, letters, and mementos from his past relationships. I had always been a firm believer in not looking for trouble, but I also don't hold people's history against them either. So, I flipped through photos, cards, and love letters, smiling to myself as pictures from John's past helped frame his present.

He and Shauna were pictured sitting side by side with wide smiles flanked by friends. The wedding reception was small but intimate. Before I knew better, I would dream of my fairy tale wedding, in my Disney-inspired gown, at a location of my dreams. There in the library I looked at those fairy tale photos with no expectation that was something I had to look forward to.

"What about her?" I asked. He really looked like he was going to be sick.

"She asked how I got married," he said.

Confused, I asked, "What do you mean *how*? How would anyone get married?"

There was a red flag waving on the parapet of my subconscious. As far as the world knew, we were married. We weren't. But everyone thought we were, including Shauna.

"She's dating a guy she wants to marry but couldn't because we…" he started to explain but I interrupted him.

"Are you saying you two never divorced? That you're still married?!"

That explains it, I thought. Shauna wanted to know how he was able to get married when she had been holding out because the two of them were still married. I sat back in the chair and rested my head on the seat trying to sort my thoughts. He's married to someone else. The world thinks we're married. I was even wearing a ring. He'd told me about his marriages, once during college, and then to Shauna, but he omitted that he never divorced the last one. In a way, I found out my husband had a wife en route to the 2012 Olympic Trials. I looked down at the ring I was wearing. He'd told me it was a three-karat ring. The platinum band was littered with pressure stacked diamonds; each diamond was held in place by the diamond placed beside it. If one diamond fell out, the entire band was at risk. Seemingly floating above the band was a beautiful princess cut diamond. On one of our early dates, John told me how he was so sure I was the "one." He had begun to design a ring just for me. He requested an extra snack napkin from our bartender and began to sketch his "idea" for the perfect ring for me. *He did this, knowing he was married to someone else, I thought to myself. Oh well, I'm in the shit now, and the only way out is through.*

"Well," I said to John, "I guess you need to get divorced at some point when we return." I said nothing more on the subject. I had an Olympic Team to make.

It wouldn't be so easy. I edited my registration to read "Tianna MADISON" and thought that would be the end of it. But like I said, if you don't tell your story someone else will, and it will absolutely be incomplete because they don't have the information you do. So, journalists did what journalists do—asked questions and pulled threads. Not sure how far these journalists were willing to go; I was certain that someone would discover that my so-called husband had a wife, but it wasn't me. But changing my name *back* to Madison had actually made it worse. Now there were questions about why I was Bartoletta first, and Madison again. And how was I supposed to explain that?

Someone did ask, and John spoke up. "I really wanted her to finish what she started under her name. She began this journey as Madison and to finally be in a position to make an Olympic team under her own strength and name is so important," he said. This was an explanation that everyone bought; it successfully presented him as the self-effacing supportive husband he in fact did not know how to be. But his secrets were safe.

Upon arrival in Eugene, we headed to Credential Pick-Up at the Autzen Stadium where I'd grabbed my athlete's credential that would grant me access to the warmup track and the stadium. John was to pick up a registered coach's credential. Rana, my actual coach, had several athletes in attendance at the 2012 trials, and any one of them could designate their registered coach's pass to him. This was the arrangement Rana and I settled on—based on what would be best for me. What was best for me was to keep John happy.

Let me clear some shit up here about the highly valued coach's credential. I, as the athlete, get to write the name of the person I want to have this pass. It's a line on a sheet of paper where I also write my name and my USATF membership number. There were two requirements in 2012 to be eligible for a "Registered Coach's Credential":

1. Be a USATF member in good standing
2. Pass a Background Check

Once those two requirements are met, the coach goes onto the coach's registry. It is not necessary for you to show proof of coaching experience; it's not necessary to be a coach at all. Only those tworequirements need to be met. Kristi, John's assistant, was tasked with taking care of the USATF membership and applying for the background check. With spending 2½ hours to get to training, another 3-4 hours at the track, and a 2½ sometimes 3-hour drive home depending on the traffic, I did not have the time to do something that people who sat in an office all day could do.

I gave John's name to Sandy Snow after handing her my paperwork. His name wasn't on the coach's registry. My skin began to flush, and I could taste bile in my mouth. I was terrified. Nothing had happened yet, but I knew how quickly it could...so I was terrified in advance. I was only about 20 seconds premature. John blew up.

He demanded to know how I dropped the ball on his credential. I informed him that it was Kristi's job. He called Kristi and loudly cussed her out and accused her of not doing her job, being lazy, and screwing him over. In an understandable but infuriating act of self-preservation, Kristi said that it was ME who dropped the ball after she passed the job back to me when she was confused about something concerning the background check. It was true that she asked me a question about the background check, but it was not true that it was suddenly back on me to handle it myself especially since I was actively driving to Daytona Beach for training from Tampa when she asked.

He hung up with Kristi and turned his ire back to me. "So, I'm just not a priority to you, is that it? You use me to get back on top just to shut me out once we're here!" I made the mistake of trying to quiet him down as the room filled with athletes, coaches, and USATF staff. "YOU CARE ABOUT THESE PEOPLE MORE THAN ME, AND THAT'S THE PROBLEM!" Leaving him standing there, face reddening with each passing moment, I walked back to the table that Sandy was manning. "Is there anything that I can do?" I heard the desperation in my voice, and I hated it. Sandy heard it too, and she explained to me about the other passes that I could pay for. There was only one problem; I could only choose one: the stadium pass or the warmup pass.

John had made it clear throughout the season that he didn't want to be "the boyfriend in the stands" even though that's exactly what he was. He chose the warmup pass; after all, it was his job to read the warmup card to me and keep track of the time. But it also meant that he didn't have access to the stadium, without televisions in the warmup area, John chose to watch me warm up, rather than watch me make the Olympic Team from the stands. With his warmup credential in hand, I was free to turn my attention to preparing for the trials.

A ROUND AND A ROUND

The US Olympic trials is one of the most stressful competitions I have ever had to endure and conquer. There is so much on the line, so much to be gained, so much to be lost, so many hopes and dreams achieved or denied depending on one's performance there. With everyone in attendance from athletes and coaches to spectators alike buzzing with energy, imagine how the atmosphere must feel. The hair on my arms stands on ends, and goosebumps pepper my skin when I'm in Tracktown USA. And the Trials are unforgiving. If you are top three in your event, you make it. If you're not, you don't. It does not matter who you are, where you came from, who your coach is, or who your sponsor is—top three make the team. Period.

And speaking of sponsors, they usually have a hospitality suite somewhere for their athletes, friends, and family members. It's a luxurious lounge where you can relax in the air conditioning, play games, eat well, drink well, and get suited with new swag. You get a gift when you enter the suite for the first time commemorating your participation in the trials. You may see your face on the wall of athletes in attendance competing under the banner of the brand. Expectation sits heavily on your shoulders as you make your way around the suite shaking hands with those who signed off on your contract. They ask how you're feeling, if you're ready, and you know there's only one answer they want to hear.

Rana and I had just finished our pre-meet session, an abbreviated workout that gives us a good sense of how I'll compete the following day based on how my body feels and moves. Based on what he saw during the workout, Rana insisted I get a massage that evening. Massages were a hot point between the three of us, Rana, John, and me. John did not want me to be touched by anyone. And when I was, he interrogated me so thoroughly about the experience that I quickly decided it wasn't worth it. Even though I was in my car for 5 hours a day to get to training, and training for another three to four on the track, I was rarely getting treatment on my body. Once, we had an active recovery day during the week where Rana sent the entire training group to a massage therapist. Because my appointment was during the time I would be on the track, I knew I would be able to get a massage and not even have to mention it later. It was heaven. My body needed the healing. I was just getting over my anxiousness about John finding out when the therapist gently grabbed my hands and began to massage my surprisingly tight forearms. "Did you do this?" she asked me. I traced her line of sight to my freshly sliced wrists.

"Yes," I said ashamed but owning it. I tried to pull my arm away, but she resisted me, her grip firm but gentle.

"Do not allow anyone or anything have so much power over you that you harm yourself," she said to me. I plastered my eyes to the ceiling, my bottom lip quivering as I struggled to hold back tears. I never saw her again. I was not ready for such a raw and vulnerable experience. I was not ready to accept the truth about anything that was happening in my life. I told Rana that I would get massages in Tampa, and he never made me another appointment—until that day before the first round of the 100-meter dash.

I pushed back. I really did not want to have this issue on the night before. *Why couldn't Rana just leave it alone, I thought.* We made it this far. We made it through packet pick-up and credentialing; I was dreading pushing my luck with a massage—from a guy. I let Rana tell John. Not wanting to seem like the controlling man he was he agreed and drove me to the Hilton to meet the massage therapist for treatment. He had his table set up in the open space between the bathroom and the entrance to Danielle Carruther's hotel room. Her room was a mess, and it was awkward stepping over her clothes to get to the table. John stood awkwardly near the door, eyebrows twitching from discomfort. Rana had told the therapist in advance what he wanted him to check out. Apparently, during my pre-meet warmup I was moving in a way that made Rana feel like I needed psoas work. The therapist lifted my shirt and began to dig in with four fingers to the left of my belly button.

John walked over to the table and put his hand on my shoulder, "You comfortable? You okay?" he asked. Not because getting your psoas worked on is uncomfortable for me (it is) but because he was uncomfortable. He was struggling to watch this professional therapist touch me which is ironic for reasons you'll understand later. John was hovering near the therapist's shoulder when the therapist asked him to move. John's face turned red and all too aware that he had an audience, he slowly exhaled the breath he was holding and took a step back. My hip flexor was tight, and it was making everything around it tight too. The therapist hiked my shorts up high enough to turn them into a bikini and placed his fingers near their edge and began to work on loosening the groin and inner hips. Moving from the outside of my thigh to the inside, the therapist was moving in a pattern that was allowing me to loosen up, I was just starting to relax when...

"You're just going to let another man touch you like that when I'm standing right here!" The outburst caught me, the therapist, Danielle, and her boyfriend Thomas off guard. Instantly embarrassed, I looked at the therapist whose hands were frozen hovering over my skin, and then at John who looked as if his head would actually explode. "I can't believe this shit, all of the disrespect, after all I do for you."

He stormed out of the room. I sat up on the table, mortified. I looked to Danielle who didn't say a word but had a quizzical look on her face. The therapist looked amused.

"I think I should go," I said to him.

"We've only done the one leg, you run tomorrow," he said, starting to get frustrated with me and the whole ordeal.

"I know...it's just...I—" I struggled to articulate a coherent thought.

"Whatever, it's only the Olympic Trials, no big deal," he said so sarcastically that I felt two inches tall. I dressed quickly, jogged down the hall, and took the elevator to the lobby where I fully expected to find John waiting. He'd be pissed for sure, but waiting on me, nonetheless. But he wasn't there. I walked through the sliding doors of the hotel's entrance to where we had parked the car; the car was gone too. He had left me. I called him; no answer. I called again; no answer.

The Hilton was one of the main hotels. Most of the athletes, coaches, and agents were staying there. I wasn't. I had rented a home not too far from the track. The family had decided to avoid the circus that was coming to town and go on a family vacation in Hawaii. The few thousand dollars I paid them to do so more than covered their vacation too. Renting houses rather than staying in hotels was important to me. Food had become the biggest game changer in my preparation. Not having a kitchen would have been detrimental to my process. And as much as I love a good hotel stay, two weeks in one gets uncomfortable fast. A house was the way to go. I was going to have to walk at least two and a half miles to get there, and that's if I didn't get lost and have to double back. I decided that if he was mad enough to leave me at the hotel, I didn't need to be in a rush to return home, so I took an even longer scenic route through campus. It was warm out, and the night sky was clear. I sat on a bench, tilted my head back, and wished on the stars.

I eventually made it to a street that looked familiar after a few wrong turns and bad directions. As I approached the front door, I saw a peculiar sight. My laptop was sitting outside.

What the...? I asked myself. I eased closer. I knew it couldn't possibly be a trap, this wasn't the movies. But it felt like one.

"Fuck," I said when I saw what was on the screen. It was a picture of a man I dated over a year ago. I had saved his blackberry messenger profile photo because he looked so good in it. John had to scroll deep through the archives to find it, but he did, and he needed me to know it. Even though the download date was clear and embedded in the file, it didn't matter. He would not see the hypocrisy of expressing irate behavior over an old picture, while he kept an entire drawer full of mementos from past relationships, maintained a closet full of Gail's clothes, and was currently married to someone else.

I rang the doorbell. He opened the door. I grabbed up my computer and went into the house.

"Where were you?" he had had the nerve to ask me.

"You fucking left me at the hotel. I had to walk. What do you mean where was I?!" I shouted.

"Well, you weren't there when I came back," he said.

"How was I supposed to know you were coming back? You didn't answer your phone!" I screamed.

"Are you kidding me? YOU RUN TOMORROW," he said, as if I was being ridiculous. I slammed my white MacBook on the counter and readied myself for bed.

✶ ✶ ✶ ✶ ✶

We walked to the track when we could. Ahead of round one, with credentials proudly displayed on lanyards around our necks, we approached the athlete entrance for the warmup track. John insisted on holding my backpack and my hand.

Holding my hand, he walked me into the track and helped me to a seat far away from other people. I don't mind seclusion in these situations, being social isn't something I truly enjoy anyway, let alone at a meet as important as this.

I ran into a colleague, Christine, who gave me a hug. John didn't have a problem with females hugging me as long as I introduced him. She made a comment about my natural hair. John told me to dump the wig, which he called my "helmet" which honestly was a lot easier to do once I saw him in it. As a joke, while I was away in Europe, he recreated a photo I had taken with Bailey, the teacup Yorkie, and sent it to me. I laughed uninterrupted for several minutes but decided if I looked as ridiculous in a helmet as he did, then it was time to let it go.

"What happened to Glam T?" Christine asked, referencing the old version of myself that took great lengths to master makeup.

Irritated at the conversation, I said, "My husband thinks I'm beautiful without it."

Christine looked at me with disbelieving eyes and said, "Does he now?" in a tone to match, before wishing me luck and abruptly ending the conversation.

I was more anxious about the warmup area interactions than I was about the first round of the 100-meter dash. I was right not to be worried. I qualified for the semi-final easily, running the fastest time of the day.

The newspapers back home were excited about this development and reached out to me through my agent for interviews. John decided that he only liked Paul Heyse of *The Chronicle Telegram*, Elyria's local paper, and gave him quotes and articles (mostly written by him) to print as my words in the paper.

The semi-final and the final are the same day, just hours apart. We drove to the track so that I could get back to the house for a quick meal and a power nap before returning for the final. The semi-final is often more intense than the final. To qualify for the final you have to place top-four in your section. That means you're not only focused on running your race you have to be aware of your place too. In a final, I simply just say, "fuck it. It is what it is. I'm going to run my race and see what it gets me." And although I can use that same mindset for the semi-final it's *place* not time that grants entry into the final. I was in a semi-final once where the fifth-place person in my section ran faster than every single person in the next section but wouldn't be able to run the final and therefore had no shot at all to make the team. It's cutthroat. It's brutal.

It was clear, I made the final, and returned home for the meal and the nap I needed before racing for a spot on the Olympic team.

Back at the track for the final, John was extra hyped up and gave me more information than I needed about the time and asked if I needed water or snacks. He was nervous. I was nervous. I had only run one race slower than 10.9 seconds in the season, and that was at my opener in Puerto Rico where I ran 11.01. I needed one more sub eleven race to make this team. I gave Rana a fist bump before walking into the call room and gave John a hug and a kiss. I turned my back to them both as I made my way through the staging tents to race.

The field was staked. Carmelita Jeter was on fire. Allyson Felix was on fire, and you could never count anybody else out of the final either. I took a deep breath, exhaled it slowly, and loaded into the blocks. As the starter said set, I held my breath and closed my eyes. The gun fired. Eyes still closed, I drove out of the blocks as hard and as fast as I could. When I opened my eyes somewhere around forty meters and I realized I was winning, I began to freak out in real time.

Oh, my God, I'm going to make this team. Five meters to go in the race. I'M MAKING THIS TEAM! my inner voice screamed.

Carmelita overtook me, as my wheels began to fall off, and won the race. I got second, but I made the team. Three things happened in that moment:

1. I recognized that I made the team and began to celebrate and fight back tears.

2. I had a flashback of Arkansas when John ripped me a new one for not celebrating appropriately or including him when he was "the one responsible for my success."

3. I remembered John wasn't in the stadium.

Deciding in a split second that I needed to look out for myself, I sprinted off the track and toward the warmup area, where John was waiting screaming with a well of tears in his eyes. I gave him a hug and whispered, "We did it" in his ear, and then I turned to return to the track for my well-deserved celebration.

But USADA stopped me. They wouldn't let me return to the track because they wouldn't be able to follow me for my victory lap with the others who made the team, who at that time were Carmelita and Jeneba Tarmoh, who actually ran the exact same time as her training partner Allyson Felix.

"What? I can't do my victory lap?" I asked somewhat hysterically. The answer was no, and they ushered me away from the celebration, bypassing the post-event press conference and all. I missed my moment. I sacrificed my moment, in that moment, to save myself later. I still don't know, looking back on it, if it was worth it.

I know that my actions on that day were misinterpreted—not unsurprising since there was no way I could actually explain myself, and no way I could tell the truth about why I made the decision I made. Carmelita voiced her disdain for my behavior by not addressing me by name at all during the press conference, instead referring to me as "that person." One of the USATF staff told me I had "missed my moment," that most of us only get that one moment to introduce ourselves to America—going into the games—and that I had blown it. I looked them in the eye, unflinching and said, "What would you have me do when you refused to let my husband into the stadium?" I had leverage, and I knew it. I was entered in the long jump and the 200-meter dash. They found a way to get John the credential he wanted the next day and for the remainder of the Trials.

ON "E"

The 100-meter rounds took all the energy I had. The high of finally making an Olympic team after failing to do so twice before, came with the reality that I'd have to do the same for the long jump and the 200-meter dash. I hated the 200 and hadn't run it since Puerto Rico, but there I was throwing my hat in the ring to make the team and potentially contest it at the Games. I thought it was ridiculous. I hadn't jumped since Puerto Rico either; if one can choose between being a jumper or a sprinter as a professional, one would choose running. It was more valuable to the people who wrote the checks. In my contract a gold medal in the 100-meter dash was worth $150,000. The long jump gold was $75,000.

I scratched from the long jump. There was no indication that I was going to jump anywhere close to 7-meters which was what it took to make the team. It wasn't worth navigating up to nine rounds and loading my legs before the 200.

Because I was scared, and because I hate the 200, I ran the rounds like an idiot. The strategy of experienced runners is to "survive and advance." My strategy was this: when the gun goes off, run as fast as you can. I went into the 200 final with one of the fastest times and 100 percent exhausted, but I lined up to take my shot anyway.

Sanya Richards-Ross and Allyson Felix were to my inside. I flashed back to that junior meet when I watched them battle it out for the "Queen of the Track" title at Stanford. I watched them as an outsider, never once considering I could be part of their company. But there I was…in the final with them. I took a moment to appreciate how incredible it was to be in such good company.

Those good feelings lasted about 60 meters. I was running the turn (as I do) when Allyson just blew right by me, as if I were standing still. It was at that moment I said, "You know what? I'm done," I throttled down and strode through the finish line. Allyson ran 21.69 seconds in the 200 that day. I didn't want any parts of that—no thank you.

Rana and John thought that was hilarious. I explained it with more energy than I used in the race. I made them laugh, and so I relaxed and no longer worried about John being upset about my wack 200-meter performance. High on victory, John texted my parents, "We made the Olympic team!" It had been months since I'd spoken to them, and even though I could not locate them in the stands at the Trials, I knew they were there. I saw them on the street once.

John texted something along the lines of, "You'll want to be part of this." He was so proud of me, but also himself. In tears, he explained to me how this was the first thing he ever saw through to the end in his entire life so far. He called all of his employees and told them he loved them, thanked them for their sacrifices on this journey, and that we'd all gather at the house, when we returned, to celebrate.

Team Processing was a dream. Once you cross the finish line at the Trials, you're given a card which functions as an invitation to "Team Processing." In the banquet rooms at the Hilton Hotel, tables were set up with Olympic partners and USATF staff. Wide-eyed, we made our way from one table to the next. We visited each one and picked up swag, got fitted by professional tailors for our Ralph Lauren opening and closing ceremony outfits, and designed our rings. I put John's initials on my Olympic Ring.

At the travel table, we discussed flight itineraries and relay camp. Jon Drummond, JD for short, who was infamous for not leaving the track at the 2003 World Championships, in Paris, when he protested being called for a false start by lying down in his lane would be our relay coach. The top six people in the final are given invitations to the relay pool; however, the coach can pull from anyone they'd like who competed at the Trials.

I was handed an athlete agreement—a contract of sorts, with a lot of small print. The gist of it was to acknowledge, with my signature, that I understood the code of conduct; and further down the page—well, past the point most people stop reading—there was a section about relays. It explained that absolutely no one was guaranteed a spot on the relay team, not even the top three who were going to represent the country in the event at the Games.

"Oh, shit," I muttered under my breath, "does Jeneba know this?"

While I was enjoying that I'd made my first Olympic team, and after Allyson kicked everyone's ass in the 200, a controversy was brewing. Although Jeneba's name was announced as the third-place finisher after the 100-meter race, officials reviewing the photo finish decided they could not actually determine who finished third after all. Even after looking at the time all the way to the ten thousandth place, it was still tied. Looking at the grainy photo finish image, they couldn't distinguish one torso from the other. So, it had been decided that there would be a televised race-off. The winner would get the spot, but Jeneba declined. In one of her interviews on the subject, she mentioned that her place in the final meant she was on the relay team, and so she was at peace with her decision. But from what I was reading on the Athlete Agreement, nobody was on the relay until JD decided they were on the relay. I hoped it would work out for her, but I had a bad feeling she'd made the wrong choice.

Not much of a texter, my father called John back. We were spending the night in a Portland hotel, making it easier to catch our early flight back home.

John repeated what he had said via text, "You don't want to miss out on this! You want to be a part of this!" John said to my father, who was now on speaker phone. "You'd be proud of the woman she's become," he said.

The woman I'd become? I thought to myself. *The woman who was currently tolerating abuse because she was winning? Her?*

"We don't want to know the woman she's become," I heard my father say on the phone.

John turned to face me as if to confirm that I'd heard what he'd been telling me all along. Nobody loves or understands me like he did, and now, straight from the mouth of my own father, his statement was validated.

"Fuck em, then," I mouthed to John. "Hang up," I said with more authority than I felt. John did, pleased, and he turned his attention toward dinner plans while I tried to hide my freshly broken and now vacant heart.

ALL THE RAGE

I have a bad temper which is often made worse by the reality that I know I should not have a temper that burns as hot as it does. So, I suppress it until I can't any longer at which point no one is safe from the vitriol or rage that's eating me from the inside out. At first, the words, "we don't want to know the woman she's become" made me sad. On one level, I understood how it must look and feel to be abandoned by a daughter—especially in that way. On the other, I expected them to know better. It was both disappointing and validating to learn they did not. With all the friction between us, I had never stopped wanting their love or approval, and the one time I needed them, they washed their hands of me too.

I went to bed most nights, since seeing them in Turkey, wondering if my dad registered the pain in my eyes. Wondering if he'd jolt awake at night and decide to extract me, even against my will, from my beautiful prison. But now it was certain, that would never happen. I could not help but feel like it was that single comment, in that single conversation, that sealed the deal of our estrangement. I turned my attention to the only remaining relationship I had—my pretend marriage.

HOMETOWN GLORY

Elyria, Ohio, my hometown, was excited. One of their own was going to the Olympics, and so they began making plans for a celebration. Because I was estranged from my parents, I learned about the celebration via Google alerts. My parents would be speaking at the event, and I was not at all sure what they were going to say given the current state of our relationship.

I emailed the mayor and asked if I could write an open letter to the city because I couldn't make it; she obliged. She told me about the banner that would hang across the main street in downtown Elyria and that anyone who came to the square was welcome to sign it. She said my parents told her they'd give it to me when we met up in London, which caught me by surprise.

Panicked now because I was certain John would think I was making secret arrangements to reunite with my parents in London, I told the mayor that we were actually estranged. There was no way they could give me the banner in London and that we hadn't spoken since March, and that they'd recently said they didn't want to. I still wanted the banner though, and so they mailed it to me in Tampa along with a DVD of the event. I couldn't watch it with John, but when I was home alone, I took the DVD out of its plastic sleeve, slid it into the player in the bedroom, crawled into bed with Bailey, the Yorkie, and watched my family.

I ran the gamut of emotions watching that video, listening to my parents, sisters, and cousins stand on the same stage in the same square, around the same fountain we'd done countless laps around throughout the years. I was homesick yet unwelcome. When I couldn't take any more, I pressed stop, put the DVD back in its sleeve, and sat outside by the pool. I had never wanted the Olympics as a kid, didn't even want them as a collegiate athlete, never had aspirations of being pro, but I walked through the doors as they were opened to me, and it felt like I was paying too high a price for it. I walked into the pantry, slid a knife out of the block, and sliced my right wrist—a few slashes—just enough to distract me from the emotional pain I was feeling but not too much that I'd bleed out or get Baker Act-ed. That would get me involuntarily detained in a mental health facility. I cut a little too deep. Usually, I made sure I barely broke the skin; blood would simply bead in the cut. But this time, blood was dripping, and as I reached for a napkin, John walked in.

"You're still doing this shit!" he screamed when he saw it. "How could you be so selfish?!? How could you do this to me? As much as I do for you!"

I had no answer, so I didn't provide one. No longer caring about making sure I didn't make a mess, I left John standing in the pantry directing his anger to the back of my head as I walked away. I was beyond giving a shit. I was leaving soon for relay camp in Monaco anyway.

HAPPY CAMPER

I arrived in Monaco grumpy from long travel in economy class. There were other athletes on my flight from Amsterdam to Nice, so we cleared customs and headed to baggage claim together. Typically, when we arrive at our international meet, we clear customs, grab our bags, head outside and immediately begin to look for a person wearing a polo with the Meet's logo on it, or a driver holding a sign with our names. I found the "meet people," as we call them, and waved the other athletes over to let them know I had found them.

"We're actually taking the helicopter," they said.

Feeling some kind of way about the meet director not making the same arrangement for me, I waited for a minibus to arrive and drive me to Monaco.

After a long day of air travel and another 30-minute ride, I arrived at the meet hotel. Bianca Knight—we called her BeeKay—was in the lobby. I gave her a hug, and she walked with me to the front desk. I gave the receptionist my passport and credit card—an American Express Centurion Card, known on the street as "The Black Card." Made of titanium, it clinked way too loudly on the counter. That got BeeKay's attention.

"Shopping on T!" she shouted. She picked up the card turning it over in her hands. "Daaamn," she said, "must be nice."

Yeah, I thought, *sure the fuck is*. I flashed her a smile that hid my sarcastic thoughts. I was only allowed to use my limitless borrowing power for gas and travel expenses related to competition or training camps, and Dennis, John's accountant, made sure that whatever I spent on the card, I repaid from my earnings.

JD, the relay coach, decided that we'd run almost the same team as the one that got the world's attention at Penn Relays. Jeneba would replace BeeKay as third leg. We did not finish the race. The exchange from Jeneba to Carmelita didn't happen. It was embarrassing to be headed into the Olympics with the hope of the States to not being able to get the baton around the track at a preparatory meet.

One thing a relay team must never ever do in the media is point fingers. In the mixed zone, Jeneba pointed to Carmelita as the reason for the botched pass. It may have been true, but that's family business, and for the first time there was friction among USA's A-team.

Rana was going to have a training camp in Austria, ahead of London, so I joined them after Monaco. I landed in Salzburg, where *The Sound of Music* was filmed. Everything was bright and beautiful, and we had a wonderful training camp.

During one of the last training sessions before we were scheduled to fly and meet the team, we did 30-meter fly testing. We stood at the starting line and ran 60 meters. The first 30 meters were untimed; the test was to try to produce the fastest time from the 30-meter point to the finish. I was battling it out with my male training partners, specifically Christian Taylor. Although he was faster than me, Christian was better suited for 400s when he wasn't in the pit. We were both running 3.0s for 30 meters, when I announced I was going to break 3 seconds on my next run. I took my shirt off and stripped down to my sports bra. Things were getting serious. It was quiet in the sprint hall. The facility had a timing system integrated into the walls. It displayed the time in a big red analog digital display. I prepared for my run. I stood in three-point stance. My right hand acted as a kickstand as I leaned forward over my left leg at the starting line. I ripped my right thigh forward off the line like Rana had drilled into me. "Knees to tits!" he shouted as I accelerated. We discovered that that was the only verbal cue that worked to make me execute the start the way I needed to. I ran the first 30 meters chanting "knees to tits" like a mantra. I transitioned out of my drive phase and into the timed zone, my mantra switched to "PISTON FEET. UP. DOWN. UP. DOWN." No wasted movement by losing control of my limbs swinging behind my body, no unnecessary airtime. I ran through the finish line and looked up at the display: 2.99 it read. Christian, not wanting to take second, and to me no less, took his shirt off too and made his way to the starting line. The group cheered as he readied himself at the start. Christian tore off the line like a bat out of hell. His time not only shattered the 3 second barrier but my time too . If those performances were any indication, we were more than ready for the Olympic Games.

What I wasn't ready for was a call from John complaining about his sexual needs going unmet and his feeling neglected while I was away in camp. He begged for me to extend him a "hall pass" which is essentially permission to have guilt-free sex with someone else. Extending a "hall pass" meant I could not in any way punish him or use this incident against him. It was the "least" I could do, according to him, with how supportive he was being while I selfishly pursued the Olympics. He was even going to *allow* me to choose the other party! And, to make me feel better, he decided to limit this rendezvous to oral sex only, and that I could listen in via Skype (I hope you can feel the sarcasm I've written these last few sentences with). I vehemently declined. But I got berated so badly for so long over the phone that I acquiesced. I was in Salzburg, Austria, on a beautiful summer day, having just run the fastest 30-meter fly ever, a week before the Olympic Games. I had better shit to do. I phoned a friend, as if I were on a perverted episode of *Who Wants to Be a Millionaire?* My friend laughed when I told her what was happening. She and I were close and have had many adventures and traded many love and war stories. She was the one person to whom I'd violate the "never kiss and tell" rule without hesitation.

I felt sub-human asking her to do this for me. John's flight to Europe was in three days. He had threatened not to come if I didn't start "giving a shit" about his needs, and I had no idea what I'd return "home" to if I let *that* happen. I'd already had all my belongings thrown into the driveway of our home in Florida several times over the last several months. Whenever John decided that he didn't have to "take my shit," I'd find piles of my training gear and pages ripped out of my training journal or warmup book, outside where, one by one, I'd pick them up, gather them back into my arms, and enter the house. On days like that I followed the script, "I want to be here, nobody loves or supports me like you, I'll do better. I love you. I'm sorry." Every time. I told my friend as much as I could without sharing the secret about the violence between us. She agreed. John was so happy that I had the most peaceful three day stretch I'd had since January. With the Olympics a week away, that three days was a reprieve from the previous seven months of stress and fear. I finally had a little breathing room, a little rest stop, before heading to London.

LONDON

Team USA had contracted the private use of a track and training facility in London separate from the one made available in the Athlete's Village. We did this for a few reasons:

1. We could afford to.
2. People liked to watch and film our relay practices and training sessions.

Having a separate facility to ourselves kept the likelihood of that happening very low. The separate facility also had another benefit; John could get access to it. The Village Track would have required Olympic Credentials which personal coaches, least of all John, would not have had. And because most of Team USA's athletes had a personal coach in attendance, the only thing they needed was to be registered with USATF and on the list with the team managers. This was a lifesaver. I did not want to spend my final practice sessions before the games stressed about John and his hurt feelings over being excluded.

It was half the reason I didn't walk in the opening ceremonies. The main reason was that I didn't want to be on my feet for as long as was required. But the secondary reason was that it would have been impossible for me to leave John sitting to watch the opening ceremonies from the couch in the flat by himself, and not hear about how unfair it was to not be able to celebrate such a momentous moment in our lives together. So, I sat and watched from the couch too, and we watched the fireworks from the tiny balcony that faced the street that led to the stadium.

Once we arrived at the championships, we didn't address the relays until our respective individual events were done. So, I didn't have to worry about that until after I was done with the 100-meter dash. Round 1 was on the first day; I was in the fourth of seven sections. To make it to the next round, I needed to finish top three in my heat or have one of the next three fastest times. I was worried about Blessing Okagbare. It's not necessary to win in the first round, but my confidence was on thin ice. I wanted a win. Blessing ran a new personal best of 10.93 to take the heat. I took second with 10.97.

Survive and Advance.

"T, I was looking up results from the last two Olympic Games and it's going to take 10.8 to get a medal. If you run 10.8, we're leaving London with a medal," Rana said to me after the first round.

I could run 10.9 with my eyes closed but haven't managed to run faster than 10.96.

I told John about this when we met up outside of the village gates post-race. John suggested that I listen to James Allen's classic *As a Man Thinketh* on repeat to help me change my thoughts so that I could start to believe that a 10.8 was possible. Before that 2012 season, I once ran 11.05, scared to death, having been thrown into the race at the last minute. My friend Sam had to break into my house and ship me sprint spikes overnight. Before that run, my personal best was 11.20. Having arrived in London and gotten settled into the flat I'd rented, I was seriously conversing with myself about running 10.8!

I took James Allen's advice and decided to simply believe I would run 10.8. I didn't overcomplicate it. I just decided that that was the only thought I was allowed to have until the final race was run.

The semifinal and final were the following day. To advance to the semifinal I needed to place top two in my heat or run one of the next two fastest times. I was in the third and final heat. I watched Carmelita run the most effortless 10.8 I had ever seen. Shelly-Ann Fraser Pryce won her heat in 10.85. I was once again in the same heat as Blessing. I really, really wanted the win. We both ran 10.92, new personal bests for both of us, but I got second which meant I was going to get an outside lane in the final. Winning the first round isn't necessary. Winning your semifinal when you don't have to is strategic for preferable lane draws.

I drew lane nine for the final. Lane nine was so far from the action it was going to feel like I was in a different race. At the same time, it freed me from the distraction of what was happening in the middle of the track because I wouldn't be able to see it.

John and I walked hand in hand to the village entrance from our rented flat. "Take your life back!" he said to me as he gave me a kiss, a hug, and a slap on the butt. Take your life back was a phrase he repeated to me often. It meant I was running my way to a new and different life—one that I would have earned for myself and I'd finally reap the benefits and fruits of my labor. I know, so ironic coming from him.

The warmup track looked like an international festival, and in a way, it was. Tents lined the outer edge of the space, each with a different country's flag flying above it. I had about 30 minutes to chill out before I needed to start the warmup. I used that time to use the bathroom, check-in, double check that I had my bib numbers, spikes, and spikes in my spikes. I sat with my headphones on and finished listening to *As a Man Thinketh* for the third time. After, I switched to an altogether different playlist—one that fueled my anger. Anger was a sustainable fuel source for me. With no shortage of life experience to look back on that enraged me, my anger fueled me forward without fail.

My phone buzzed. And buzzed again. And again. And again. John was blowing up my phone with text messages. I smiled thinking the messages would be a series of *I love you, you got this, rip some tits off*, and *snatch wigs off bitches* sort of messages. I opened the conversation.

"That's it! I've been disrespected for the last time! I did all this work to get you here, and they give me the worst seat in the house. I'm so high up I can't even see the race. It's like I didn't play a part in this, like you did this all on your own. Fuck this."

We got two free tickets for the Games and only for the days we were competing. So, if you made the team in the 100, you got tickets as you progressed through the rounds. Like will call, you had to go meet the person at the designated spot to get your tickets. We did not have a say in where those comped seats were. We are not extended discounts to buy tickets for friends and family. I wasn't sure what he wanted me to do about it but doing nothing was also not an option. I flagged down my agent, Paul Doyle, showed him the messages, and asked him to handle it.

Rana was upset, of all the people to bitch to about bad seats, hammering the phone of the person about to run for an Olympic medal should have not been an option. But I'd been here with John before and knew how nights like that ended, so I begged Paul without telling him why to fix that for me. He assured me he would. And they both, Paul and Rana, told me to forget about it and focus on myself. Happy to finally have permission and the space to do so, I did.

The Olympic Stadium was lit with electricity. I stood at my blocks noting how close the sideline television cameras seemed to be to me in lane nine. I set my blocks. It was time.

"Ladies, stand behind your blocks," the starter said as the cameraman walked from lane to lane pausing for our introductions to the television audience. It seemed like forever had passed when the camera made it to my lane. By that point I was so wracked with nerves and fear I hardly noticed.

"On your marks." Left-handed, I have always entered my blocks on the left. I don't even know if that matters but loading in from the right felt weird and I wasn't about to introduce any potentially aggravating elements right now. I took a deep breath and released it slowly.

"Set." I held my breath, closed my eyes. This is it. Take your life back. Run for it.

The next moment I was aware of happened 60 meters into the race. Allyson and I had hit each other. She was on my inside, lane eight. IF WE CAN HIT EACH OTHER, SHE'S TOO DAMN CLOSE! My brain sent a warning sign to my legs, and I found another gear to pull away from her.

That was it. The race was over. Beside Allyson, I couldn't feel or see anything that was happening in the race. We all stopped just short of the bank of photographers set up along the perimeter of the track and looked up to the jumbotron for the results.

Shelly-Ann won it; 10.75 was her time. Carmelita took second with 10.78. There was a pause as third place took longer to appear. With anticipation, I willed the jumbotron to display my name. It didn't. Veronica Campbell Brown was third in 10.81. I stuck out my bottom lip in pouty disappointment. I had no idea what place I had gotten; I just knew I wasn't leaving with a medal. That sucked. By then I could see that I had taken fourth, but my time had not yet come up on the screen.

I clapped my hands together in delight. The board said 10.85! I had run 10.85! I lost, but I kind of won! I didn't think I could do it, and I did! I have never been disappointed finding out I could do something I wanted to do but didn't think I could. I celebrated as if I had won gold. It's hard enough to line up in a final as intense as that, it's even harder to deliver your best performance at the exact moment you need to. Medal or not, that's a victory. John and I met beneath the stadium. Paul had come through with much better seats for John, and now John was with me in the clerking area. I got dressed, and we walked hand-in-hand through the Olympic park. We stopped for dinner at Mondo, a little-family-owned Italian restaurant along the way. We had made fast friends with the owners and had essentially hired them to prepare my meals––none of which were featured on their menus.

I'd have one day of treatment and recovery before I was on the clock for relay duty. But I woke the next day and could not move. My body screamed in protest. I wanted nothing more than to remain in bed. But that would have been the worst choice. I got up, cooked breakfast, and was about to hail a cab to Team USA's track when my phone rang which was unusual. Only a handful of people had my number and those who did were almost all John's associates. They'd contact him directly. I usually didn't answer calls from numbers that I didn't recognize, but I couldn't be sure it wasn't Team USA staff or drug testing, so I answered. Sandy Snow's unmistakable voice said hello. She asked how I was doing and how I felt after last night's final. I told her all was well, that I was sore, but otherwise doing okay. She said she had a question for me.

"Okay?" I grew concerned.

"Is there something you'd like me to know?" she asked.

"About what exactly?" I asked in return.

"I got a letter today from someone claiming to have information regarding you that could affect the relay. Have you had a positive drug test?" She asked.

"What! No! Who would tell you that? Who would lie on me that way?!" Sandy wouldn't tell me. Angry, I reassured her that she had nothing to worry about when it came to me. I didn't take any supplements at all; there was no doubt that I was clean.

I hung up the phone perplexed. "What was that about?" John asked walking toward me. I told him. "Your fucking parents," he said pounding his fist into his hand.

"Why would they do that?" It didn't make sense to me why they would travel to London to watch a relay they'd get me kicked out of by creating a cloud of suspicion around me. But John was convinced.

His phone rang. He had been expecting Dennis' call as they dealt with a lawsuit concerning former clients who sued him for losing $1.2 million of their $3 million investment in 14 months. He had informed his former clients that he'd be declaring bankruptcy. The pending bankruptcy had added an additional layer of stress to our experience at the Olympics, as John was worried about American Express rescinding his Centurion status because of it. With my $20,000 salary and the prize money from meets that wasn't paid out immediately, a lot of the trip was being charged. We'd be in trouble if AMEX chose to shut down the account, and it was my understanding that they could choose to do so at any time.

Sandy's call sent him over the edge. I listened to John screaming into his cell phone and waited for his fiery rage to burn itself out—grateful that, for once, his anger wasn't directed at me.

I eventually made it to the track and got treatment from the team chiropractor and massage therapist. Beth Mignano had magic hands, and I felt good as new after I got off her table. We had another great meal at Mondo that evening, and the next morning I was ready to step into relay mode.

Allyson and Carmelita were present but wouldn't be doing handoffs. They both were in the 200 and were free to focus on that. Although there was no set order, according to JD, Allyson and I had never practiced anything other than second and first leg respectively. Carmelita had not worked on anything other than fourth. That's not to say that the other alternates did not practice those legs; I'm saying that, unless JD decided I wasn't running at all, I was running first, Allyson second, and Jet fourth. That didn't mean that we were the lineup either. It meant that JD had identified which legs we were and practiced us accordingly. There would be no reality in which I switched to third leg. BeeKay was a different story. She came in with a spirit of service, clapped her hands together, and announced she would run whenever and wherever the team needed her. She probably did more handoffs in different positions than the rest of us combined. It was inspiring to watch.

JD had us gather around on the infield near the second exchange to let us know he had made a decision. He had decided the lineups. It was decided that Jet and Allyson would sit out of the first round. Their 200-meter dash final was the night before, but Team USA had enough world class sprinters to make it into the final without them. JD informed us he was open to hearing anything anyone wanted to say, but that we needed to remember it was his call and his call alone in the end. I wasn't worried about my spot, but I was holding my breath while he told us.

"First round is Tianna, to Jeneba, to Bianca, to Lauryn."

We nodded at each other smiling—no surprises there.

He continued, "Barring any mishaps in the 200 or the first round, the lineup for the final is Tianna, to Allyson, to Bianca, to Jet."

I smiled. This was the team I wanted. I was just about to flash BeeKay a smile when Jeneba hopped up from the ground; she was irate. She had given up her spot on the 100-meter team because she fully expected to be running in the final. She had placed fourth at the trials. She argued how BeeKay shouldn't have been there in the first place, having placed fifth in the final with a slower season's best than hers. BeeKay stood up, not the one to tolerate disrespect sitting down. BeeKay informed Jeneba that JD was the coach, and he had decided she was the best person for the job and that given how Jeneba's handoffs looked in training and her subsequent failed pass in Monaco, BeeKay said she agreed with JD. Jeneba picked up a spike and threw it. BeeKay side-stepped the wayward shoe, and advanced toward Jeneba. I grabbed Jeneba, turned her, and asked her to come with me, half dragging her across the infield. We sat inside the field house.

"This can go one of two ways," I said to her. "You can get your ass kicked out of the first round too by carrying on like this or you can run the best damn leg you can and prove them wrong."

I decided to omit what my biggest fear of all was, that we'd have another Monaco situation and not make it out of the first round at all. I appealed to her Christianity, since she evoked it when she deferred her spot to Allyson after the trials.

"What God has for you is for you. Come on." I wrapped my arm around her shoulder, and we walked back out to rejoin the squad.

I was worried about Jeneba. I didn't need to be though. When the first round came, she handled herself like a professional and ran an incredible second leg. Our time of 41.64 was .7 seconds faster than the next fastest time, and we did that without our additional 10.7 and 10.8 sprinters.

Happy with my performance in the 100 but still disappointed it didn't result in a medal, I was looking forward to the 4x100 relay final. I did not want to leave London without a medal.

G.O.A.T.

"T, come here." Rana flagged me over to him in the warmup area before the 4x100-meter final. "Walk with me."

I found his presence in the warmup area soothing. The walks around the track meant the world to me. Sometimes he talked to me about the things I needed to execute reminding me of my cues, and how I deserved to be there, and how I've put up with and overcome so much. Other times we said nothing at all and just strolled giving me a place to move nervous energy without needing to articulate it.

"This is gonna piss you off. Jamaica decided to put Shelly-Ann on first leg. They said putting her there would scare you, and you'd run a leg so bad that it'd be too big a deficit to overcome." He looked at me with a quizzical expression.

"The fuck!?" I said, insulted. "Who told you this?" I demanded to know.

"I just know," he said.

We walked past Jamaica's team tent—their flag visible.

"I just want to rip all these fucking flags down," I said through gritted teeth.

Rana smirked, patted me on the back, and told me to begin my warm-up.

Warming up allowed me to convert my anger into fuel. I was calm by the time we entered the call room—the place where all the teams were held before entering the stadium. It was here they checked uniforms, bib numbers, and confiscated electronics we tried to sneak inside.

We sat on plastic chairs, legs bouncing with nervous energy.

"Man, I'm gonna take my cruise after this," Jet said dreamingly.

"I am not a fan of cruise ships. Saw *Titanic*; I am not the same," I said laughing.

BeeKay chimed in with what she'd like to do at the end of the season. I knew I had limited options and resources to do anything as cool as the others, so I said I just wanted to sleep. Jet said there were two types of people in the world: the kind that like Red Vines and the kind that like Twizzlers. I told her I was Team Twizzlers.

"T, why you never wear the briefs?" BeeKay asked me as I was adjusting my boy shorts.

The day before we had to decide as a group which style of the Team USA uniform we were going to wear, I begged them to not choose the briefs. The answer was complicated, I've loved running in briefs since high school. Sure, my butt had filled out way more since then, and the aesthetic is different, but I felt faster in them. I'm sure it's irrational, like my disdain for socks and how they feel like ankle weights to me. BeeKay was waiting for an answer. It was just us girls, so I decided to tell them the truth, as embarrassing as it was.

"John doesn't let me shave. So, yeah, the world does not deserve that." I laughed at the ridiculousness of it.

"Let you?!" BeeKay shouted.

"A fetish I'm happy to oblige," I said. A statement only half true.

"To each their own I guess," BeeKay said.

Carmelita and Allyson sat smiling silently shaking their heads. A quick look around the call room made me realize we were the only team relaxed enough to be carrying on a casual conversation. In fact, we were the only team talking at all.

We headed into the tunnel that led to the stadium. I asked Allyson how she was feeling. She had had a lot of races in her legs and sometimes struggled to accelerate well off the line. But once she was up, watch out. She told me she was feeling pretty good. I told her I'd get her the baton.

We walked out of the tunnel as a team and ran to our respective positions. Allyson, Bianca, and Jet rushed to measure out their spacing, and put down tape. I set my blocks carefully in lane seven. Jamaica, led off by the two-time Olympic champion who had won the 100 meter dash days before, was on my inside in lane six.

I didn't have a problem with Shelly-Ann, but she was mistaken if she thought she was just going to roll me up as if I were standing still, as if I had no say in the matter. Nah. No ma'am.

"Stand behind your blocks." Again the cameraman drifted from lane to lane for our television introductions. I could hardly contain myself. I felt like a caged animal pacing behind the bars or a horse just before the starting gate sprang open. I could not wait to tear the turn up.

"To your marks," the starter said, raising his gun.

I loaded into the blocks, and just before I lowered my head I looked up at the runner in the outside lane. *I'm coming for you Germany. Go get her ass.*

Those were my last thoughts before the starter said, "Set!" I held my breath.

"BAM!"

The gun went off, and so did I. Flying around the curve like my life depended on it, because, well, it kind of did, I got to Allyson sooner than she or I had anticipated. I nearly ran up her backside, but I got her the stick as promised. I was so close to Allyson during the handoff that she spiked my leg; I didn't care though.

I screamed, "Go!" at her back as she sprinted away. I turned and jogged back toward the finish line. Bianca had the baton. Then Jet had the baton, and then she pointed it at the clock. We were the Olympic champions setting a new world record! A record set in 1985 when I was two months old by the German Democratic Republic team; a record largely believed to be untouchable because of the prevalence of performance enhancing drugs during that time; a record we destroyed by over half a second! I would be leaving the Games with a gold medal. The relief I felt was indescribable.

Later, while sitting in the waiting room ahead of drug testing in order get our world record ratified, I noticed blood dripping down my leg.

"Oh, that's right," I said out loud but to no one in particular, "She spiked the shit out of me." I wiped the blood away thinking about how drastically different the experience of pain and hurt are when you're winning.

COOL RUNNINGS

I was done with track after the London 2012 Olympics. After we returned to the flat, I put the medal on the table, walked down to the corner store, bought a bunch of junk food, and pigged out to a Harry Potter marathon. I was happy to not be leaving empty-handed. But I wasn't sure that medal had been worth what I'd gone through to get it, and I was not interested in grinding for another four years to do it again—just to feel like that.

I sank into a depression when I returned home to the US, only leaving bed to feed the dog and myself and to use the bathroom. I was watching the ticker scroll on CNN on one of my bedridden days when I saw it. "Olympian Tianna Madison sued by parents for libel and defamation," scrolled across the bottom of the screen.

"WHAT THE FUCK IS THIS?!" I shouted so loud I scared the dog. I jumped out of bed and called John. "WHAT THE FUCK IS GOING ON!" I shouted into the phone. "MY PARENTS ARE SUING ME!?" I was inconsolable. John told me his "people" were on it, and I opened my computer and scoured the internet for more details.

Nothing that I had thought would happen after winning the Olympics actually happened. There was no tour of the late-night shows, no windfall of endorsement deals, and no checks. We didn't get invited to the ESPY's, and I was so embarrassed by the lawsuit my parents had filed against me that I would have said no to any media opportunities offered anyway. Of all the things that I had gone through, put myself through, or that had been done to me, that lawsuit was the most damaging. My ability to earn beyond my $20,000 salary was crushed by brands not necessarily wanting to be associated with "the daughter who gets sued by her parents." Except for Nike.

Everyone else was wondering how shitty of a person I had to be to get sued by my own parents. The whole world was asking. The comment section of each article that reported on this story was filled with people guessing what kind of people we were, calling us racial slurs, and using this case as a reason to validate their low opinions of black people and their families.

Did I deserve this? I asked myself, trying to find a way to see this from my parents' perspective.

I had done very shitty things and treated them poorly for most of the year. They didn't know that each time I did, I was saving myself from something more horrible. I found the case online, filed in Ohio. It was largely based on something I had written during training camp in Austria.

When I arrived in Austria, my accommodations weren't ready. And so, after a long day of travel, I had to sit outside of the Hofbräu while the adjoining inn got my room together. The weather was beautiful, but I really wanted to nap, shower, and unwind. Finally, someone gave me a key to a room, and when I entered the room, it was occupied by two men. I closed the door, marched back to reception desk, informed them of the situation, and took up residence on the same bench outside the Hofbräu.

At the same time, John had been complaining about his needs not being met. I had been in Europe for weeks now, and he was pressuring me to give him permission to sleep with someone else.

"You can choose the person," he said as if that somehow made it a better situation. He was meeting me in Europe in three days for the Olympics, and this was where he was at. Furious, I pulled out my laptop and wrote about everything I was pissed about, from my entire life that brought me to that point. My anger was largely directed at my parents, specifically my mom. I believed that, had our relationship been better, had she treated me better, managed my money better, done anything or everything better, I wouldn't be sitting in Austria, on a bench, fake-married to a man demanding a "hall pass," because I'm "not around," as if I were on some spa vacation with girlfriends and not making money or preparing for the Olympic Games. How was that my life? It felt really good to get it out on paper. My mistake was letting John read it. He told me that it was the most amazing piece of writing he had ever seen and that I should send it to my parents and maybe it would make me feel better. The second mistake I made was actually agreeing to it. The third mistake was related to the first mistake because he forwarded it to a journalist. I had to act like I didn't care that my words were in the hands of a journalist, otherwise I'd revive the accusation that I was choosing my parents over him, the only person who loved me, took care of me, and didn't take from me. With the Olympics around the corner, I wanted as smooth a ride as possible. Some time had passed. I was settled into my room when John called to tell me the journalist was worried about legal exposure, that some major accusations were raised, and that he had reached out to the Madisons. They denied the entirety of the contents of the letter.

I was infuriated all over again for two reasons:

1.   I raised questions rather than accusations. The tone of the questions raised was definitely accusatory, but I framed it that way to avoid making definitive statements of which I was *pretty* sure but not 100 percent sure of.

2.   I had not lied. I may have been a shitty, nasty, bitch of a daughter, but I did not lie.

But that was what my parents had claimed in their lawsuit against me, and that was now how the world would view me after making my first Olympic team, making the final in the 100-meter dash, running a personal best when it mattered the most, holding off Shelly-Ann on the first leg to help my team win gold, and break a world record. Yeah, for all that I had done, I was not sure I could or would ever understand or forgive this trespass against me.

Two more things happened that led to my desire to step away from the sport after the Olympic Games. Rana had taken a job in the UK. He would be relocating the group to Loughborough. John wouldn't let me get an apartment in Daytona Beach 2½ hours away; there was no way he was "letting" me move to the United Kingdom. Second, Dr. Phil…yes, THAT Dr. Phil…wanted to know if he could assist me with my family issues. I could not shrink myself small enough.

John thought quitting was a bad idea, and he suggested that maybe I just needed a break. So, after a few calls, I joined the bobsled team. I was miserable. Not used to team dynamics, I needed to not only learn the technical components of being a brakeman but the socio-political savvy of getting myself into a sled. I loved to slide, but bobsled was meant to be a break from drama and pettiness; instead, Lake Placid was the same shit in a different toilet. But it was a great place to hide from the world, tucked away from ravenous journalists itching to pull the threads at the fringes of a family in crisis.

I left the team halfway through the season because the coaches refused to race me because I refused to gain weight. I had decided that I would return to track for outdoor, and if I put on the weight they were asking me to, I'd struggle to get it back off in time to have a good season. Because I was a lighter brakeman, we had to add weight to the sled itself which made our sled heavier to push. None of the drivers liked the idea of that. I tried to plead my case, pointing out that it shouldn't matter so much with the high velocities we were producing. The numbers didn't lie; but if the driver didn't want you in their sled, you weren't sliding. Thinking I had better things to do with my time than waste them freezing on the sidelines, I returned to Florida. I didn't leave my bobsled experience empty-handed though. I'd leave with a World Cup bronze medal, a new friend named Emily, and the sneaking suspicion that I could and should return to the long jump.

ENOUGH

As much as I had tried not to gain weight, I gained enough to cause me issues when it came to getting back on the track. Still not recovered emotionally or mentally from the toll the previous year had taken on me, I tried to ease myself back into training. I injured myself lifting in my first month back. Not used to wearing straps, I was awkwardly strapped to a bar with 200 pounds on it for a power clean. I got it up—after all, mass moves mass, right? But I was off balance when the bar reached my chest and instead of releasing the straps and dropping the bar, I tried to force it up and finish the lift with a catch. I could feel the discs in my back shift as I did so. I lowered the bar to the platform and tried to walk it off. I went on to do a set of box hops and finish my workout. I drove home, slightly uncomfortable, took some ibuprofen, and went to bed. The next day I could hardly move. I went to practice, struggled through the warmup, and spent the afternoon in a hyperbaric chamber. On my way home, I stopped at Books-a-Million to browse for books to add to my collection. I needed to pee so I cut my trip short to make the drive home, which was only 15 minutes away. I felt the urge to pee one second and was peeing on myself the next. I tried to do a Kegel exercise to stop the flow of urine. Nothing happened. I tried to lift my pelvic floor, no response. I was frightened; I could feel my legs but couldn't hold my urine, couldn't do a Kegel, couldn't do anything.

I called Loren Seagrave, my new coach, who reached out to St. Vincent's, a hospital partnered with USATF. I flew to Indianapolis where I learned that I had protruding discs in my back. My lumbosacral joint, the L5-S1 was sitting to the left of my spine. Forcing my body under 200 pounds off balance was stupid, and I had damaged the nerves in the area too. I was put on prednisone, and just like that, my season was over. All that was left to do was sit around and heal. I was uncomfortable and in pain all the time. John offered me a painkiller I'd never heard of...hydrocodone. He instructed me to take half a tablet just before eating, and to enjoy the ride. I was hooked.

Weeks turned into months, and I sank deeper and deeper into depression. I ate my misery by the pound, washed my sorrows away with alcohol, and questioned why I was living at all. John had been growing frustrated with me too and had begun giving me lectures about the dangers of one-sided relationships which he claimed ours had become since I wasn't running or earning any income. If he was going to be doing the "heavy lifting," the least I could do was take care of *his* needs. *Great, I've decreased in value*, I thought.

I'd decreased in value to John, and also to Nike, who had reduced my salary due to the injury.

I'd had enough. I organized my closets, folded my panties in my panty drawer, cleared out my nightstand, and cleared my call log and chat roll. I wanted to control what I left behind when I killed myself. I had settled on hanging. John had a full-garage gym, and I could hang myself from the cable crossover machine. I debated writing a letter, but what was left to say? *I'm really sorry that I no longer have value?* I had told John I didn't like marriage. I didn't like the power imbalance or the expectation he had of me to be subservient. It was fully counter to my true nature. I told him I didn't want to be married anymore. He chuckled. He told me I could leave any time, because—guess what—we weren't actually married.

But after an hour or two of serious searching and looking into how I could leave, I realized that I couldn't. I had no money. John and Dennis, under the guise of settling my IRS tax debt from 2007, when just one injury changed the entirety of my financial future, were managing my earnings. Club 360 Management, although loosely affiliated with me, was owned by John. All the income I earned went to accounts there. From there, Dennis would forward a couple hundred dollars to my personal accounts of which he was also an authorized user. John would also give me a couple hundred dollars cash so all I'd get was about $12K a year no matter what I'd earned, unless I asked to purchase something specific and needed more money. I was told that with my lack of spending, the remainder of the money was going toward debt, student loans, and a savings account. Over and over, John would tell me and anyone who would listen, how he was the only one in my life not taking from me, and everything I earned was sitting right there in the bank. I was free to call Dennis and ask for its status at any time. But when I did, Dennis called John, and then John called me asking why I was questioning him. Couldn't I see that it worked? Did I forget how I got that gold medal? The nerve of me, who was doing nothing more than sitting on the couch, questioning him who was working so hard for the "family."

I was back to my original plan to take my own life. I stood in the gym staring at the Cybex Cable Crossover machine. I was going to attach the strong 100 percent leather belt to the pop up pull up bar. We had aerobic step-up boxes that I could stand on and kick away. My toes would just barely graze the floor as long as I got the belt secured properly. The irony of hanging to my death as an African American was not lost on me. The jury in the George Zimmerman trial had just found him not guilty on all counts. Trayvon was walking home. I had told John that I was going to stop walking Bailey for a while. We lived in Avila in Tampa, home to Tony Dungy and Jon Gruden, among other notable residents. I'd walk Bailey in the morning sometimes before the sun had fully risen. As one of the only black residents, I'd told him I was scared. Here in Florida, all it took was for one of the neighbors to feel threatened by me, and they could kill me, and I had no reason to believe there'd be consequences. What if Bailey got off her leash and ran into a yard, what if while bending over scooping up poop near a bush they thought I was "casing the place." John told me I didn't have to worry because I was with him. He wanted me to believe that I didn't have to worry about my blackness because I was covered by his whiteness. I was reminded of a time we went to a party for Dennis and his accounting firm. Dennis and John's mutual client flew up from the Cayman Islands to attend the party and conduct other business.

When John and I walked into the party together George exclaimed, "Here comes John and his nigger."

In response, John had his assistants keep me company at the bar far enough away from George to be out of earshot when he called me a racial slur, but close enough to watch him laugh with John and Dennis throughout the evening. His whiteness did nothing to protect me then. And yet when we travelled together, I never got questioned about which cabin I was traveling in or my Diamond Status. When I was mistreated in a clothing store, John came back with me and made them regret it. My value was tied to him, and he had voiced that my value in his eyes had diminished. *What then?* I didn't want to find out. I thought about my parents, my sisters, my niece, and nephew. I grieved for them and myself, stood up on the aerobic boxes, secured the belt to the bar, and the belt around my neck.

I was pulling the belt tighter when the house phone rang. *Fuck!* I thought. It was going to be John on the other line and not answering was not an option. I undid the belt. I'd have to answer the phone; that would buy me a couple more hours of quiet time if I answered. If I didn't answer, he would call my cell, and when I didn't answer that, he'd call the house phone again, repeatedly. At that point, he'd either hop in his car and drive home, or send someone over. I wasn't sure how long it would take for my heart to stop beating. If he was already calling from his car, he could get to me fast enough to revive me, and then what? No, I had to answer the phone.

He was at the office and needed a favor. I decided to do the favor first, affording him that one last thing before I left. It took me hours, and I ran out of time to hang myself. I could hear the gate creaking open, and I remembered that the belt was still hanging from the gym equipment. Rushing out to the garage, I removed the belt just as the garage door opened, and John pulled inside.

His usual routine upon coming home in the evening was to walk in, change clothes, and head back out into the garage for a workout. This usually gave me another hour of downtime. Frustrated with myself, I added some cuts to my wrists and promised myself to hold on. I had only one more day that I needed to live.

But that day passed and the next and the next. Eventually, put off by my depression and weight gain, John sent me to a therapist. She was a black female cognitive behavioral therapist named Dr. Raena. Her office was in Lake Mary which meant I had to drive an hour-and-a-half with an injured back to see her so that no one in Tampa would know. I sat on the couch across from her with an expression as blank as I felt.

"Do you know why you're here?" she asked me.

"My husband told me I needed to come," I said to her in a flat tone.

As far as I knew, whatever he had said to her on the phone about why I needed professional help was a complete fabrication, and her job was to help convince me that it wasn't. I didn't trust her.

"Did he tell you what he told me when he called?" she asked.

"No, are *you* even allowed to tell me?" I asked her with a challenge in my tone.

"He is not my client, you are. I can tell you," she said.

She told me that he had called explaining that he had a wife that didn't know how good she had it, that he was the perfect man with a perfect body, who was "ripped to the gills" and all his wife did was sit around doing nothing and getting fat while he busted his ass at work. He was sexually unsatisfied, and he deserved to be in a marriage where it was give and take, not just take, take, take, take, take. I wasn't surprised to hear it. Everything he said to her, he had already screamed in my face. I said nothing.

"So," she continued, "that was weird. What's going on?"

It took me a few visits to understand that she didn't buy anything he was selling. But once I did, it was like a weight had been lifted off my shoulders, and I unburdened my heart and spilled my guts on that broken down couch.

"That's a lot," she said, when I came up for air. "How are you coping?" she asked.

I didn't want to get Baker-Acted for admitting to a suicide attempt, or that it was still on the table, but I did confess to being a cutter. She didn't judge me, but she did make it clear that I should not ever resort to harming myself. There are plenty of other effective coping mechanisms that are actually productive in addressing the issue I may be cutting for. But she also understood it might take me a while to get there. She handed me a handful of rubber bands.

"Put this around your wrist, and when you feel the urge to cut, snap the rubber band instead." Now that that was covered, she moved on to her next question.

"When did your father die?" she asked.

"What?" Her question caught me off guard. Why would she think he was dead? I definitely didn't *say* he was.

"You have only ever mentioned your mother in these sessions. I assumed he was either dead or not in your life at all."

Damn. Was I really that fixated on my mother? What was it about her that hung over me even now...going on two years with no contact? She suggested a book for me to read titled, *Toxic Parents*, by Dr. Susan Forward. She wasn't sure if it described my exact situation but thought I could find some helpful methods for dealing with the estrangement.

"Tell me about your husband."

I groaned and began to relay the story of how we met and what had transpired over the last two years. I stopped short of admitting to physical abuse. Knowing I was a reader that had a growing library on the second floor of the house, she recommended another book, *Who's Pulling Your Strings*, by Harriet Braiker. She had a feeling that a foundational issue of mine was that I was being manipulated by the people in my life with no tools to guard against it. She didn't know John beyond the first phone call, but she was trained in recognizing behavioral patterns and identifying their catalysts.

I'd drive home from our sessions more hopeful than I had been in a while. When I got to my exit on the highway, I'd shift gears and start to think about what I'd tell John about the sessions. He'd ask me to recount everything that was said by Dr. Raena and me, in as much detail as possible. I knew that I did not *have* to do this. But I couldn't not do it either. And so, I lied my ass off. Every single time. Eventually, John declared my therapy as a failure and instructed me to stop going. I did, but I already had the tools I needed to cope with the estrangement from my family and the dynamics of my marriage. I no longer wanted to kill myself. Dr. Raena had, in fact, succeeded in helping me see the inherent value I had as a human, and she provided me with a way to learn the skills I need to survive my life.

RETURN OF THE MACK

Because Rana took a job with UK Athletics after the Olympics, I had to solve the issue of finding a new coach. I settled on Loren Seagrave after weighing my options in the area. He was at IMG in Bradenton, Florida—a much shorter commute than driving to Clermont or Orlando would be. In one of our first meetings, I told him I wanted to return to the long jump in the outdoor season. I didn't think I could be ready for indoor season, so I'd take my first jump—in two years—that outdoor season after we'd have a whole fall to prepare. I told him that I believed I was ready to give it another serious shot.

Why did I think this? Bobsled. I may not have had the opportunity to race in competitions extended to me when I was on the bobsled team, but I took a lot of reps in practice. When I watched the video of my pushes, I noticed that I was absolutely nailing the jump into the sled after the pushing was done. Not only was I nailing the takeoff into the back of the sled, the step before takeoff (known as the penultimate step) was fast and efficient. That was something that I had struggled with in the long jump after Rana made me fast. The penultimate step has to be your fastest step. So, the faster you get, the faster the penultimate step has to be. If you're really fast on the runway, the force and effort required to make that second to last step even faster than that was wild and scary. But I had found one thing that was scarier than that, trying to jump into the back of a bobsled that was increasing in speed and traveling downhill on ice. Suddenly the long jump wasn't scary at all.

Sad that Rana had taken a job overseas but happy for him and his family, I told him I wanted to stay in touch. I had hoped that he could continue to write my program. It felt like a cruel gift from the Universe to be gifted with a coach—who turned my whole career around in just one year after seven years of floundering—and only allow me one year to have him. I told him I would email him every week, and I did for a while.

The best part about training in Bradenton was not spending 5 hours in my car every single training day. This left me more time in the day to do other things. Loren suggested yoga for active recovery, and so I found a studio in Sarasota just 15 minutes away from the track. I'd go on regen (short for regeneration) Thursdays, either before or after our general fitness work. Marie Myrbakk was the owner and instructor of the studio. Entering for the first time was like being welcomed home after a lifetime of wandering.

I started with yin and restorative yoga. We didn't move much which was great because I didn't want to. Instead, we used blocks, straps, bolsters, and gravity to help us release sore or tight muscles. Soft music played during the class, and Marie moved about the room as if on air speaking softly to us. Sometimes she'd recite a poem, a prayer, or yogic philosophy, but every time I received her words, it was like a gift I would always hold on to.

Those "dharma drops" as I dubbed them aroused a hunger in me that only more yoga could satiate. I began to seek her out for more classes and services. She offered private sessions where we could focus on specific issues, poses, or progressions.

"It's your time, you can use it how you want," she told me when I was deciding if I wanted to take the leap. I wasn't yet sure about adding another active component to my week. I wasn't sleeping. I hadn't slept in so long, one of John's doctor friends wrote me a prescription for Xanax which had proved to be the only thing that knocked me out and kept me out for at least six hours. I told Marie I'd think about it because I wasn't sleeping and wasn't sure if I should add something else to my schedule or just nap.

"What about Yoga Nidra?" she asked me.

"Never heard of it, what is it?" I asked.

"Yoga Nidra actually translates to yogic sleep. It's essentially a guided meditation practice that places you in a state between consciousness and sleep. It's said that 30 minutes of Yoga Nidra is equivalent to three hours of sleep," she explained.

"That, I need that," I said. And so, every week I practiced Yoga Nidra with Marie, who had no way of knowing she was saving my life and my season.

But there was an unintended side effect of being exposed to those dharma drops, it reignited my Buddhist practice. I was reminded again of The Four Noble Truths:

1. There is suffering. *Hell, yeah, there is.* I thought. In the seven years since I was first introduced to them, I'd found ways to suffer even more.

2. There is a cause to suffering. *I could name a few contributing factors to my suffering right now.*

3. There is an end to suffering. *God, I hope so.*

4. The end of suffering could be found in the eightfold path. I decided to commit myself to walking the eightfold path. And my first order of business was to stop clinging to what was no longer mine.

So, I stopped emailing Rana. He wasn't my coach anymore. He wasn't writing my workouts, he was no longer replying to my emails, and he wasn't coming back. I'd have to figure it out without him. I had to let him go.

I turned my attention to my new team, Loren Seagrave, Steffen Visk (my strength coach), Josh Lifrak (my mental conditioning coach) and Jorge Giral (my physical therapist) at IMG Academy. We had some big hills to climb. The first was the weight I gained during my year of depression, and the second was returning to the long jump. Running indoor was part of the plan. Because I had no marks from the previous season, the meet directors were not interested in giving me lanes, so we put together a mini circuit of meets.

I asked John to let Loren and me handle it, asking him to stay home and focus on his work, rather than tag along to these tune-up meets. He didn't like it, but there wasn't enough glory in traveling from college meet to college meet for him to fight me on it. So, Loren and I got to know each other better, traveling and competing at small meets. I was a far cry from the world leading sprinter of 2012, and I was sad about that. After seven years of struggle, I had one glorious year, my coach left, I got injured, and there I was again back at square one.

There were two reasons my return to track and field was self-funded. After the 2012 Olympics, I signed with Nike again. Nike uses two different contracts. A short form contract that states the terms in an abbreviated document. Signing this allows payment to process while Nike's legal team produces the long form version of the contract. The long form states the same terms as the short form but also details the bonuses and reductions. I spent the winter on the bobsled team but got injured late spring trying to prepare for my return to outdoor track. I was already competing in Nike gear in the 2013 outdoor season and had already signed the short form contract when, after they were made aware of my injury, they attempted to reduce my contract by 50%! Their claim was that I had not met the minimum number of meets required to avoid that major reduction. The short form contract mentioned no such reduction. Nike argued that the long form contract did, the contract they had not yet sent me, that I had not yet signed. I wrote a strongly worded email explaining that it was ridiculous to hold me in breach for a provision in a contract they had not sent, that I had not seen, and that I had not signed. They argued that signing the short form version was in effect agreeing to the terms of the long form. Nike ignored me and tried to demand that I not only accept half my salary moving forward, but to make sure I only competed in my Nike gear. John had one of his attorney friends write Nike a letter—one I felt was the same strength as mine but, you know, maybe I should have created a letterhead to be taken seriously.

I told Nike that I would not be competing in their gear and that I was no longer so desperate for money that I'd tolerate such unprofessional treatment from them. I hired a former training partner, Tori Polk, to design my uniforms. I spray painted my spikes black and went about my business of making a comeback.

John was frustrated with me too. I didn't look like I did in 2012; it was two years later and my body had changed. He'd show me naked pictures he had of me from then, with cuts I no longer had.

"You're too big, you're too big," he'd say pinching the skin of my underarm. "You can afford not to eat; you'll be ripped in the morning."

My eating became disordered again, and my energy erratic, while I maintained my training and ragtag competition schedule. I still wasn't getting faster, or I was getting faster but I just wasn't 2012 fast. John decided that it was because he wasn't as involved as he had been—my struggles were proof positive that he was the X-factor in my successes; and so I said he could be involved. Even though nothing actually changed with how I was training and competing, he was more amicable, and it was *that* that changed everything.

Until we arrived in Boston for a meet, my first pro-level meet since beginning my return back, John had taken to posting up at the bar at Abe & Louie's, a high-end steakhouse with a good bar, to unwind and sip his old-fashioned. It wasn't far from the Charlesmark Hotel where we were staying, right at the finish line of the Boston Marathon—the site of a horrific bombing just a year before.

I asked John to make us a reservation for after the meet. I told him it was the smart thing to do since most people in big cities celebrated Valentine's Day by going out for dinner. We'd be competing for tables with the entire city if we didn't get ahead of it. When he returned, I put on our favorite race eve movie, *It's Complicated*, and we drifted to sleep.

The meet was stacked. Mary Cain, 17 at the time, broke her own junior world record in the 1000 meters. And I was set to line up against a solid 60-meter field. Although my times were trending in the right direction, nothing was happening that indicated I'd run spectacularly or even pull off the win, but I wanted to take my shot. I won the race in 7.17. I was elated! John was pumped and so was Loren, so John invited everyone in our support circle to Abe and Louie's. The place was packed; Loren and another guy, who was tagging along, looked concerned about the likelihood we'd get seated. I asked John about the reservation. He said he didn't make one because he was "friends with the bartender," and he told us he was going to handle it. We watched him wade through the crowd of people making his way to the bar. He flagged his "friend" the bartender down, who looked up briefly, acknowledged John's presence with a slight nod of the head, and continued serving his drinks. The hair started to stand up on my arms; I had a bad feeling.

"Hey, Man!" John shouted again. "Anything you can do for me?"

The bartender, his arms moving rapidly around his station, gave him a "what exactly do you think I can do?" look. John walked back to us and ushered us to the part of the bar where patrons stood and sipped. There was a ledge for resting your elbow or glass, but it was too small to rest a plate on.

I did not want to stand for the entire evening, and I was starving. Loren asked for the extra barstool of a party of three seated at a four top.

"Here, sit. You've earned it," Loren said to me as I got situated on the stool. John looked embarrassed; it wasn't a look that people who don't know him well would recognize though. He had started to twitch, slowly at first, but now every few seconds both his eyebrows would raise as if he were surprised. The time between his eyebrows doing this nervous dance was decreasing. I decided to play it cool.

"I can just order and eat like this if you don't mind," I said to John.

"No, he's gonna get me a table," John said.

"Sure, I can order and start eating and then when a table becomes available, I can just take the plate to the table."

He found this agreeable. I ate my whole meal on my lap. The guy who joined us left to find somewhere else to eat, and Loren was happy with his drink and leaning on the ledge.

By the time we returned to the hotel John was drunk and furious.

"Why are you such a bitch?!" he shouted, his speech slurring.

This wasn't unexpected. I saw the embarrassment, and people who are uncomfortable with themselves, or who don't properly process their feelings, like to discharge it onto others. I replied calmly, but it didn't matter. He escalated himself, and in the tiny rooms—standard in that boutique hotel— there was nowhere for me to go and no way for me to avoid him. He stood up and began walking toward me but was only trying to reach the door. He said he was going for a walk and hoped I had a different attitude when he returned.

I exhaled. He didn't take his coat, and it was freezing outside. He wouldn't be gone for long, but something told me to get out of there. I grabbed my bag, threw the remainder of my toiletries in it, and sprinted out of the room to the elevator. Praying to a God I didn't even believe in, to keep me out of John's path. I emerged out on Boylston Street with no idea of what to do and with no place to go. Too ashamed to call Loren, who was likely drunk himself, I wandered the streets with my Nike rolling bag for an hour. Cold and with frozen tears on my face, I started looking for a place to sleep. Looking for a hotel on Valentine's Day night proved damn near impossible or too damn expensive. I eventually found one—the room was barely the size of a closet but was big enough for me and my bag. I went to sleep, met John in the morning, and flew home.

We returned to Boston a few weeks later for USATF Indoor Nationals where I'd win again, running 7.08. That win qualified me for the indoor World Championships in Sopot, Poland. I'd take home the bronze medal again from that championship behind Shelly-Ann and Murielle Ahouré; I'd run a season's best time of 7.06.

I was emotional after that race. It took nearly everything I had to get there after how the season started. Winning the medal meant a lot to me; it meant I wasn't dead yet. It meant that my success wasn't tied to Rana which I had been convinced of when he left. It meant I still had it in me. I took my victory lap where there was only one other person in the stands who knew what I had to overcome to get there. I reached up and took his hand.

"I'm proud of you," John yelled down to me. "You're a beast!"

Shifting to outdoor, Loren and I prepared me for my first long jump competition. Then Rana returned, not permanently, but he was back in the States for a while for warm-weather training camp in Daytona Beach. I asked if I could hop in on some jump workouts while he was there. He said yes, and I drove to Daytona Beach for training just like in the old days.

His jump squad had short approach jumps on the day that I joined their training session. Christian Taylor sailed through the pit, seemingly jumping the same distance from the short approach as he could from a longer one. Shara Proctor, a long jumper for Great Britain who also trained with Rana took off the board, getting more height than I ever had in my life. I skidded across the sand, with no height and no form, just speed. Christian suggested a mini competition they called "Diamond League." There was nothing to it other than jumping, marking the jump with a small cone, and then trying to out jump the person the next time. Typically, the women would keep a separate cone from the men, but secretly everyone would try to out jump everyone else regardless of sex or gender. British Paralympian Stef Reid also joined in on the fun. I jumped after Shara but before Stef. Never having jumped well from a short approach, due to my inability to lean on my speed, I had no delusions about beating Shara. I took my jump, eyeballed the mark, dusted the sand off my thighs, and stepped back from the pit to give Stef room to jump. Stef sailed past my mark by two feet. Before he could help himself, Christian's mouth fell open in shock briefly before he regained his composure. I finished the rest of my jumps and Stef continued to outjump me.

"Hey, T," Christian called to me as we were packing up. "Are you sure about returning to the jumps? Sprinting is going really well, and you know I just don't want to see you…you know, not be, maybe…um…not your thing anymore."

I cracked him a wiry smile. "I'm sure," I said.

Two months later, I jumped seven meters for the first time at a Diamond League competition in Oslo, Norway. I won the Diamond League trophy and ended the season ranked number one in the world. Plus, as the cherry on top, I won the 100-meter dash at USATF Nationals for the first time.

THE GREAT WALL

I had momentum. And I won my battle with Nike too. They reinstated me to my full salary, finally sent me the long form contract with an additional year due to their "lost" season. It helped to end the season as world number one and a national champion in two different events.

Seventeen years after taking my first long jump ever, I had finally crossed the seven-meter barrier. Jumping 23 feet was almost every female jumper's wish. But I not only wanted more of those, I wanted to make the World Championship team and go for another world title 10 years after my first. Again, indoor was part of my plan; and as had become my new normal, my indoor season started off a little rocky. I ran the 60-meter dash at the Millrose Games in New York on Valentine's Day. I ran 7.17 taking third behind Murielle Ahouré of the Ivory Coast and Michelle-Lee Ahye of Trinidad and Tobago. It was a bad loss. Murielle ran 7.05! Frustrated, I headed to Athlone, Ireland, intent on running a close to perfect race so that I could see a time in the 7.0's again.

We stayed in what looked like the Irish equivalent of a roadside motel. I had heard Carmelita Jeter was running but hadn't seen her. Turned out, she was staying at a luxury hotel elsewhere. This fueled me. Here I was national champion in the 100 and the 60 from the season before, and world number one in the long jump staying with a roommate I didn't know at a roadside motel. It was just the fuel I needed. During my pre-meet workout I walked the length of the race over and over. Reinforcing the cues, I needed to execute at each phase in the race I was confident that my race would be the best I'd run in a while.

I was right. But the world would never know it because although the gun went off, the clock never started. I nailed the first ten meters covering the distance in 7.5 strides (a pretty good indicator that I'd set up my acceleration well). I stayed patient through my drive phase and didn't rise into my upright sprinting position until close to 40 meters. At that point, I ripped my thighs up, and forced them back down more like pistons in an engine rather than cycling on a bike. With my stride frequency revved as high as I could get it, I ran through the finish line. I'd won by a couple meters. But no time appeared on the clock. It had malfunctioned. But I knew it in my bones that that was my race. My agent, who was also the meet director, asked if I wanted to run again, but I knew there was no way I could duplicate that effort. I settled for the win, and the check and returned home to prepare for nationals. I won the national title in the 60-meter dash, winning in 7.08. Running 7.0 in the 60 was a pretty good indicator that I'd jumped close to seven meters. But I'd learn a couple years later, when someone ran the video of my Ireland race through a biomechanical analysis software, that I had run sub 7! Damn.

Winning the 100 meters at nationals the year before but losing to Brittany Reese in the long jump, made me want to go for the double again. Brittany had a bye to the World Championships as she was the reigning champion from the previous edition of the World Championships. But she wasn't the type to not go for the win simply because she didn't have to. I needed to be prepared for that, and I needed to build on my indoor speed. The 60 is not a shorter version of the 100; they required two very different approaches.

The 60 is almost completely about your ability to accelerate, or "get up to speed" and then the race is over. The 100 is about your ability to accelerate, plus your ability to maintain your top velocity, and your ability to control your deceleration. So as much as a good 60 time makes me feel optimistic about the 100-meter dash, they are two different animals.

I became neurotic about succeeding at both the 100 and the long jump. I simply had to win, I had to. The difference between my life when I was winning and my life when I wasn't was so drastic that it created a necessity and an urgency so profound, nothing else existed. But I had taken this singular focus and narrowed its aperture so much that I must have shut John out too. And that was never a good thing.

"You think you're hot shit now," he said to me.

Maybe it was something about my tone or maybe it was the more frequent flexing of my independent thoughts that had begun to rub him the wrong way. I don't know. But he didn't like it. And I didn't care. He hadn't hit me; we hadn't hit each other in a long time. *We're due*, I thought. Leaning on my education when I was in the social work degree program at Tennessee, I had no delusions about actually believing the promises we made each other that those incidents would *never* happen again. Occasionally, when I looked at my medals, I'd see the incident behind them. Not the achievement. Whenever I look at the bronze medal from Turkey in 2012, I'm reminded of the beginning of the estrangement from my family and choking John in the hotel room. I do not look at my medals with pride when they represent so much pain.

I told him I was leaving.

"Fine! Go sleep on Loren's nasty-ass couch in his dirty-ass house! Good luck!"

I ran up the stairs to the spare bedroom where I kept my luggage and grabbed a bag. I ran to the other spare bedroom that had all of my training gear. I hardly wore things that weren't active wear anyway. I threw random things into the bag from each section of the closet, sports bras, shorts, long tights, tees, tanks. I was moving fast. I heard John's footsteps on the stairs, closed my bag, and ran out of the room. I had side-stepped him and was heading down the stairs. But he got a grip of the bag and dragged me back with it.

Fuck the bag, I thought and let it go. I tried to make my way down the stairs again. He reached out and grabbed my arm. I tore it away. He grabbed my ankle—I fell hard. I contemplated whether I should continue trying to make my way down the stairs head-first. I did, I tried. I tumbled down a few steps curled in the fetal position. I stood up and ran. I needed my wallet which was in the bedroom, and then I could go for my keys which were in the kitchen—in opposite directions.

I grabbed the wallet and sprinted out of the bedroom across the foyer but never made it into the kitchen. John grabbed me and tackled me to the floor. I began to kick and scream at the top of my lungs in a voice I did not recognize. He flipped me over so that he was straddling me and pinned my arms down with his hands. I could smell urine; this was where we kept Bailey's potty pads. Bailey was hiding, likely shaking to death in her bag in the closet, where she always ran to when things like this happened. That fight felt different. That fight was going to hurt. I wiggled, I squirmed, I shouted, and managed to turn to my side. He grabbed my hair and began slamming my head into the floor. He was saying something, but I couldn't hear him over my own screaming and crying. We were closer to the dog's potty pads now, and just to make it clear what he thought of me and my "hot shit" status he rubbed my face in the fresh urine on the pad. Enraged I found the strength to scamper out of his grip. In my hysteria, I made the dumbest decision ever; I ran back into the bedroom. I grabbed the cordless phone off of John's nightstand and tried to lock myself in the bathroom with the phone to call 911.

The lock didn't work. The two of us were in the water closet—the size of a public bathroom stall at best. His frame filled the doorway and blocked my exit.

"I'm gonna call 911," I threatened, clicking the phone on.

"Go ahead, you'll only damage your reputation as a so-called role model and star athlete, and you'll validate your parents!" he shouted into my face.

"I don't care anymore!" I screamed back at him.

"When did you ever?" he shouted pining me to the back wall. "You've only ever cared about yourself…you selfish cunt."

I braced myself against the toilet for leverage and used my leg to kick him away. It surprised him enough that there was now room to his right for me to squeeze by him and out the bathroom door. I leaped for it, my body leaving a shoulder-shaped dent in the drywall as I scurried away, phone in hand. I dialed. *Fuck it*, I thought. I *can't keep doing this*. I pushed the "talk" button. It rang once. I hung up terrified. *I wasn't safe enough to call, he could cut me off midway. I could be dead before they arrived. What's the point?* I thought. My priority shifted to surviving the night. I stood up, unsure what to do next—costly hesitation. John pushed me onto my back on the bed and was advancing toward me.

Suddenly I heard my father's voice in my head. "Why aren't you fighting, T? I taught you how to fight. My only rule was that you never use your skills to start fights, but you have always had my blessing to finish them. Always. Fight."

I used my core strength to get back upright and landed a left jab to his chest to create some distance. That gave me enough space to deliver a front-snap kick to his face and another left jab to keep him from advancing. Shocked, he stood in front of me holding his nose that had started to bleed. I squared up, which surprised both of us. I thought I'd run, but apparently something deep inside of me was done running. John took a step back. I took a step forward. I was in southpaw stance now.

"You fucking bitch," I said to him through gritted teeth.

Stepping forward with my right foot, "You scared?" I asked. I shouldn't have been taunting him, but I was finally in control of the situation, and control felt like a potent drug to me in that moment.

"Hey, we need to be adults! We can be adults about this!" he shouted, his voice muffled by his hands still covering his face. "I think you broke my nose!" he shouted again. I took another measured step forward still in a boxer's stance.

The phone rang. It was 911. I answered the phone and explained that the call was accidental. We had been trying to order a pizza and hit the wrong speed dial button. All was well, I told the operator.

"We good?" I said to John as I hung up the phone and placed it back on the nightstand. He nodded his head.

"I'll get you some ice."

Not wanting to concede so easily, John spoke up, "I wish you stood up to *your parents* like you stood up to me!"

I didn't take the bait. *Me too*, I thought.

Because if I had, there would have never been a Tianna and John.

I went to practice the following day with a ruptured ear drum, struggling to hide my occasional clumsiness, passing it off as needing to see the chiropractor to correct my misalignment.

"You're a beast," John said in a text message after my workout. "Your mental strength is ridiculous!"

My jumping was going well but my speed was not there. Two weeks out from nationals, I emailed Rana out of desperation and asked him what I could do every day for the next two weeks that would help me show up at the championships more ready than I was now. He sent over two-week's worth of workouts and wished me luck.

I ended up running 10.94 for fifth place at nationals. I wasn't mad about my fifth-place finish though, I had been *hoping* to run sub eleven seconds in the 100, not expecting to. My dream of pulling off the double were dead though, and so I focused my attention on the jumps. There were two flights, and I was in the second with Brittany Reese. *Good*, I thought, *right where I can see her.* I opened with 7.02, but the jump was over the allowable wind. That distance would still be good for placing, but it didn't qualify for world rankings or performance bonuses. Brittany opened with 6.97 with a headwind which is technically a farther jump than the one I produced when adjusted for the wind. It was going to be a close competition. I buckled down. I jumped 7.12 meters for the second jump. The wind had changed directions and was blowing in our faces. Brittany, with unlucky timing, had to jump into a headwind nearly four times the strength of the wind I had on my attempt and only managed to jump 6.43.

Feeling pretty good, I decided to go for it. Confident now, that I had the speed to jump big because of my 10.94 time in the 100, I sprinted down the runway with nothing held back. I fouled the next two jumps. The fifth jump felt different, bad even, and it hurt at takeoff. I landed hard, my momentum rocking me forward as I rolled out of the pit. I landed well past the world record mark indicated on the performance board and right around 25 feet. I looked back at the official: red flag. I had fouled. It didn't count. I checked the plasticine, the clay that indicates the foul and by how much, barely a toe. *I can jump 25 feet,* I thought as I dusted myself off. My 7.12 jump was a personal best though. I won nationals, qualified for the World Championships, and was going to get a shot at reclaiming my world title—10 years after the first.

I arrived in Dalian, China, with Loren and our training group for camp. Darya Klishina, a Russian athlete, was my training partner and had become a friend over the past year. Where I used power and aggression, she used grace. We were opposites and always enjoyed each other's company. We had a good training camp in Dalian, and I was always grateful for my alone time, especially ahead of a championship.

I had made arrangements for John and me to stay at the Holiday Inn in Beijing. We had credentials to grant us full access to the meet hotel, meet transport, and warmup area, but I preferred to have separation between myself and the bustle of the athlete villages or athlete hotels. I don't know what it is about international Holiday Inn's, but I've yet to stay in one overseas that didn't rival a Hilton at home. Our two-room suite was not only generously appointed, it was cheap.

The day before the long jump was to begin Team USA made arrangements for us to take a tour to a very popular section of the Great Wall of China. I really wanted to see it, and so did John. Together we loaded a bus with other members of Team USA and made the trek to the wall. I was really excited about touring this section of the wall, until I saw it. Between the overwhelming and seemingly endless number of stairs, and the number of people attempting to ascend and descend them, all I could imagine was tripping, falling, and rolling my ankle the day before my competition. I told John that I wanted to walk about to the first set of steps, and take a picture, but that we could wait for the team to return in the café. I wanted to experience the Great Wall of China, but I needed to spare my legs. I wanted to win more.

The final was two days before my 30th birthday and 10 years after the last time I had been in an outdoor World Championship final. I wanted nothing more than to get that gold medal back. I wanted it so badly that I had ordered my iPods, headphones, and anything else I could, in gold with the words "#AndTheNew" engraved on each. It was a homage to my favorite sport, boxing; "and the new..." was something the ringside announcer would say if the winner of the match was not the reigning champion. In that scenario, it could only go one of two ways, "and still" or "and the new." But since Brittany, who was not competing and had undergone surgery, was the reigning World Champion, that night there would be a new one, and that new one would be me. I would accept nothing less—not with all that I'd gone through to get there.

I opened with a foul, and so did my former training partner Shara who was still coached by Rana Reider, Rana, having left the UK was now a coach for The Netherlands national team. Ivana Španović of Serbia opened with 7.01—a new Serbian national record. She was in top form. I got closer to Ivana's mark, jumping 6.95 in the second round that moved me into second place. Shara answered with 6.87 for third place. Ivana fouled her next two jumps; she was really going for it now and trying to get everything out of the takeoff to stretch the tape.

This was the approach I would take if I put a big jump out early too. My third-round jump was 6.87, but Shara answered with a leap of 7.07 and broke her country's national record too. I was now in third place. Unacceptable. My fifth jump was horrible. I jumped 6.62, a laughable distance when one needs to jump over seven meters. Ivana, forced to stop risking jumps because Shara took over the lead, jumped 6.86. Shara answered with yet another jump over seven meters. I opened the fifth round with a jump of 6.94, still struggling to reach the seven-meter mark. Ivana jumped 6.98, and Shara fouled. The sixth and final round had arrived—due to the reverse order of the top three, I jumped first, Ivana second, and Shara third.

I took a deep breath. *I'm not leaving here without the gold medal.* I jumped 7.14. I knew before I landed the jump that it was big but waiting for the distance to appear on the digital performance board was agonizing. If I thought that wait was bad, I had to sit through two more jumps, Shara's and Ivana's. Ivana jumped 7.01 again. She was securely in third. Her coach threw her flag over the railing, and she began to unfurl it. I held my breath for the duration of Shara's attempt and only let it out when I saw the red flag indicating she had fouled. I had done it. I had won the World Championship title—10 years after my first.

"Tianna, Tianna! How did you rally on that final jump to take the victory?" a reporter asked me in the post-event press conference.

"I told myself I was not leaving here without that gold medal, and I made sure that was the case," I told the reporter smiling with self-satisfaction.

John was quiet for the entire time through drug testing and the ride back to the hotel. "Why did you say that?" he asked me.

"Say what?" I said. Between the mixed zone and the press conference I had said a lot, none of which I could remember.

"That you rallied because you told yourself you weren't leaving without the gold medal," he reminded me.

"Oh," I said, "because it's true. I wasn't." I said nonchalantly not recognizing the tension building in the back seat of the cab.

"So, you did it all on your own, huh? That's what you think?"

Uh, yeah, I thought. "Of course not," I said.

"Then why did you say that?" he asked again.

"I don't know. I wasn't thinking, I'm sorry," I said trying to mask my irritation at not being able to enjoy anything I've accomplished without him feeling left out.

My phone was blowing up! Since 2012 I had been sharing my number more with service providers who helped me in my training and recovery and my training partners. As long as I told John who was calling or texting and agreed to read messages sent or received it was fine. I smiled scrolling through my WhatsApp messages.

"What are they saying?" he asked as we arrived in our room.

I pulled a 100-ml container of Tennessee Whiskey out of the mini fridge. I was going to celebrate with a drink and my "zero fucks" cocktail of a Xanax and half a hydrocodone.

"This one says, 'that was brilliant! I'm in awe of you!'" I located a tumbler glass in the mini bar.

"Who sent that?" he asked.

"Kai, my massage therapist." I answered pouring my drink into my glass.

"Don't you think that's inappropriate?" he asked again. I took a sip.

Here we go, I thought.

Kai was an excellent massage therapist who was the husband of my equally excellent yoga teacher Marie. John had met Kai but disliked him instantly for reasons only he knows, and because he knew he touched my body as my soft tissue therapist.

"Men don't send messages like that to another man's wife unless they're fucking."

I laughed before I could stop myself. These accusations were getting boring.

"Give me your phone,"

I did.

He began texting furiously. He handed my phone back. He had attempted to text as me but instead started his text from my phone with "this is Tianna" which is usually a dead giveaway that it's not. The messages said that I didn't want him to contact me again, that I was uncomfortable with his inappropriate behavior, and that I was demanding to be removed from his website, plus he would get a letter from my attorney when I returned to the States.

I refrained from taking my prescription cocktail so I'd have a clear head for the evening. When John fell asleep, I picked up my phone again in an attempt to undo the damage he caused. I texted Marie, my yoga teacher, who told me that she was done with me, and that she wasn't going to let her husband tolerate that level of disrespect from me either. I wanted to tell her what was happening. I wanted to explain just how much she was keeping me alive, but everyone has a breaking point. And unlike me, she absolutely did not have to tolerate it and neither did her husband. In that year alone John had ended my relationships with my mental conditioning coach, my yoga teacher, and my massage therapist—all the people who had helped me get here. Some thanks they got.

As always, all things were new the following morning. We were headed to Zurich for the Diamond League final (which I already had in the bag but needed to show up for). After the meet, I posted to my Instagram account, which I had successfully argued for opening the year before under the condition that he and his partner, George would have the login credentials. The picture's caption said the words "Triple Crown." American Pharoah had just done it in the world of horse racing, and I had just done it in the world of athletics, winning nationals, worlds, and the Diamond League. George called John and snitched on me. John hung up the phone and turned to face me.

"You really can't help yourself, can you?" he asked. "You think you know so much better than me how to run your social media account? You think you know better than the team that I pay over at UNATION? You're so fucking smart. You don't need me! Is that what it is? Fine you can be on your own then, I'm going home. I'm calling Mikey, and I'm on the first flight out."

I just stared at him. I knew this fight wasn't going to get physical. That stopped when he found himself on the other side of a fist for once. But he was loud, and the windows were open, and even though it didn't feel like it at times, I was a professional. Athletics was my profession; and his acting like a damn fool in the Movenpick Hotel was uncouth. He stormed out of the room.

Good riddance. I turned back to my magazine, wondering what these people around John get out of being his minions, when I saw first-hand how they were treated too.

He returned with a sheet of paper that he shoved in my face. I grabbed it and started to read. It was a chart, a timeline, really, divided into three segments: before John, with John, and after John. He listed two medals under the section of the timeline labeled "before John." He listed four medals under the section labeled "with John."

"A dumb bitch could see she was better off, but not you," he said.

I stared at the page. It felt heavy. In seven years, I had won just two medals in the first two seasons. I spent five years struggling. Then I met John and in the course of four years had more accomplishments than I had in the previous seven. Was he right? Was he the difference?

SHAME, SEX, AND XANAX

John was counting the remaining pills he kept in unmarked glass vials on his side of our master bathroom. Percocet, hydrocodone, Xanax, oh, my.

"Damn," I said absent-mindedly. *I'm high and know that I shouldn't be. I know. I need to stop popping pills. I know that I'm playing with fire, but the alternative is sobriety.* Being sober *and* present is an unbearable thought.

"How are these going so fast?" he asked. I shrugged and took a long sip of my double shot of Jack Daniels and relished the fiery cinnamon burn on my tongue.

"You think the housekeeper is taking them?"

"Hmmm," I murmured into my glass. I really like our housekeeper, but I have no intention of owning that it's actually me popping pills like Tic Tacs. I most definitely will not say it's me, but I'm also not going to say it's her. So, I settled on babbling acknowledgements while he drew his own conclusions.

Nights at home with John were like a box of chocolates. You never knew what you were going to get. Most nights I'd prepare dinner while John finished up his workout in the garage gym. He'd come in, grab a towel, take a dip in the pool, shower, and join me in front of the television where he'd pick at his dinner, and together we'd watch whatever show we had recorded on the DVR or a movie. When we were both sufficiently tired, we'd relocate to the master bedroom and settle in to sleep while watching Hogan's Heroes; the light-hearted episodes lulling us to sleep. Other nights were so volatile I'd lock myself in one of the three fully furnished yet unused guest bedrooms upstairs. I always chose the red room. It was the furthest from the master suite, had a heavy door with a working lock, and was situated over the garage. Being over the garage was important to me because it alerted me to his departure and eventual return without me ever needing to leave the safety of the room.

Sometimes, if things were really bad, I'd wait until he departed in a fit of rage. I'd grab my keys and I'd leave too. Once I stayed at a hotel I could pay cash for, another time I spent the night in my car at a rest stop, and yet another I drove from Tampa to Bradenton showing up unannounced at Coach Loren Seagrave's house he shared with his wife Marsha.

But now, I don't bother leaving. I just raid the medicine cabinet, swallow the pills, wash them down with whiskey, and wait for the high. I know the risks of mixing opioids and alcohol. But death, should I bring that upon myself, doesn't feel like such a bad outcome.

John's voice always snapped me back into the room and out of my head which is somewhere in the purple clouds floating across the bathroom ceiling.

"I'll confront her tomorrow," he said, "about the pills."

"Sounds good," I said. "Let me know what she says. Don't be surprised though if she denies it."

"I know, right? Everybody lies," John said, slightly exasperated as he squatted to return the refilled bottles to their designated space in the cabinet under his sink.

As I stood in the bathroom with him, glass tumbler in hand, I took another long sip.

"Yes. Everybody does," I said standing face-to-face with John now that he's upright. We lock eyes and for a second we see each other clearly. We know that we are both full of shit; we also know that we are committed to pretending otherwise.

"There's a new episode of *The Voice.*"

"Do it," he says, eyes twinkling, dimples deepening, as a smile grows across his face.

I take another sip and a deep breath, "This is the VOICE!" I sing the shows jingle at the top of my lungs.

"Why are you so good at stupid shit like that!" he said, laughing.

I'm laughing the carefree laugh of someone who is high but is pretending not to be. Together, we grab the puppies who have been lounging silently around our ankles, and we make ourselves comfortable. Me on the couch, John in his yellow chair. I'll be asleep in three minutes tops if all remains as calm as it is now.

I grabbed a throw blanket and burrowed deeply into the couch. Bailey hopped up on to the couch and spun in two slow counterclockwise circles before curling up in my lap.

The Voice singing show was on, and I shifted the dog napping in my lap to stretch my limbs.

"You are built for sex," John said, eyes peeking from behind the beer he's finishing in his favorite short glass.

"What's that even mean?" I asked in return. Thinking, *aren't all humans built for sex? What makes me different?* I don't have to wait long for John's answer.

"You've got a tight stomach, a tight pussy, small waist, and a big butt. You're the perfect specimen. I wish Antonio could see it."

Antonio is a mystery to me, a supposedly good friend of John's who I've only ever seen in the homemade porn films John showed me of Antonio having sex with John's friend, Gail.

Oh yes, let me tell you about Gail. I met Gail on a weekend when John and I had been dating long enough where I'd spend the entire weekend at his home in Tampa, and then drive back to Sanford, Florida, on Sunday night—a two-hour trip. The first time I visited John at his home I was stunned into speechlessness. It was one of the most beautiful homes I ever had the pleasure of stepping foot inside of, and my love of real estate has put me in a lot of homes.

You could tell that he was extremely proud of it as he walked me through room after room sharing details like, "This wallpaper was imported from Italy and is Venetian. It was a bitch to install because it's all one sheet, see?" He pointed up, my eyes following his fingers, tracing an invisible line up a wall that had none. The master bedroom was a study in the "art of retreat," set back and at the farthest point of the house; one enters the bedroom through double doors which open to a sprawling space of milk chocolate brown woods and cherry reds. The dome, that housed the ceiling fan that floated over the large bed, looked as if it had been commissioned to Michelangelo or belonged in a side hall at the Sistine Chapel. The walk-in closet had floor-to-ceiling shelving and storage that was large enough to fit a full chest of drawers in the center, plus a place to shine, clean, and put on your shoes. In a small corner was a travel bag for a dog where his Teacup Yorkie, Bailey, was hiding, shaking so hard from anxiety caused by my intrusion into her space that the bag was shaking too. Knowing it's best to let a pup warm up to you in their own time, I turned my attention to the clothes. There were a lot of women's clothes. I could tell they were an older woman's clothes from the style. *But whose were they?* I wondered. So enamored by John and the tour, I crafted a story. I told myself not to ask him about it because apparently whomever they belonged—an ex or deceased wife, an ex-girlfriend…he wasn't quite ready to tackle that particular problem. And I'm not the type to demand closet space on my first visit.

The weekend when I met Gail, John had introduced her to me as his best friend. He said that he could see us taking to one another and maybe even becoming friends separate from him. She came just as John finished preparing dinner. That particular evening, I sat at a stool at the kitchen island with its Louis Vuitton-like checkered pattern and prepared to dig into a giant baked potato layered with ham, bacon, shredded cheese, and a dollop of sour cream. It was a lot of food, but I could and would eat it all.

"Watch this," I heard John whisper to Gail from where they sat behind me at the round kitchen table. "She'll eat this whole thing."

"How?" Gail asked.

"You'll see," John replied.

I finished the potato off, and John asked me to stand, lift my shirt, and show Gail my abs which to her surprise I still had after eating so much.

Gail stood and said she had to get some things from the closet. John looked up at me and asked if I could take Bailey out for a walk around the neighborhood. Bailey finally warmed up to me after several weeks, and when she heard the word "walk" she came flying into the scene from her safe space in the closet. I grabbed Bailey's harness and leash and watched Gail disappear with John in tow into the master bedroom.

Oh, I thought, *all those clothes were hers—a very much not- dead and very much not-ex anything.*

The next time I saw her was on a homemade sex tape John showed me. The scene was the master bedroom, but the man was not John. They were just using John's room, his furniture, his camera, and maybe his girlfriend. Still uncertain of Gail's role in John's life, this video provided even more evidence that everything was not as it seemed between the two of them.

The man was Antonio, and he was the one on top of Gail.

"I'd love to see you two together," John said looking longingly at the video.

My stomach clenched tight as it dawned on me that he was talking about passing me to his friend and potentially adding me to his sordid video collection. I laughed it off, hoping he'd start laughing too at the absurdity of such a comment, but he didn't. He looked at me with a solemn expression, turned off the tape, and left the room. He asked if I was coming, and I followed him back out of the master bedroom, past the double pane glass doors that led to the outdoor oasis and pool, through the kitchen, and to our respective places on the couch and yellow chair to watch an altogether different kind of movie together before bed.

So, when I heard the words, "You're built for sex," and that he wished "Antonio could see it," I knew exactly what that meant. There are only so many times and so many ways I could say no. Each of them infuriating John to the point of rage. I passed yet again on his request, and John's dancing brown eyes narrowed into dark beads.

"When a relationship is *this* one-sided, when all you do is take, the least you can do is give the other person what they need," he said coldly.

"You need me to have sex with your friend. How is that a need?" I asked.

"It's about fantasy. Partners are responsible for making the other person feel wanted and appreciated—help them live out their fantasies." He grew louder and his face reddened as the reality that I've denied him of this yet again sunk in. "You're an ungrateful cunt," he said standing up.

"Where are you going?" I asked, squinting to see the time on the microwave from across the room.

"What do you care? You don't care about me," he said as he headed back to the bedroom to grab his jeans.

"I care!" I yelled across the house. "But there are other ways to show it that don't include fucking your friends!"

"Just know this, Tianna," he said grabbing his BMW key fob when he returned to the kitchen, "what you won't do, another woman will be happy to."

"I'm sure," I said defiantly, knowing that that wasn't the end of the conversation. This was a reoccurring fight.

He stormed out of the house, as I poured a double shot of Jack Daniels Fire into my empty tumbler glass and headed back to the bedroom to pop a Xanax. With any luck, I'd be long asleep before he returned. I had to train in the morning.

WINTER SIXTEEN

I was not the same after 2015's Zurich Diamond League Final. John's diagram of my career accomplishments before and with him did it. My spirit was finally broken. I had become suicidal over the offseason. Heading into 2016, an Olympic year, I was still suffering from depression and was prescribed Celexa, due to an additional diagnosis of PMDD (Premenstrual dysphoric disorder). Plus, I had graduated to the entire hydrocodone pill, sometimes popping two, and a higher dosage of Xanax. The only thing that always made me feel better, albeit temporarily, was winning. I did not believe that Loren, with all he had going on at IMG and his speaking engagements around the world, had the time to do what was required to not just get me on the Olympic team, but to win. I wanted back on the relay which meant I needed to get back to top form. So far, the only man who succeeded in doing so was Rana, and so it was Rana I called.

He came over to the house to sit down with us to discuss coaching me again. "I don't know," Rana said, "Carmelita's been calling, and I think one US sprinter is where I'd like to keep it."

I wanted to throw up. *Jet had John Smith, leave Rana to me. Damn.*

"Thirty thousand dollars!" I shouted, "I'll pay you $30,000 to coach me—please!"

I had never paid a coach more than $12,000 for the year, and my contract's usually included a $10-$12k coaching stipend as well but this was how desperate I was to be back in his program. He agreed. And it would require me to move to The Netherlands for weeks at a time, travel to warm-weather training camps, and meet them every day at IMG when they came to Florida for warm weather camp. "Yes, Yes, Yes!" I shouted. I was ready.

"Wait, will you have conflicts of interest?" I knew who else he was coaching and wanted his word that I'd get the same coaching as they did. His word, he gave.

I arrived in The Netherlands in the winter; it was rainy and grey. I'd be staying at Rana's house, and riding to and from practice with him. I enjoyed the time I got to spend with him and the conversations we'd have. All of my coaches I had any significant success with spent time with me away from the track and allowed me to know them. I, in turn allowed them to know me, and as a result the trust between us helped solidify the working relationship.

We trained at Papendal, and I don't know what it was about the campus, maybe how it's nestled away in the forest, or maybe it was the people, but I'd never felt more at home. I loved going to practice. I'd wake up, cook myself breakfast, and wait for Rana to say we were leaving. We'd go to the track, talk on the drive home, or not, and return to the house where I read in my room and watched *Big Bang Theory* from start to finish. On nicer days, I'd go for walks exploring the village. I learned the bus route and began to take the bus to the City Centre, taking myself out to eat, and to the movies. I loved my freedom, and even though I was living in my coach's house and carless, I had more freedom than I'd had in a long time. I was not particularly interested in giving that up.

I returned home just long enough to wish I was away again before heading to warm-weather camp in Stellenbosch, South Africa, where the Dutch Federation often went in the winter to train. I had never been to South Africa before, and I didn't want to leave. I thrived there. With a set schedule for training and lifting every day, I had more freedom to read and explore. I started to write again. I opened a Pages Document on my MacBook, titled it *Gravity*, and began to put my life story on paper.

John called every morning and every night and demanded that I send him photos of my naked body to reassure him that I wasn't on vacation getting fat. He had begun to complain about how much I was away. Suddenly it was me giving the speeches about doing what was required to get the goal. I thought that using his own words back to him would help him receive the message, but I was mistaken. All he heard was that I didn't miss him, and that I didn't want to come home. He wasn't wrong. He tried to convince me that I was not good beyond four weeks away from home—that after four weeks, the toll of being away started to affect my mental health. It didn't. That was gas lighting and Projection 101. The truth was, after four weeks, *he* couldn't handle my being away from home; it was he who started to deteriorate, pick fights, and get moody. He worked hard to make me miserable, and once I'd snap he'd say, "See! This is too hard on you!" But it wasn't, and I made the most of my time in South Africa—training and learning to enjoy life again.

The 2016 Indoor World Championships would be in Portland, Oregon, and I really wanted to make that team for a third time. Because I was with Rana again, I thought I could possibly win my first individual sprint gold medal.

I told Rana, but what is a coach supposed to say to one athlete who says they want the same gold medal as another athlete they coach? That athlete was Dafne Schippers, the Dutch sprinting phenom. The Dutch Federation hired Rana, in no small part, to take her sprinting to the next level. Dafne and the Dutch Federation were the reason I got to live in The Netherlands, train at Papendal, and go to South Africa. I couldn't exactly make any cases against why she'd be a priority. It's the reason I asked him about conflicts of interest in the first place. But where I had gotten used to Rana's meticulous attention to detail in 2012, this time around was different. He was different—still a great coach because I watched him every day be a great coach, but to me, with me it was different. In a microscopic, inexplicable way I could only slightly sense. Like the faint smell of incoming rain on the wind.

I drank my disappointment away and chased it with prescription pills. My indoor season was horrible. The Celexa, that was keeping me from suicidal ideation, also kept me from reacting to the gun, or reacting to anything at all. I knew that the indoor season could end up disappointing, and I knew John didn't handle those types of losses well. So, I did something I learned from him—I hedged and told him I was finally ready to get married. Legally.

TILL DEATH

I could only put it off for so long. There are only so many times one can dodge the question, and only so many creative ways in which to answer in the negative. I ultimately lost this battle, like so many other battles for my soul that I've lost to this point.

Damn, this mirror is so clear. My high-definition reflection looks on from her judgmental perch.

What are you doing? She asks me.

What I have to, I say.

We were in Sacramento, California, a brief overnight stop on the way to Portland, Oregon, for the 2016 indoor national championships which would serve as a qualifier for the IAAF Indoor World Championships to take place a week later.

I knew this upcoming competition wouldn't go well. My coach, who I'd meet up with in Portland was training me so that my body would be at peak fitness and top speed in June, for the Olympic Trials. It was only March. The Rio Olympics were that summer, and I needed to have a good showing there. But right now, my legs were currently loaded from the intensity of training camp in South Africa, The Netherlands, and those trips accompanying long haul flights. The medication I was on to control my depression had made it really hard for me to care about finishing first.

It was John who had been anxious for the season to get started. I get it; there's no high like the high of competition or winning. But it's not time to win, and *he* doesn't lose well—correction—he doesn't react well when I lose, and I lose a lot. The truth is there are only two competitions that matter to a professional track and field athlete in a year like this one: the Olympic Trials and the Olympic Games. Any competition before or after only serves two purposes—practice and prize money. But when you've been grinding in silence for months and months with no way of knowing if the work you're doing now will pay off later in the year, it's all too easy to rush in before you need to, to line up before you're ready.

That's rich, my reflection says to me. Of course, the irony of my rationalizations isn't lost on me. I can almost see the phrases: *before I need to, before I'm ready, and rushing in*—bouncing against the walls of my consciousness looking for a place to land.

Shut up! I snap back at the mirror through gritted teeth. *You know exactly why we're here. I put this off for five years and now,* I hesitate before continuing. *Now, the only way out is through.*

Sounds to me like you're trying to convince yourself. My reflection's eyes dart inquisitively around my taut face.

I don't need to be convinced, I nearly growl the words. *If it's the only move I can make…how can it be the wrong one?*

My reflection concedes the point by pursing her lips and narrowing her gaze.

"Now, where's my lip gloss?" I say out loud to myself, snapping into a character I play often and know very well. I root around in my makeup bag which seems to have become bottomless.

Mind chatter now calm, I sneaked a glance back up at the mirror. My tie is askew, my collar flipped. My lip gloss, as if by magic, appeared in front of me, on the ledge framing the mirror where it's been this entire time.

I retied my tie.

I popped and fixed my collar.

I applied my lip gloss, then carefully kissed a folded tissue to remove the excess. If I didn't, I may not hear the end of it, and today would be the worst day to be called a whore—one of his favorite quips about women who, to him, are wearing too much makeup.

I checked my reflection one last time.

You know you're fucked right? My reflection said once more for good measure.

Yeah, I know. I said in rare agreement. *But come on, or I'll be late; it's time to get married.*

I chose Sacramento because it was in California. I chose California because it's the only state that issues confidential marriage licenses. This was an important detail to address—the confidentiality of our union.

As far as my parents knew I had gotten married in 2012. As far as the public knew, thanks to an anonymous overzealous person who updates my Wikipedia page, I had gotten married sometime between the 2012 Indoor World Championships and the 2012 Olympic Trials. Truth is, we didn't tie the knot until March 9, 2016. And when we did, it was at the county clerk's office in Sacramento, in secret, and I asked for the abbreviated version. It took less than ten minutes.

I said, "I do."

He said, "I do."

He wrote vows. I didn't. Which is why I campaigned so hard for the short version claiming, that "I've waited so long to marry him I couldn't wait a minute more." After, as I always do when we travel together, I pulled up the website for *Diners, Drive-Ins, and Dives*, to find a Guy Fieri-approved spot to commemorate our nuptials.

After breakfast, at a place whose name I no longer remember, whose food, although delicious-smelling, remained largely untouched on my plate, we grabbed an Uber back to the bed and breakfast. I remember finding it online and booking a romantic package. A nod to the ever-shrinking part of me who had planned her dream wedding *once upon a time* and could visualize the wedding reception. I'm not that girl anymore, not at all a believer in unconditional love and fairy tales, or even marriage. I know, because on that very same day, in a different browser window, I clicked "new private window" and searched "Florida divorce."

Packing our things, I tossed my new name around my mouth as if deciding if I liked the taste, as if I hadn't been using it for the past three years. It's different this time. It's legal. I have actually become HIS wife in the eyes of the law—a promotion of sorts.

Finally in Portland, I turned my attention to USA Indoor National Championships. Sluggish to get out of the blocks because of my medication, I powered my way to the finish line to advance out of the semi-final and into the final round. I took third, running 7.17 behind Barbara Pierre who had run 7 flat and Tori Bowie who had run 7.15—only the top two qualified for the Indoor World Championship team.

I'd be sitting at home. I was right about one thing though, that the marriage would dampen the disappointment of the loss a bit. John was way less upset than usual. I, on the other hand, was devastated.

"Maybe you need to look more like Tori Bowie," John said to me.

He unlocked his iPhone and scrolled through his photo album. "You're not this lean anymore," he said to me showing me a picture of my naked body from four years ago.

"I'm going to censor it and send it to Rana, tell him to make you look like that again," he said to himself still working his phone. The iPhone whoosh tone of an outgoing text told me that was exactly what he did. My road to Rio was going to be a difficult one, and I was not off to a good start.

SUMMER SIXTEEN

I lost every meet in the lead up to Rio, and I was at my wits end. I had been voicing my disappointment in what I perceived as a shift in Rana's coaching style toward me. I was expressing my concerns again over espresso in the cafeteria at Papendal, when he turned to me and said, "If that's how you feel, we can hug and go our separate ways."

I had hoped that we'd be a successful enough team for me to make my own Olympic Team, but this conversation, and his reaction to it did not feel good and I was not at all confident. My jumping was going horribly, and he seemed to not be worried about that at all!

The only thing keeping me sane was my new friendship with my AirBnB host, Andrey. Andrey was Russian and in the ballet; it was how he came to be in Arnhem, the city where the training center was. I only had to text him when I would be back in town, and he made his entire house available for me—even allowing me to store extra luggage in the basement. He was a godsend. And his home became my safe haven and base from which I could fly back and forth to meets on the European circuit.

The DN Galan meeting in Sweden was my final straw. It was the only final of the season I had made so far. This was the only glimmer of hope I'd gotten for what I'd hoped would be a successful season. But Rana had left. He was not in the stands going into the final three rounds, and he didn't tell us that he'd be leaving. Shara and I struggled through the remaining jumps, and I walked past Rana without speaking as he reentered the stadium with his athletes who were running the 200. I called John from my hotel room, told him I believed I was on my own to make the Olympic team and flew home, back to the US the following day.

I was going to have to fix myself. Rana was not going to attend the trials, because they conflicted with the European Championships which he had to attend as the coach for The Netherlands. I would have to manage making the team on my own. John saw this as an opportunity to step in as coach. The schedule was unfriendly for someone attempting to do the 100 and long jump double. But I had been simulating the schedule in training at USF day after day and was confident that I could do it. I'd do my entire warmup and then complete six full approach pop ups. I'd then do my sprint workout, and return to the pit to complete short approach jumps.

This difficult double was an interesting story in the lead up, and NBC did a feature (mistakenly crediting John as my coach) explaining how we had worked out the logistics for such a tricky schedule at such a high-stakes meet. John was extremely helpful though, and his attention to detail was valuable in managing the meet for me.

I qualified for the final on the first day, jumping 6.77 for the auto qualifier to the next day's final. The long jump final was contested at the same time as the first round of the 100-meter dash. My plan was to make the team on the first jump, run the first round, and pass the remaining of the jumps round by round to save my legs as much as possible for the 100-meter semifinal and final the day after that. I jumped 7.02 on my first jump. Confident that I would place in the top three, I jogged over to the 100-meter dash with my spikes in my hand. I put my spikes on near the starting line, took some steadying breaths, and got ready to race. I won my heat in 11.03. I came back to the long jump pit, looked at the standings, and passed my next two jumps. Brittany had jumped 6.99 and was capable of jumping something ridiculous at any time, and that's exactly what she did on her fourth jump—umping 7.31! I was so pumped up from her jump, I stupidly tried to answer on tired legs. I jumped 6.82 and passed the rest of my jumps. When Brittany returned to her bag to put her sweats back on I looked at her and shook my head. "What!?" She said with her signature sly smile. "You're so disrespectful!" I said to her laughing. "There was no need for you to do me like that, you see me huffing and puffing trying to manage the 100 and the jumps at the same time! Damn! 7.31! All that wasn't even necessary!" We laughed together and congratulated each other. Mission Accomplished! I was on my first Olympic Team for the long jump.

The 100-meter team was going to be hard to make; it was especially difficult on loaded legs I had completed multiple jumps which wreaks havoc on the body and two rounds of the 100. I was exhausted but I had prepared for this by myself on the USF track. There was nothing left to it but to do it. I had taken second in my semi-final behind English Gardner. I ran 10.79; she ran 10.74. More exhausted by the time the final arrived, I told myself I had nothing left to do but this and set one goal for myself—cover the first 10 meters in seven strides. That was my only goal and the only thing I felt I could control and execute. I stood behind my blocks waiting for the announcers to finish presenting us.

"On your marks," the starter said.

I exhaled slowly and loaded back into my blocks.

"Set!"

I raised my hips. "BAM!" I was off, my only goal to get to 10 meters in seven steps. I felt brave enough to open my eyes around 60 meters, I could see English just a hair in front of me, and I could feel Tori on my left. I dug deep on my tired legs and bounded through the finish line. The three of us were in a race of our own. English won in 10.74, Tori and I ran 10.78, but I took second when they extended the time to the thousandths. I had done what I came to do.

Relay camp was held at Prairie View A&M, and team processing was at the Convention Center in Houston Texas. There were no real surprises or mishaps until I got an email from Sandy saying that John would not be able to get access to the warmup area once we arrive in Rio. I did not make it this far to have it derailed by what would most likely be the worst fight we've ever had when I'd have to call and explain to him how he'd have to watch me compete from the stands. There was nothing he wanted more than to have a credential, to be in the warmup area, and to feel a part of the action. I had figured out over the last couple years how to manage my own behavior so that I could manage his, only to have something like this happen at the last minute and threaten everything I had trained so hard for.

Sandy had explained to me how everyone knew he wasn't my coach, and so she didn't think it would have been detrimental to my performance. She was caught completely off guard by what I said next.

"Okay, then I'm not going." There was no way I could make that call to John. No way. I didn't care that she wouldn't understand my reaction. I knew what would happen if I told John he couldn't get access and I decided to look out for myself.

By the end of the same day, she informed me that since I was a medal contender in three events, they would make sure John had a credential. I had found a condo directly across from the swimming venue on Airbnb and booked it immediately thinking it could not get any better than to be basically on site. I was wrong. You could not get within a mile of the condo except on foot or via official transport. Only residents of the building could pass the security checkpoint; they had decals on their windows issued to them by the government that allowed them entry. The host of our Airbnb, Sergio, was an attorney and staying with his in-laws not too far away. The Olympics were his opportunity to make some money for his family. He brought along his friend Jorge who spoke better English than he did to see how we were settling in. Understanding that only Sergio could drive in and out, John hired Sergio to drive us to and from the track giving him a crisp $100 bill each time. Sergio used his attorney chops and talked his way past each checkpoint dropping us off directly at the athlete entrance every single time. When we were ready to be picked up, John texted Sergio via WhatsApp and he was there within minutes.

The 100 was terribly disappointing. I was in 10.7 shape and didn't make the final. I was in the middle of a PMDD episode—my limbs and joints felt heavy, my brain was in a hormonal fog. I could not pull it together. As much as my mind wanted to hit the override button, hormones are undefeated. I could not overcome it. I was ninth, and only eight advanced. My shot at getting that individual medal was gone; it was only going to get harder as I got older. I felt that loss deeply. Back in the warmup area I cried and mourned not only the loss but the fact that I would now likely end my career without ever earning an outdoor sprint medal. John saw me crying, told me I was embarrassing myself, and to get my shit together before people saw, and so I choked my feelings down and gathered myself.

I came out of my cloud of depression just in time for long jump qualifying. The automatic mark for entry into the final was 6.75, but just four women cleared that barrier. I jumped 6.70 to advance to the finals in fifth position. Qualifying always seemed to be a struggle for me. I think the knowledge that it's not a final, and the need to jump a specific distance shifted my focus to outcome rather than the process or the steps I needed to execute. I'm rarely ever successful being results driven, but when I focus on the process, I'm hard to beat.

I told Rana, who was finally back in my presence after nearly a month apart, that I was going to foul my first jump. The track was fast. I was fast, and he didn't know what I knew because I had been training alone. My usual approach wasn't going to work. I needed his eyes to make the adjustment, and I needed him calm. So, I warned him beforehand. I fouled by over a meter. I took off exactly halfway between the takeoff board and the sand and landed between the 8 and 9-meter indicator lines on the performance board. Make the adjustment for the foul and that's a 7.20-7.50-meter jump in the works. I jumped out of the pit excited. Robyne Johnson, Team USA's long jump coach, looked concerned. John was stunned, and Rana was standing pumping his fists. He knew what the night had in store for us. Ivana of Serbia opened with 6.95. Brittany fouled, and Malaika Mihambo of Germany opened with 6.83. I jumped 6.94 for the second round. Brittany answered with 6.79 and Ivana and Malaika both fouled. I jumped 6.95 on my third round, and now Ivana and I had the same jump, but I was leading because I had the farther second-farthest jump. We call that the "countback." After the first three jumps, the top eight jumpers get three more attempts with the jumper in eighth placing jumping first. In reverse order, Brittany, Malaika, Ivana and I would round out the field. Brittany fouled her fourth-round jump. Malaika jumped a personal best of 6.88; Ivana jumped 6.91. I jumped

6.74! *Stay in it.* I told myself. *You only need one.* Brittany was up again for her fifth jump, she jumped 7.09 to take the lead, and she made sure we knew it.

"This is my runway!" she shouted.

Oh, for real? I thought to myself.

Malaika jumped a new personal best of 6.95 which was also equal to my farthest jump in the competition. Ivana jumped 7.09 for a new Serbian national record.

I was up. I took a breath and the "big-ass" step backward Rana told me to take as the adjustment for my big-ass foul. 7.17! I took the lead. There was one round to go. Malaika jumped 6.79 and would finish in fourth. Now, no matter what happened now I had an Olympic medal, but the question was which? Brittany jumped 7.15 coming within two centimeters of my jump. Ivana jumped 7.05. I had already won, when I stepped back on the runway to take my final jump. Struggling to keep my emotions under control, I wanted to take my last jump almost like a victory lap. I jumped 7.13. I was the new Olympic Champion.

I woke up the following day sore but happy. My left ankle was throbbing which wasn't unusual after a long jump competition. I stood up. Nope! I sat back down on the bed. My ankle was swollen, and I could not put pressure on it! The first round of the relay was in a few hours! I hopped in my NormaTec compression boots and elevated my legs. *Hold on for one more race today,* I said to my ankle. One more race.

Sergio dropped us off at the athlete's entrance, and I tried not to limp to avoid freaking anybody out. I got my ankle taped nice and tight and walked a slow lap around the warmup track. "Thank you for your sacrifice," I said to my ankle. I know it sounds silly. But I wanted to express gratitude rather than frustration with my body. I wanted that kind of energy. As I progressed through my warmup, my ankle felt better and better and by the time I was walking to the blocks I, and my ankle, were ready to roll.

Our first-round team was me, Allyson Felix, English Gardner, and Morolake Akinosun. My exchange to Allyson went as I expected, so I turned around and began to make my way back to the finish line where I'd meet Morolake when she crossed. But as I was shuffling back to the finish line where I'd meet back up with the team, someone in the stands shouted "LOOK!" and pointed down the track toward the second exchange. I looked toward the finish line; other teams were finishing. None of them were Team USA. What happened? Was Allyson or English hurt? Should I run down there? Should I wait? By the time I had decided which way to go, Morolake was crossing the finish line with the baton. Afterward, she immediately turned around and walked back toward Allyson and English who were walking the homestretch. I met them too.

"First of all, is everybody okay?" I asked.

They nodded. Allyson looked like she was in shock.

"No injuries?" I asked.

Everyone shook their heads no.

"Good," I said. "Let's just get through the mixed zone and back to the warmup track."

Lewis Johnson of NBC was the first person we encountered in the mixed zone. He showed us a replay of the botched exchange. The video showed Allyson being hit by Brazil's outgoing runner which succeeded in halting her momentum. English had left on time but with Allyson decelerating rapidly and English approaching the end of the zone, Allyson in a moment of panic and desperation basically tossed the baton to get it to English and it hit the track. They scrambled for a moment and regaining her composure Allyson picked up the baton, passed it to English within the zone which was the only reason we were not officially disqualified. We were able to finish the race. That was enough evidence for us. We rushed through the mixed zone to file an appeal. Allyson may have panicked, but she also saved the relay.

Duffy Mahoney, Chief of Sport Performance at USA Track and Field knew the rule book inside and out and set off to file the appeal. Allyson was struggling to contain her emotions. Wanting her to feel safe enough to release them, I took her behind a tent in the far corner of the warmup area. I told her I would sit with her while she cried, that we didn't have to say anything at all. I wished someone had done that for me after the 100, instead John had admonished me for being embarrassingly unprofessional for crying. Heart break shatters differently and more deeply when forced into silence. I didn't want that for her. It wasn't her fault *and* she had kept her wits about her enough to pick up the baton and keep going. She *saved* the relay. She said she was ready to return to the team. When we rejoined them, Duffy was back with news.

We were going to have to run again, solo. The same quartet, in the same lane, by ourselves this evening just before the evening program began. If we ran a time that displaced the eighth-place team in the final, we were in. Brazil had been disqualified, and China was now on the bubble.

I gathered the group. "Ladies, I had a long night last night, I'd like to go to sleep. Everybody rest, eat, stay off social media, and I'll see you back here in a couple hours." I gave them each a hug. John called Sergio, and he promptly whisked us home.

Rested, fed, and back at the track a few hours later, I gathered the ladies again. "Okay, we're entering a potentially hostile situation. Be prepared for that. We got the host country disqualified. And I know you went on social media because I couldn't help it either, so you know Jamaica and China are talking mad shit right now. It's likely we'll get booed. Let's just get the job done." But it wasn't hostile. The crowd actually cheered for us when we emerged from the tunnel. I jogged to my starting blocks. One lonely block was set in lane two waiting for me. I had been curious all day about that, but now I had my answer—one block, one lane marker, all eyes on me.

A random thought surfaced. *What if I false start? I don't false start,* I responded. And set my blocks. I'd learned from my mental conditioning coach, Josh Lifrak that you can challenge your own self-doubts. That the presence of a thought doesn't automatically make that thought the truth, or even real. And it's not important to understand where it came from. It doesn't matter in the moment. I was prepared, so I knew better. I don't false start. Self-doubt: handled.

"Take your marks."

Technically the starter could have used the singular, I thought loading back into my blocks. I tightened the grip on the baton. As a left-handed person, starting with the baton in my right hand feels weird, and I am always slightly worried that I'll leave it behind at the starting line.

"Set!"

I raised my hips. "BAM!" The gun fired, and I exploded out of the blocks as if shot by a cannon. With no runners to walk down and break the stagger on, I had no way to tell if I was rolling or not. I just kept trying to find a new level deep within. By the time I passed the baton to Allyson, I knew I had given it everything I had. I watched the exchange between Allyson and English that time, and after I saw that it was made, I jogged toward the finish. Morolake crossed the finish line in 41.77, the fastest time overall. We were going to have lane one for the final, and we were going to be ready.

In the warmup area ahead of the final we learned that English didn't have her spikes. Clamoring to find Nike spikes in her size Allyson offered English a pair of hers. They were too big for English, but it was our only option.

We were in the call room beneath the stadium. It was the final staging area before we were to be walked out onto the track. They had just informed us that we would go out one country at a time, stop on the X, and pose for the cameras before jogging to our respective position. I listened quietly and waited for the official to finish speaking.

"Ladies, nah we ain't doing that. There is no way in hell we are going to prance out there and strike a damn pose! This is fucking war! Those mother fuckers over there," I pointed at Jamaica, "have been talking about how pressure bursts pipes, that we choked and were handed this gift, as if we didn't run faster than they did by our damn selves! Hell no. This is war, and I've never seen a soldier posing pretty before battle."

That did it. The squad was fired up. We stepped out of the tunnel looking like reformed gang members who weren't afraid to call on their banging past if needed. I told Allyson that we would have the race won by the end of her leg, but that I would catch two women on the turn. She clinched her jaw and nodded her head. This relay was as good as handled.

I wasn't worried about lane one at all. First, we're all running 100 meters, but second and more importantly this was my opportunity to play my favorite character Ms. Pacman and eat everybody up. That's exactly what I did. Allyson and I had our trademark pass, Allyson to English was made. English nearly ran out of her borrowed shoe to get Tori the baton well ahead, even as their exchange made me hold my breath—41.01, the second fastest time in history, from lane one. Honestly, it could have been a new world record if the last exchange between English and Tori had been as solid as the others. But I wasn't going to complain. I left the Rio Olympics with two gold medals!

HAWAII

I returned to Tampa with two gold medals, a worn-down body, and an exhausted spirit. Home just long enough to grab a different bag and head back to the airport so I could finish the rest of my season in Europe.

"You know what's weird?" I said to John as he rummaged through the pantry and I through the refrigerator. "After London I wanted nothing else to do with track and field; I was done. After this one, I just felt fired up! I think all I'll need is just a vacation to recharge, and I'll be ready to get back into it!" I said excitedly. It was true. I was so turned off by my road to my first Olympics, I quit the sport and joined the bobsled team.

"That's a 180 from last time. Where do you want to go? The Lake House? Key West? Safety Harbor Spa?" he asked me.

"Hawaii," I said. I have wanted to go to Hawaii since I was a kid and my parents dropped us off with a family friend for a week while they had what seemed like the best vacation ever, without us. Back then, I wanted to go simply because I wasn't invited. As an adult, I wanted to enjoy the beach and the hikes. I imagined renting a villa on the ocean and spending my time reading, writing, sleeping, and recovering.

"Hawaii." John repeated, "Not quite," he said under his breath, but mostly to himself. Louder, he turned to face me and said, "You didn't earn enough to go to Hawaii."

Dumbfounded, I stared back at him, the Olympic Champion with not one but two gold medals sitting behind us on the kitchen table—too fresh to have been put away on the living room mantle for display. The long jump gold by itself had earned me a six-figure bonus, and yet, I didn't earn enough?

"I can't go to Hawaii. I have a job. You think I can just leave whenever?"

This was a rhetorical question, and even if it wasn't, I knew better than to answer. I was confused. Although only he and Dennis had access to my money, it didn't make sense to me that I could not afford a trip to Hawaii. It didn't make sense to me why he, the owner of the two businesses he was referring to, couldn't take time off if he wanted to, and why it didn't occur to him to let me go by myself!

Of all the things and all the ways my body and spirit had been broken by that man, it was denying me a vacation to Hawaii that did it. It was in that moment, standing in the kitchen, staring my husband eye to eye that I was certain of two things. The first was that I would never be or do enough in his eyes, ever. If two gold medals weren't enough, nothing was enough.

In fact, I had overheard him on the phone telling someone that it should have been three golds if it weren't for my fucking period. When someone would congratulate him on "our" golds, his response was, "It should have been three."

I did get unlucky with the timing of the 100-meter dash. I had been suffering from severe PMDD, premenstrual dysphoric disorder. It's PMS with the added experience of depression. For me, my PMDD spells range from drastic mood swings to suicidal attempts and deep depression. The 100-meter dash fell right in the middle of a PMDD episode. Earlier in the year I was taking an SSRI called Celexa to help balance me out. I kept track of my cycle on a calendar and would begin to take Celexa two weeks before my period was set to begin to help me avoid that pit. It worked, but I decided to forego taking my medication when earlier that year I failed to make the world indoor team in the 60-meter dash. I could feel the medication keeping me from accessing the level of intensity I needed to be competitive. I heard the gun go off and thought, *That's the gun, I guess I'll run now.* And by the time my brain got the signal that it was time to sprint, the field had already gapped me. I felt like an elite athlete trapped in the body of someone who gave zero fucks about competition. Screaming on the inside to "TURN UP!" only to be blocked by a medication whose sole job was to keep me from high highs and low lows. I made the unilateral decision to deal with my depression and suicidal thoughts on my own, hoping that my success on the track would keep both at bay. For most of the season that was true, until the Olympic Games.

But as soon as my period started, just before the long jump final, the fog lifted. I felt like a new woman, and I was out to avenge my 100-meter loss by taking it out on the long jump field and the relay. It was a largely private battle and although it was kind of true that my period was responsible for my performance in the 100, I wasn't thrilled that he was telling people about that, especially framed as "it should have been three."

The second thing I was made aware of that day was that I was near the end of my career, only getting older. At some point, I'd have to retire, and once I did who or what would I be to John then? What value would I have to him if he could no longer cash my checks? I did not want to find out and the reality that I was somewhat of a public figure was keeping me relatively safe. He spoke often about being "behind closed doors" and the skill of having one image for the public and another behind those doors. I was too familiar with what happened behind those beautiful wooden doors, and I did not think I would survive a life with him behind them full-time.

The rejection of a Hawaiian vacation without an invitation to discuss it further made it clear to me that there was an expiration date on our time together. Something shifted inside me standing there in that kitchen, a film was removed from my eyes and I saw the precarious situation I was in clearly—perhaps for the first time—and it scared me. I knew in that moment, for as much of my authentic self I had already killed or allowed to die to make it that long, I was certain that beyond 2017 I'd be completely gone, perhaps not physically— but unrecognizably beyond reach.

He didn't know it, but that brusque dismissal of my request to take time away to recharge so that I could return to the business of high performance activated the countdown clock to the end of our marriage. I didn't know when the end would come, or how it would happen, I just knew it was coming.

I walked past the medals in their sustainable wood cases and headed up the stairs to pack my bag for Europe. I had a victory tour to enjoy. Contrary to what was happening at home, there was a world waiting to celebrate me, with me, and I was happy to join them.

HOW DO YOU KNOW?

I did my best to recover after the 2016 season. I embraced the staycation visiting the Safety Harbor Spa, staying at the new Four Seasons Resort at Disney World, playing with my puppies Baxter and Bailey, and writing. I had written a book titled *Why You're Not a Track Star,* the year before, and although a short read, I was extremely proud of the content and thought it needed to be shared with young athletes. I printed a hard copy for John and emailed copies to George and other members of his team to get their opinion. I thought they could and would help me figure out how to disseminate it. Between UNATION, which was meant to be the next hottest social media platform, and High Street Financial, which had publishing capabilities, I thought I was on my way. Not long after presenting John with his copy, I found it with rings of coffee stains on the cover from his mini-espresso cups. I threw it away. He didn't mention it, and I didn't mention it, and no one I emailed the copies to bothered to read it either.

I was bored. Needing something to do, I enrolled in Bob Hogue Real Estate School. John's mom, Zita, was a realtor and had done really well, and having been a fan of all things real estate I was excited by the possibility that we could spend time together and maybe even start a new company flipping or developing properties. I spent most of my off season studying and taking the online courses.

As it always seems to do, the return-to-training date was upon us. I would be flying through Amsterdam and connecting with the team again in Stellenbosch, South Africa, for a month for training camp. I could not wait. Stellenbosch was the wine country of the Western Cape. The food was delicious and inexpensive, the people friendly, and the accommodations well-appointed. It would be summer there when we arrived, and I loved the hot weather. It was in South Africa where I learned that black people could get sunburned. My shoulders burned, turned charcoal black, and then peeled before I understood the importance of slathering myself in sunblock. Most importantly, in South Africa I felt as far away from my problems as one could be, without leaving the planet—free to train and do whatever whenever I wanted. I just couldn't go too long without checking in with John via WhatsApp, and I was good.

I felt a weight lifting off my shoulders when the wheels touched down at the Cape Town airport. My driver, arranged for me through American Express' concierge service, picked me up and delivered me to my cute little

Airbnb downtown, situated above shops and restaurants. The first thing I do upon arrival in The Netherlands, South Africa, or any of our destination training camps is go grocery shopping. Feeling quite at home, I dropped my bags in my flat, unpacked my reusable Albert Heijn grocery totes, and walked to the grocer—face up, letting the sunbathe me in hope.

Rana's group "The Tumbleweed Track Club" tagged along with the Dutch Federation who had hired Rana as their coach. I loved the environment. We worked hard, both on the track and in the gym, and pushed each other the entire time. Were we without drama? No, but most of it was overshadowed by the knowledge that we were doing good work. And as long as we continued to do good work, and as long as I was confident in the coaching, I could tolerate a little drama. After all I was well aware of how much I could actually put up with. My training partners had no idea what real drama looked like.

By the end of the first week in South Africa, I had established my routine, made friends again with servers at my favorite cafes, scheduled appointments for facials and manicures for the duration of camp, and learned how to order pizza, you know…for my cheat day. I was experiencing freedom I had not felt in a long time, and with each passing day I grew both in the knowledge that I wanted to retain it and depressed that I couldn't. I committed to enjoying the time that I had and making the most of the camp.

Two things happened when camp came to an end. The first, I got an email that my real estate course was set to expire and that I needed to finish the class and schedule my exam or risk needing to do it all over again. The second was that I was asked to run the 60 at the Armory in New York. I began to cram to finish the course and study for my real estate exam which I scheduled for the day after I returned to the US. I wanted to decline the invite to run at the Armory. One thing I knew I should NOT do was try to run in a race after four or five weeks of the training load that I had been under. I tried to explain this to John, but he insisted I take the meet…that *he* was ready to get back into it. So, I obliged because I knew I had to.

I could feel how heavy my legs were when we arrived in New York. My stomach was in knots, anxious about the inevitable subpar race I was going to run. It was an 11-hour flight back to Amsterdam from Cape Town, then another seven from Amsterdam to the US, then another two from the port of entry to Tampa. I was fried, jet-lagged; but somehow, despite all that, I sat for my real estate exam and passed! Passing the exam gave me a much-needed boost, but that was short-lived when John demanded that he and Dennis decide what I would do with the license now that I had it.

As the Olympic Champion, I was invited to a press conference ahead of the meet. Omar McLeod and Dalilah Muhammed were also at the press conference. Tired, bitchy, and over the energy required to play pretend I sarcastically answered nearly every question with the answer, "my husband," with the same delivery as Marshawn Lynch saying, "I'm just here so I won't get fined."

John beamed from the back of the room soaking up what he thought was genuine praise from a doting wife. No one asked me any follow up questions.

"That was one of your best press conferences," John said to me over lunch afterward. I chuckled to myself, *Of course he would think that, of course.*

I knew from the way my body felt during my pre-meet warmup later that evening that I was flat. There was no spring in my steps, my block starts felt sluggish, and I was hitting hurdles on my hops that I would usually clear by over a foot. I tried to prepare John for the reality that it could be a bad race the next day by explaining the load I was under.

"Why are we even here if you can't win?" he asked me.

"Because you wanted to come," I said back. "I'm doing this meet for you. Neither me nor Rana thought this was a good idea," I continued.

"So, you're not even going to try? You're wasting time and money?" he started to escalate himself, as usual.

"Of course, I'm going to *try,*" I said, trying to cut the building tension.

"Well okay then," he said more calmly, as I uncoiled the HDMI cable I always traveled with, connected the laptop to the TV, and started a movie.

We arrived at the Armory early. I like to soak in the atmosphere for 30 minutes before starting my warmup. This meet also featured age-group races which meant a lot of people were in attendance, both as participants and spectators. This left very few places for us to post up so I could get my 30 minutes of down time in. We were directed by a volunteer to office space in the building. I chose a corner cubicle with a rolling desk chair to relax in. Spinning around in the chair, I looked at the walls of the office. Posters and photos framed the little work area. One poster in particular caught my attention. "How to know you're in an abusive relationship," it was titled. Still spinning in the chair, I squinted my eyes to read:

1. **Intensity**, someone you just met exhibits the following behavior: lying or exaggerating. *Hmm,* I thought. It was a running joke between him and me that he was the King of Hyperbole. I kept reading. **Insisting you move in, get married, have kids, trying to win over friends and family.** *Hmm,* I thought again, remembering back to the beginning when he told

me on an early date he had designed a ring for me, or how four months in he insisted I move in without actually helping me move out of my sister's apartment. He bought me new clothes to keep me from going back for my own. Over the top gestures and bombarding rounded up the description for intensity. *Check and check.*

2. **Jealousy**, *check*. At every meet I was accused of having slept with someone. I thought back on all the times he scrolled through my old emails, tweets, and photos.

3. **Control**, *check*. My toenails had to be certain shades of red. I was not allowed to wear short shorts, or flip flops, or leggings outside of training. I no longer had control of my social media accounts, and no more blog; if he felt like changing my number he did. My stomach clenched when I got to the bottom of the control paragraph and read the line about sexual coercion. *Damn it*, I thought. Check.

The list went on covering **isolation, criticism, sabotage, blame, and anger.** All eight signs of abuse, we had thoroughly covered. It wasn't that I did not know, but seeing it spelled out so clearly on that poster, on that day, changed me. It felt like a higher power was finally saying to me, "I see you. Do *you* see you?"

I did see me.

I lost that race to Allyson Felix, as I predicted I would. John was as upset as I knew he would be, but I didn't care about any of that. I sat him down when we returned home and asked for a divorce.

IN CRISIS

"There's no way you're happy. There is no fucking way, dude," I said. "Happily married people don't do what we do to each other. You deserve to be happy, like I deserve to be happy."

John had always said that cheating was stupid when you could just sit down like two adults and be honest with each other. I was done with marriage. I told him as much in 2013, and even though we weren't legally married then, we were living as man and wife—a trial run of sorts in which I gathered enough data to know shit was for the birds.

I know, I know. "With the *right* person it's a totally different experience," they say. I know that, on an intellectual level, but I'm not in a rush to find that out.

"Okay," John said. I couldn't believe what I was hearing. He told me many times over the past five years that I could tell him when I wanted "out," and he'd call Dennis and start the unwinding process.

He flipped open his Moleskine notebook to a blank sheet of paper, uncapped his black Sharpie pen, and began to jot down figures. Apparently, he was creating a rough sketch of an invoice. He and Dennis would have to calculate what he was owed, and once they had done that they'd make sure I got the rest of my earnings.

What he's owed? I wanted to dig into this peculiar statement and this invoice he seemed to be drafting but the man had just said "okay" when I asked for a divorce; I thought it smarter to take my win and leave well enough alone.

"We'll need to wait until September," he said looking up from his scribbles. "You don't want that kind of disruption before World Championships, do you? Your contract expires in December; if you don't medal that can be the end, You're old now."

Ooo, I thought, seeing the red flag of passive aggressiveness waving. The age reference was a dig at me, a low blow of sorts. I did not have, nor did my sponsors have, any reason to believe that after winning my first Olympic Gold medal 10 years after my first season as a pro, and running 10.78 at 31, that I was too old to renew or sign me to a new contract. But it's Nike; they've done people dirtier for less. He was right. I hated disruptions. I'm toddler-like in that way: mess with my routine—prepare yourself for a tantrum.

"It's March, how do we make it to September?" I asked baffled. "Do we live separate lives until then? Do we pretend everything is fine publicly? Do I move upstairs?" Question after question bubbled to the surface.

"Behind closed doors, hunkered down, do what you want, but we've got the season to think about. So, I'll still be traveling to all the meets and handling your warmups."

It dawned on me just how much money I would make between March and September—another $100,000 in salary and whatever I earned from medal bonuses, prize money, and appearance fees on top of that. It slowly dawned on me why he *really* wanted to make it to September.

"No. I can't do it," I said. I had been on the verge of tears from the beginning of the conversation and now, the thought of another six months as miserable as I was, it was just unbearable.

John stood and returned with a three finger pour of Tennessee Jack Daniel's Fire. The weight of the crystal tumbler brought me comfort for some reason. Salty tears mixed with cinnamon when I licked my lips. "You're not a quitter. You don't quit anything. You're going to quit this? Quit on me?!" John began to cry. "We said our vows not even a year ago! You promised me! And you're quitting on me?" the accusation stung.

I knew when I repeated my vows after the officiant when we were married that I didn't mean them. I was almost certain John didn't mean his either but there he was across the table crying with me. He refilled my glass, another three-finger pour which I immediately got to work on. I was tired of walking on eggshells, the gaslighting, behavior so modified I didn't recognize myself anymore.

I had been getting more and more glimpses of my true self. Every time I meditated, every time I attended a yoga class, or practiced yoga Nidra, almost like a ghost passing peripherally through my line of sight, I'd catch a glimpse of her, and I'd see that she was suffering, and the question in her eyes was, *Why are you staying?*

The answer was that I had nowhere to go. I had access to none of my money. I signed it over years ago, naively believing Dennis, the accountant, and John, a financier, when they said they knew how to help me settle my tax bill and pay off my debts, so that I could feel the freedom of enjoying the money I earned. John told me about making his first million and how it felt. I had earned $1 million between 2012 and that conversation, but I experienced no freedom. I hid packages that came for me upstairs in bedrooms he never entered. I had an American Express Black Card I was only allowed to use for travel and gas. He'd even gone so far as to question my purchases from Target.

From bankruptcy in 2010 to a millionaire on my own efforts in 2017, I felt less free than I did on the day the judge discharged me. I stayed because as beat down as I was, as exhausted and broken as I had become, what waited for me outside the walls of Avila? Was it a world that rushes to support a battered black woman? Was it a world where I could start over again at 31-32 years old? With no degree, no money, and no support? The idea of stepping out was even more terrifying.

He refilled my glass again.

"No, I'm good," I said through eyes burning with tears. I was tipsy, maybe bordering drunk already; there wasn't any food in my stomach to absorb the alcohol—my appetite surpressed by stress. I wanted a clear head for this conversation, so that I'd remember it in the morning. I had a Percocet and a Xanax waiting in the top drawer of my nightstand to swallow as soon as that conversation ended. I had been checking out of the world more and more lately. I was flirting with addiction and I knew it. Track and Field was the only check on my drug use. I knew from my rate of consumption that I had a problem. What started as half of one hydrocodone, and half a Xanax had turned into a cocktail—no longer getting away with halves and washing it down with whiskey.

I knew the danger of doing so and was choosing to do it anyway, hoping that whether I lived another day or died would be decided, not by suicide, but by overdose, maybe even in my sleep, if I was lucky.

"Just drink, we're sitting here talking this out," he commanded.

The drink halfway down, I bolted out of my seat into the bathroom just off the dining room and threw up. I hate throwing up; I hate throwing up so much that I immediately cry and howl while wrenching my guts out in the porcelain bowl. John followed me into the bathroom and rubbed my back.

"Shhhh....shhhhh you're okay," his voice was soft, my tears slowed. Another cramp gripped my body, and I heaved over the bowl again.

"I'm here to take care of you," he bent lower to whisper in my ear. "I'm the only one who has never taken from you, the only one who cares about you. I'll take care of you."

John rubbed my back one last time before grabbing my hand and walking me to the bedroom and tucked me into bed. "I love you, Punkin," he said to me before leaving the bedroom and settling in on the couch in the living room. I could see the silvery blue light of the television play off the Venetian plastered walls as I drifted off to troubled sleep.

I woke the following morning to breakfast in bed. The smell of applewood bacon wafted into the bedroom when John entered. He extended a plate toward me with my favorite honey and brown sugar sausage links each wrapped in a halved flour tortilla, held together with a toothpick—a snack I created by accident a year ago that was now a staple in our house. He left again and returned with espresso.

He leaned over, kissed me on the forehead, and told me he was headed into the office. That wasn't unusual;his behaving this way after I'd asked for a divorce the night before was. I liked being alone in the house though, and I wasn't particularly interested in revisiting the previous night's conversation either. He said September. I'd just have to figure out how to make it.

I kept my cell phone on silent and in the drawer of my nightstand. Leaving my phone out would have been too much of a temptation for John to riffle through texts, emails, and anything else he wanted to search if I had something to hide.

After our particularly bad fight in Beijing, the same night that I had won my second Outdoor World Championship 10 years after the first, I realized that I would never have anyone outside of John and his minions, after John threatened my massage therapist and his wife. When we returned home from China, I created a Facebook page to find Chuck again. Chuck was one of the only people I knew who has had the same phone number since 2004. I was hoping that I could find his Facebook profile and reach out via messenger. I didn't know for sure what I wanted from him specifically. It wasn't like I could call him. I couldn't be sure that Dennis or John weren't monitoring the call log when they paid the phone bill. That had happened once when they asked about a charge because of an international call. I couldn't be sure it didn't happen all the time, and I did not want to risk it. I was pleasantly surprised at the ease of locating Chuck's public profile. I was even more surprised to see his phone number listed there. *Who puts their cell phone number on the internet?* I thought. Both shocked and grateful that he was in fact just the type of person who would. I added his number to my phone under John Preston, the actual name of Mr. Big, a *Sex and the City* character. I didn't dare send a message, but I opened WhatsApp and clicked on his name. His profile picture was the front of a hotel I recognized immediately.

The last time I saw Chuck, in person, was three years ago, by chance, in Switzerland. We sat outside at a table "catching up" while I lied to his face about how my life was going. Seeing this as his profile picture brought me to tears. I felt like a kidnapped child who had just learned her parents had never stopped looking for her. Depending on your settings, WhatsApp will tell you the last time a person was active. Chuck had been active on the app less than 30 minutes prior. I hugged the phone to my chest. For the first time in a long time, I felt close to someone who knew me, who had loved me, and had not given up on me.

When I was finally brave enough, I opened WhatsApp and composed a message to Chuck. "Hey!" was all I could manage to say. I stared at the phone waiting nervously to see his status change to online, to see the check marks turn blue, to see that he was typing a response. "Hey, Kid," he replied. All these years later and every conversation started the same. "You okay?" he asked. I took a deep breath and typed, "No, no I'm not."

I dropped my phone when it buzzed. Snapping me out of my past and back into the present. My phone never rang. No one else, outside of a handful of John's employees, had my phone number. When John knew I was home, he typically called the landline. The phone's buzzing jarred me out of my emotional stupor alerting me to a series of texts from John.

"Me and you. Hawaii Vacation." the first said.

"Depart September 14 – Return September 28. I would like to purchase tickets to Maui ASAP, two weeks in Hawaii, guaranteed." said the next.

"End of season celebration, start of holiday fall season celebration. We can brain-storm together hotel, fun stuff, site-seeing over the next few months." said the last.

Annoyed that Hawaii was a totally doable trip once I asked for a divorce, I read the messages again. *Wait a minute*, I thought, looking at the proposed dates of the trip. John was a smart man. Once on a flight when I was struggling with an equation in my Mensa puzzle book, John looked over my shoulder, shook his head.

He said, "The answer is two."

Thinking he was just throwing a random number out to derail my train of thought, I dismissed him.

"No, check it," he said, referring to the answer key at the back.

I did. The answer was two. He had looked at the equation for all of 15 seconds tops and knew what it was. I crumbled up my sheets of scratch paper equally amazed at how easy it was for him and surprised by how rusty I was with math.

He'd set the dates for our Hawaiian vacation for two weeks in September. September— the month we had agreed to get divorced.

Fuck! I thought slamming my phone down. He had no intention to let me leave.

SET THE DATE

Reality settled over me like a weighted blanket. My head began to pound again; I was hungover from the night before. That whole "sit down like two adults and unwind the relationship" speech was bullshit. If he was going to grant me a divorce, he wouldn't be planning a vacation—and not just any vacation. He was planning THEE vacation, I really wanted to go on, in the month he was meant to be granting me a divorce. Frightened, I felt like the final lock on my multi-padlocked cage had been secured. *Was there really no way out?*

"Hi," I typed a message to Chuck.

"Hey, kid," he replied almost instantly. I went on to tell him that I needed his opinion on the events of the night before and the texts from John that morning. Our text conversation was interrupted by a phone call. It was Chuck.

"What are you saying to me? Are you saying he got you drunk?" he asked me, his voice two octaves higher as he struggled to contain his anger.

"I don't know if that was intentional! I can't say, maybe he lost track of how much I'd had." I heard myself doing what I'd always done, explain away the hurt, rationalize the abuse, give him the benefit of the doubt. I stopped talking.

"You have two choices. Listen to me. You have two choices. One, leave or two, I'm coming to get you," he said in a tone I had never heard before.

"You'd never make it past the guard gate," I said, thinking about the guarded entries to the exclusive Avila community. I already knew option one, leaving, was out of the question.

"That leaves option one," he said again in the same tone. "I'm going to call you back in a few hours and when I do you better have the date you're leaving ready."

We ended the call; speechless I opened the calendar app on my phone. I'd needed time to prepare. If I'd left right then and there, I'd have $500 to my name in an account that Dennis also had his name on. The BMW I drove was in Club 360 Management's name, but John was the owner.

Club 360 was my dream project—a club for girls and young women that encouraged them to be multi-dimensional, to develop healthy self-esteem, and to hold a zero-tolerance policy for negativity. I had passionately explained this to John on one of our drives together to Daytona Beach back in 2012, and he told me that he would do everything he could to help me realize that dream. As much as my heart wanted Club 360, it was hypocritical of me to launch it. Instead, it was hijacked, and Club 360 Management became the name of the vehicle that would keep me forever separated from the money I earned. Club 360 started as an act of service and love but turned into a symbol of my own oppression.

Scrolling through my calendar I landed on May 1. The first Diamond League was scheduled for May 12 in Shanghai. In fact, I had already had my plane tickets for Shanghai out of Atlanta. If I played it right, I could leave on May 1, and just leave the country. Shanghai Diamond League and Kawasaki, Japan, were the first two meets on my schedule. After that I could fly to The Netherlands and get based there. Because I was paid quarterly, my $62K quarterly check would get paid out April 1. The thought of emailing Nike and asking them to hold my payment or direct it to a different account was frightening. After all, I'd tried that before years earlier when I'd tried to leave the first time; it didn't end well for me and I sent an embarrassing email to both my manager and Nike saying, "nevermind," but I could get my fourth quarter check. I'd have to survive for five months. Chuck told me that he didn't care where I went, but I needed to get out of Tampa, and if I needed to come to Alabama, I was more than welcome for as long as I needed or wanted to stay. As terrifying as even thinking about these plans were, I began to see that this was not impossible to pull off. I called Chuck back so that he wouldn't call me at an inopportune time.

"May 1st," I said when the line connected.

"May 1st," he repeated back to me.

"Okay," I said.

"Okay," he repeated, "I love you. I'm proud of you. Start planning."

I hung up the phone and looked at the time. I opened a new text, "Do you want me to have anything ready for you when you get home?" I sent the message to John. He replied in the negative and said that he had a gift for me.

When he came home a few hours later, John handed me a print-out of an order confirmation page. He had finally purchased the Walt Disney Annual passes I had been asking him to do for four years. I put on a fake smile, gave him a real hug, and thanked him for the passes.

"Want to go to Epcot this weekend?" he asked me, waiting with anticipation for my answer. We went to Epcot like others go to their favorite restaurant. We'd drive up in the evening just before sunset, walk straight to the back of the park for the World Showcase, and drink our way around to

Italy, stopping in Mexico for an opening shot of Tequila, and in Germany for a deliciously sweet shot of honey bourbon, finishing with deep red wines in Italy. I enjoyed those visits so much. Time after time, Disney World has proved itself to be a guaranteed escape from my real life.

"Sure," I said, my tone betraying me.

"I thought you'd love this! You love Disney! We go so much, an annual pass just makes sense, plus no black-out days or nuthin', Punkin."

All true, and all things I've said to him year after year when arguing my case for the passes. Hearing him spout it back at me in that "this is a no brainer" sort of way after years of telling me "no," infuriated me.

"I am so excited; it's just my head hurts still from last night." I held his gaze and searched his eyes for any indication that he felt any kind of way about the night before. Unflinching, he suggested I take "half-a-pill" and lie down. "Okay," I said, as I turned my back to him and popped a whole Percocet, climbed under the blankets, and waited for my deliverance.

COUPLES' THERAPY

"Will you come to therapy with me?" John asked. He had finally found a therapist he liked—a black woman named Dr. April. He originally sought her out to develop better skills as a boss and leader. He believed some of his personal fears and demons held him back from being the best he could be. I resisted the urge to say, "no shit," and applauded him for not only recognizing he could use some help but for taking action, which was the step most people got hung up on. He beamed.

"You know, when you talk to me like that. When you treat me like a king, I could run through walls." He'd been seeing her for a few months and had asked her if she could see him, then us together, and then me by myself.

"What's the point of therapy when we're getting divorced in September?" I asked with zero fucks left to give and forming a secret escape plan. I had expected to feel terrified but not empowered. That was a surprise. Empowerment felt like a drug, and the high felt so good that I was becoming a little reckless.

"You're still on that? What else can I do, I'm doing Hawaii. I got you the passes!" His temper flared.

In that moment, I remembered something I had read while looking up resources for domestic violence victims. The most dangerous time for someone in an abusive relationship is when they leave. I checked myself and was a different person when I spoke again.

"Of course, I'll go with you. I'm sorry." He pulled out his phone to check a message before telling me the time and date for the appointment he had already set.

It took me two couple's therapy sessions to learn just how dangerous of a situation I was in. A huge fan of therapy, I was careful not to hold back. I wanted Dr. April to hear and understand fully what was happening between us.

"John, why do you want to stay married to Tianna?" she asked him. I wasn't paying attention to his answer, I zoned out after he mentioned "our" Olympic runs and "our" medals. "Tianna, why do you want to stay married to John?" she asked me.

"I don't," I said.

"SEE!?" John shouted, "She's not even trying!" He was right, I wasn't. Dr. April dug a little deeper.

"Why not?" she asked.

"Well," I sat up taller and upright against the well-worn couch. "For starters, I don't want to be with anyone who wants me to be afraid of them. I want my freedom. I want access to the money I've earned. How's that for starters?"

Dr. April took her notes.

"John, do you want your wife to be afraid of you?" she asked him.

"Of course not!" he said, appalled.

"You've got to be fucking kidding me, dude!" I shouted back before I could stop myself. I really needed to reel it in and stop poking the bear if I wanted to make it to May 1.

Dr. April rearranged her sweater as we began my one-on-one session. I didn't trust her. She had been John's therapist for months, and I saw no change at all at home; in fact he was worse. I weighed what was safe to share and what wasn't. After all I wasn't actually her client, John was. After a few quiet moments Dr. April flashed me a disarming smile. I relaxed a bit feeling like I was in a safe space.

"I have never seen a man more in love with his wife than John is with you," she said to me.

Shocked, especially since I had just finished detailing the physical fights and domestic violence incidents we'd had. That was her takeaway after that? No thanks, that smelled like a trap and I wasn't stepping in it. The rest of the session went smoothly because I decided to be as agreeable as possible.

Later that evening I told John I didn't think I needed therapy anymore. I had decided to stay married. A few days later John brought up Antonio again. I didn't have it in me to say no.

MARCHING ORDERS

It was March, and I was several days into a training stint in the Netherlands and I was in trouble. Dennis told John I had just completed a transaction via LegalZoom. John called me immediately. I was between workouts at training camp in the Netherlands so I answered the phone.

"Are you trying to do a LegalZoom divorce?" John asked me without saying hello.

"Legal Zoom does divorces?" I asked him, laughing it off.

"I don't know!" he said. "Is that what you're doing?" he asked again.

"Why would I do that? You wouldn't even respect divorce papers I would have printed from a website would you?" I asked laughing.

"No, you're right I wouldn't," he agreed. I told him it's probably some recurring fee for something to do with Club 360. I assured him I'd look into it and that he did not have to worry about me trying to secure a divorce online. Satisfied, he told me to have a good day and hung up the phone.

I returned to the open internet browser on my MacBook Pro. The charge in question was not a recurring fee for Club 360 at all but the incorporation and filing fees for a new company Team TB, LLC—a new company for a new life. I clicked the next tab I had open, a Google search page. "Best lawyers for high-conflict divorce in Tampa," was typed into the search box. I sat back in my chair as I reached for my half-eaten Stroopwafel. *Close call*, I thought as I took a break from plotting my way out of John and Dennis' death grip on me and my money.

One time the USOC sent $10,000 directly to my personal Regions Bank account. I had earned a $1 million since 2012, and this $10,000 was the most I had ever seen in my bank account. I had an idea to siphon the money into a brand-new account, one that belonged to me and only me. I opened the account online and transferred the entire amount to the new one. The status was pending confirmation which was likely to happen during business hours the following day. I was back home training at USF until the Dutch Federation arrived for another warm-weather training camp at IMG. I was warming up on the track when my music was interrupted by a call.

"Where are you?" John asked without saying hello.

"I'm at the track, USF," I said.

"I'm coming, don't move," he said. I did move. Whatever was about to happen I did not want the track to be where it did. I waited in the parking lot.

"I told you not to move!" he shouted. "Get in the car!" He was pissed. "You sneaky bitch, and you wonder why I don't trust you!"

Nope. Never wondered that, actually. "What are you talking about?" I asked, not thrilled to have my workout interrupted for nonsense.

"Dennis told me you're moving money around."

Fucking Dennis. I didn't know which of the two I hated more. In my opinion, Dennis was the type of guy who would smile in your face and tell you he's looking out for your best interest but then turn around and ask for instructions on how to best screw you over. I hadn't seen John this mad in a long time.

"I'm not sneaking. I can't sneak when you and Dennis are monitoring everything. I just wanted to add a savings account," I said coolly.

"No, you're planning something, but guess what, you're going to get us all screwed. Good luck with the IRS! Get out. Close the account!" I got out of the car. And walked back to the track, packed my things, and drove home.

I looked at the status of my new account. "Closed," it said. But I hadn't closed it, and the $10,000 was there. Furious, I drove to Regions Bank, the branch I knew Dennis did business with in Seminole, Florida, and demanded to speak to the manager. The manager's smile disappeared as she got closer and noticed I did not look particularly friendly. I followed her to her office.

"Tell me how and why this account was closed," I said, sliding the supporting documents, which I had printed at the account's creation, in her direction. She stared at the paper, turned to her computer and punched her keyboard.

"I believe we were directed to close the account," she said.

"By whom?" I asked. "I believe, I'm the only person here who can direct you to close an account in my name. So, by whom?" I was barely in control of my anger. She knew she'd messed up, and now her only goal was to not say anything at all.

So, I spoke again. "So now the question is what legal action can I take against you and Regions Bank?" I sat clenching my teeth. She had no idea how her actions had or could have affected me. "Or, you can give me my money right now, and be done with it." She gave it to me in a cashier's check. A few days later John asked what had happened with the account, and if I had closed it. I told him his friend Dennis had it closed somehow and what happened to it after that, I had no idea. The cashier's check for $10,000 was safe in my secret storage unit down the street.

HOUSTON, WE HAVE A PROBLEM

John was as happy as I'd ever seen him. As far as he was concerned, "we" were back! I saw this as an opportunity to pounce. We had just watched *Hidden Figures* together, the story of three black female mathematicians who worked at NASA during the Space Race. I envied Janelle Monáe's character, Mary Jackson, and her ability to unapologetically pursue the paths that called out to her. As far as I could tell, based on the film, she was who I wanted to be. I had an idea.

"John, I think I know what could shake me out of this funk I'm in," I said to him while we lounged in front of the television.

"Yeah? You've been a bitch," he said.

Not taking the bait I continued, "Yes, I know I just need something to shake me up a bit and give me some perspective, make me train even harder so we can win gold this summer."

I had his attention with the reference to gold medals and because I used the word "we," so I continued. "Space has always been able to do that for me. How about I take a trip to the Houston Space Center? I could fly up and back or spend the night and fly out first thing in the morning. I just know I'll return a better wife to you, which is what you deserve, and a more hungry athlete."

I hated how manipulative and secretive I had become. I was turning into him in order to leave him. I had no idea where the bottom was.

"That's a great idea, Punkin!" I knew he'd think so, I'd said all the right things. "Try to find a ticket so you don't have to spend the night. I know how you hate being away from home."

I didn't. I loved being away from home, but that was his way of telling me I could not spend the night.

I really did want to go to the Houston Space Center; however, just as important as it was to see Mission Control with my own two eyes, I knew that Chuck and his Alabama State Track Team would be in Houston at the same time. I needed to give him documents for safe keeping. Upstairs, hidden beneath spare pillows and blankets were articles of incorporation for Team TB, LLC and other documents formalizing its creation. I'd already opened up two Wells Fargo bank accounts, depositing $100 in each one to start them and keep open. I directed all business and banking correspondence to the address where Chuck lived. When he checked his mail, which wasn't often, he'd take a picture of it and send it to me that way. I'd review it, give him instructions if necessary, and then delete the picture. Paranoid about every single thing I did, I didn't want to risk mailing my documents for fear that someone would see me at the post office.

I rented a storage unit up the street from our house on Bearss Avenue and began to move things out of the house and into the storage unit, a little at a time, every morning before driving to Bradenton for training. My hands would shake as I waited for the always slow-automated gate to open so I could be less exposed in my car on the street.

A few days later, I told John it was impossible for me to get a flight back that same night. He wasn't happy about that, but the idea that I would return home a problem-free wife was too good of an opportunity to pass up.

I had a great time at the space center. After spending all day there by myself or trailing school kids' field trip groups to listen in on their guided tour, Chuck asked me to meet him at the track where they would be competing. I vehemently declined. No fucking way—a single photo of me could surface right now.

"It'll be fine," he said.

"How do you know it will be fine? Do you know what's at stake for me right now? Is it really worth risking blowing up my entire plan? Do you not get it?" I was furious and scared, and starting to second guess my plan of trusting him with so much. No one, who wasn't in the situation I was in, could fully appreciate the dangerous game I was playing.

"It's just a shakeout. There aren't many people here, and I'll make sure you're safe. Then we can go to dinner after." Chuck had ridden with the team on the bus from Montgomery to Houston and was dying to get a break from that mode of transportation. Reluctantly, I agreed.

John called during dinner like I knew he would. I was enjoying lamp chops with mint jelly, sweet potato casserole, and grilled asparagus—my usual when I visited Ruth's Chris Steakhouse. I told him about my day and how I felt like a new person after spending all day at the Space Center. I told him I'd gotten him a cool gift, took a souvenir photo, and that I missed him and would see him in the morning. He asked me to check my arrival time so he could pick me up from the airport. I told him I'd call him when I was back in my room and ready for bed. Chuck and I finished dinner, and he waited in my room as I said good night to John. After hanging up and feeling guilty for being such a liar, we caught a late night showing of a new movie, *Get Out*, a film that revolved around an interracial couple. The black boyfriend would be visiting his white girlfriend's family for the first time. I left the theater shaken, but sure that I was doing the right thing by "getting out."

Rosa, our housekeeper, picked me up from the airport. "Tianna, can I ask you a question?" We had only been in the car for a few minutes, but she looked troubled.

"Of course, anything?" I said, meaning it.

"Are you leaving?" I knew what she meant but played dumb.

"Leaving?! You just picked me up!" I said forcing myself to laugh.

"Porque I was talking to mi esposo and he said I should just ask you, you know you can digame right?" She turned to face me, both hands stayed on the steering wheel at 10 and two.

I turned to face her too, "Why do you think I'm leaving?" I asked her.

"Your upstairs closets. They more empty." Damn, I knew John would never bother to go upstairs, let alone check my closets but I had definitely overlooked the possibility that the housekeeper would not only notice but feel compelled to ask me about it.

"Oh no, no, no…I'm spring cleaning. Just getting rid of clothes I don't wear anymore that's all," I said.

"You'd tell me, right?" she said with a note of sadness in her voice.

"Of course, Rosa, somos amigas. We're friends," I assured her. Hell no, I wouldn't tell her. She told John months before that she had found an empty emergency contraception box in my bathroom upstairs, giving John an excuse to start accusing me of cheating again. When the truth is I simply had no desire to get pregnant. She was most definitely not on my team.

I scoured the internet for an attorney and settled on one who specifically referenced high-conflict divorce and narcissistic personality disorder. I knew my husband well, and I knew this was not going to be an easy ride. Her office was too close to one of John's offices for comfort, so I hid the car behind the building whenever I needed to meet with her. There was so much paperwork, so many questions most of which I didn't have the answers too. I was afraid that asking too many questions of Dennis about my Regions Bank accounts would arouse suspicion. It was my attorney's request for documentation that led to me snooping around John's home office. That was where I found his divorce certificate and settlement from his second marriage to Shauna. I hadn't seen it before, but this was what my attorney had asked for. I scanned and emailed the pages as I read them. The last page stopped me in my tracks:

"Husband agrees to return to wife 3-karat platinum diamond ring"

My ring. The ring I flashed so proudly in 2012, the ring I won my gold medal and broke the world record in. The ring, that John said he had designed for me, was actually Shauna's ring. Because I'm left-handed, my ring—excuse me, Shauna's ring—had gotten banged up a bit and had lost a tiny diamond from the band. John took it to Mayors for repair, but he told me after a few months that if I wouldn't mind letting it sit there that would help him because he didn't have the disposable income to pay for it at the moment. I, of course, said that was fine. I went to Swarovski Crystal at Citrus Park mall and purchased rings that looked similar enough to replace the other in the meantime. I never saw the ring again, and I had just learned why.

My training group had just arrived in Florida to train at IMG which was only about an hour away from home in Tampa. One day, I pulled my coach, Rana, to the side. "I've decided to leave John and may need some cover while I meet with my attorney." Saying it out loud in that way made it feel more real, and suddenly I wasn't sure I could pull it off. But Rana said he had my back and whatever I needed he would try to do.

It was happening. I was doing it. I was preparing to take off.

APRIL SHOWERS

I got paid April 1. Like clockwork, anytime a deposit hit the account, Dennis would send John an email notification listing the amount. I walked out into the gym to ask John a question. I found him sitting on his knee extension machine with his phone in his hand, "God, I needed that," he said shaking his head from side to side.

"Needed what?" I asked him, thinking that it must have been something big for him to have a reaction like that.

"Dennis said your Nike money hit the account. I needed that!" he said again.

"You mean we," I said finding his choice of phrase troubling. "Are we hurting for money?" I asked.

"No, no…just it's nice when people pay on time," he said. He put his phone down and resumed his lift. I forgot the question I had gone out to ask and returned to the house. I was leaving him in exactly one month, and he just banked another $57,000 of my money. But there was no way around it. Seeing how tightly Dennis and John monitored my accounts, there was no way I could have explained away why the Nike money was a month late. I was too afraid to try to pull off that level of deception.

Plus, I had bigger worries. John had been pressuring Paul to give him my summer meet schedule so that he could pick and choose which meets he wanted to attend and buy his flights as soon as possible. I was hoping that as always my meet schedule would come together at the last minute; hopefully I'd be long gone by then. My other concern was the IAAF World Relays. They were set for the week before I was planning to disappear. I was living two lives already, the one that was meeting with her attorney and making plans in secret and the one where I was happily married. I hated needing to layer the lie on top of high-pressure situations where high performance was expected. It was depleting. But there was no way around it. I flew into Nassau, Bahamas, early, enjoyed the beach, relay practice, and the media, particularly my beach interview with Trinidadian sprint legend Ato Boldon for *Inside Athletics*.

John arrived the day before the meet and within hours had a meeting with "some guys" at the bar. He told me that the USATF Foundation was looking at him for a seat on the Board of Directors, which I found ridiculous but didn't and couldn't say so out loud. I was John's only connection to the sport. My success on the track somehow made him an expert by association.

He would tell clients in intake meetings at his financial company, "If I could do this for my wife, imagine what I could do with *your* money, applying these *same* principles."

He asked me to come down and say "hi" to the guys. It would make for a better setup, and then I could excuse myself and go back up to the room. They introduced themselves. John introduced me to them. Someone said something about Rio, and one of the board members said, "Oh, you were there too?" I looked at John, not expecting the USATF Foundation's Board to not know who made their last Olympic team. The USATF Foundation is most known for its distribution of elite athlete grants. Their organization awards grants for up to $30,000, a life-changing amount of money for so many of us. One must apply for these grants, and they award them based on performance (are you a top performer?) and a board of directors' vote (do all the board members think you deserve it?). Now I was learning that, not only didn't this board member have a clue who I was, he also didn't know that I had earned 8 medals so far for USATF. I now understood why I never got those much-needed grants.

"Yes," I said. "I competed in the 100, long jump, and relay," I said hoping this would jar some kind of memory.

"Yeah?" he asked. "How'd you do?" *Wow. These are the people who disperse the grants. Laughable.* I thought to myself as I dispensed with the niceties and said, "Two golds." And I excused myself back to the room.

An hour or so later, John returned, "What a bunch of idiots." he said.

Good, I thought to myself. I wouldn't have to worry about John on the board after the divorce then. But a few minutes later he informed me that a bunch of USATF "guys" were going to come to the house for a party when we returned from the Bahamas. And by "bunch of USATF guys," he meant Tracy Sundlun—a very active member of USA Track and Field and some of his buddies.

We made the 4x100-meter final easily, and I couldn't help but think how the prize money from this race would be the first prize money in five years that I'd get to see in my own account, in my own name. I was excited and ready to run for the win. The winners split $60,000 and, even divided six ways for the entire relay pool, that would go a long way in helping me get back on my feet.

The lineup for the final was me to Jenna Prandini to English Gardner to Morolake Akinosun. English and Morolake weren't strangers to each other.

English passed to Morolake for the first round and the solo run of the 4x100 at the Olympics the year before. It would be the first time I was passing the baton to someone not named Allyson Felix, but I was confident.

"To your marks!" the starter said. I checked my grip on the baton like always.

"Set.....BAM!" Off we went. I was just at the spot in the turn where I could see Jenna waiting for me when I started to fall. It happened in slow motion. Yet it took me 30 meters to hit the track and another 10 to come to a stop after contact. My skin burned; my body ached. I did not understand how that happened. Sure, the track was wet, but that's what spikes are for. I remember wondering if this was a bad omen for my leaving. No one came for me, not a single official, not a single person from Team USA came for me. I rolled to my back, stared at the sky, and mused about how this was absolutely a perfect diorama of my life. As always, no one was anywhere to be found when I was down. My teammates made their way back to me eventually as I was helping myself up. My torso was sore, as if I'd been punched. Once again, we learned that it was the Brazilian team with their wild elbows, that tried to take Team USA out of the race; this time they succeeded.

I was upset for my teammates and for myself. What an easy payday it could have been for all of us. What a chance to feel good about what was going to happen next for me but nope. That's too easy. And as far as my life goes...easy isn't a visitor that comes around often.

I walked back to the warmup area, disappointed. Paul, my agent, rushed to me and asked if I was okay. Rana, who had been in the stadium but was coaching the women's Dutch team that finished fourth, said he wasn't sure if the Dutch would have been mad at him for jumping over the rail to check on a Team USA athlete while he was wearing his Dutch National Team kit. I just looked at him with a blank expression and continued walking over to John, who also hadn't bothered to rush to me.

"You didn't run the turn right, and that's why you fell," he said with the conviction of a person who doesn't know a fucking thing.

"No, I was hit by Brazil," I said, pissed. He was so convinced that the fall was my fault; he wasn't worried about whether I was okay or not.

"Again?" he asked. "Aw, man, I'm so sorry, Punkin. Can I get you anything?" His tune had totally changed since I was no longer to blame. *One week to go,* I told myself. *One week to go.*

Back home in the US, Tracy Sundlun and a bunch of employees from UNATION came to the house for a party when we returned from the world relays. They schmoozed, drank, and talked about how their companies could help each other. By the end of the evening, they all but declared their love for each other and toasted to good business ahead. I hoped, like most things that happened over this many drinks and empty promises, that this was a relationship that would burn out quickly. I'd be wrong. That evening John shouted excitedly! "Ooo, you get to go to Japan!" Paul had sent him my entire meet schedule. Now, he'd know exactly where I'd be and when for the rest of the summer. I was going to get free in a week, but I would not have the luxury of feeling safe all summer long.

THEREIN LIES THE ANSWER

"Happy wife, happy life" they say, don't they? I was much happier when I returned home from Houston. It had been a long time since I had felt empowered. I had my incorporation papers for my new LLC; I had spent time at the Johnson Space Station dreaming about the stars. Astronomy always lifted my spirits, and I got to see my best friend and get much needed encouragement to keep moving forward.

I felt the fear, but I was doing what I needed to do, for myself anyway. I was leaving, and as a result, my interactions with John were more palatable. I became more agreeable. "Sure, I can do this for you," I'd say out loud. *Because this is the last time I'll have to,* I'd say under my breath.

All month long I had taken comfort in knowing it was my last month. As I suspected, my improved mood completely altered John's. We weren't fighting anymore. As far as he knew, couple's therapy had worked and that I had meant it when I said I wanted to stay married. He'd say I simply "flipped the switch." He was right about my having a switch; I can turn my discipline off or on. I can decide to stick with a person or cut them off. I can go from scared to death at the starting line to beast mode and earn a medal. John loved and hated that about me. He loved it when I flipped those switches on other people. He hated when I did it to him, until now.

He was walking taller through the house and smiling more. He was treating his employees better too. It seemed to me that he truly believed that he had finally turned his bull-headed wife into the submissive he felt he deserved.

I was mulling this over while nursing a glass of Jack Daniel's Tennessee Fire when I was proven right.

"Antonio's in Orlando" he said randomly in the direction of the television. Antonio was John's "friend." The one he has on video having sex with his other friend Gail. The man John wants to watch have sex with me. The man who has unwittingly been responsible for some of the worst fights between John and me.

I took a long sip from my glass. My mind was racing 100 miles per hour. *How do I do this?* I thought to myself. *I am so close to being free.* Saying "no" would most definitely initiate a blow up—especially because I had been so agreeable, so submissive. To deny him this again, especially now, would be confusing, frustrating, and infuriating for him. Saying "no" would be like signing a death warrant for me.

But how can I say yes to this? I had only recently recognized that I was worth fighting for, enough to leave all of this behind. Can I really go back on that and treat myself and my body as if it's nothing more than a living sex toy? Can I do that?

What if you don't? A sharper, more clear voice cut through my mind's chatter. *The most dangerous time in an abusive relationship is when you're leaving,* the voice reminded me. It was true that before I declared to both John and the therapist that I "wanted" to remain married, things had been escalating. Not physically, but the threat was there. Like the movie, Jaws, we didn't need to see the shark to know that any moment in the water could be our last.

"Oh, yeah?" I finally answered.

"Yeah, he could be here within two hours," he said.

So, Antonio is on call. My mind began to race again. This told me a few things. First, my new agreeable and submissive persona gave John the confidence to pull this stunt. I wouldn't have been surprised if Antonio was actually in Tampa already. The second thing, saying no wasn't going to be possible. I could feel it in my gut that saying no *this* time, with all that has transpired between us, would lead to a fight I might not survive.

So, I said yes. "So, this weekend or what?" I asked, knowing the answer.

"Tonight," he said.

Trying to sound braver than I felt, I laid out some conditions for my participation in my body's violation.

"I don't want to hear him, and I don't want him to talk to me. I want to wear my sleep mask because I don't want to see him. It can't be on our bed. And I need you to pour me another glass of whiskey, while I go shower. A double!"

John hopped into action faster than I'd ever seen him move. He handed the drink to me and ran out to the garage to text his friend.

Back in the master bathroom, I opened John's cabinet, my fingers lingered over the bottle that held the hydrocodone before I grabbed the one that contained the Percocet instead. I unscrewed the lid with shaking fingers, took and swallowed one, and placed the jar back on the shelf. I was closing the cabinet, when I changed my mind and grabbed the hydrocodone bottle too. I took half of one and placed the bottle back on the shelf and closed the cabinet door. I took a swig of whiskey, turned the shower on, and walked out of the bathroom to my nightstand to take a Xanax. With the shower still running, I walked into the kitchen and grabbed a tortilla shell. Eating something would get my stomach acid working and help the drugs kick in sooner.

I had less than two hours before I sacrificed my body on the altar of my future freedom.

John had set up his massage table, and set out towels and a bottle of Astroglide, his lubricant of choice.

My stomach dropped, but my drugs were kicking in. I started to feel separated from my body. If there ever was a time to be distant, this was it.

"Punkin, you ready?" John called from the kitchen. That was my signal to strip naked, climb up onto the massage table, and lie down. Chest up, legs spread.

I heard them. And my body immediately tensed. I closed my eyes and dreamed of far-off places, breathing slowly and deeply.

I jumped when a cold hand touched my skin, then another, then another, then another. Four hands felt like four million. Grabbing everything, touching everywhere, no inch of skin unmolested.

John whispered encouraging words in my ears. I could hear him talking to Antonio, "Her body is amazing, isn't it? Look at her." I heard Antonio make an affirmative sound and I tensed again. "Don't speak," John reminded him.

My legs were parted for me. I could not bring myself to participate in that way. The massage table creaked as someone climbed up on the table. Two thoughts crossed my mind: which man is it? And will it hold our weight?

John was near my head and was massaging my breasts, so the man on the table was Antonio. *Here we go,* I thought, my breath caught in my chest as he penetrated me.

Maybe it was minutes, maybe it was forever. But they were finished. They'd both had their way with me, and as I lay on the massage table—high, blindfolded, and profoundly sad, I spoke.

"Thank you, for not hurting me."

A lone tear slipped past my mask. *What a fucked up thing to say,* I thought to myself. And yet I meant it. The two satiated men left the room, and I slowly climbed down off the massage table and due to my dangerous mix of drugs, alcohol, and shame I stumbled back to the shower.

Was that rape? I asked myself as water washed over me. *Can't be, you agreed to it,* I answered. But the last time I felt this way, I *had* been raped. When I moved to Orlando in 2009. I had the same conversation with myself after that too. *Was that rape? Well, I shouldn't have let him in. I shouldn't have had so much to drink.*

The water was scalding hot, that pain welcomed on my skin. It didn't matter what I labelled what just happened as. My choice was do it, or risk everything else.

Which wasn't a choice at all. Therein lies the answer. My only peace was that it wouldn't be long before I'd leave that place forever.

MAY 1ST, 2017

I could feel him stirring in the bed. I rolled onto my side facing him to take in his face. I'd always loved his nose, and he'd always laugh when I'd stare or wax poetic about my obsession with it. His face was in shadow when he rolled out of bed. It wasn't even 5 a.m.

"You going to the office?" I asked in a voice broken with sleep.

"Yeah, I can't sleep, and I've got some fires I need to put out," he replied.

It wasn't unusual for him to leave home so early. He'd often wake me, calling home from his office landline phone after his arrival as if to assuage fears I didn't have about his true whereabouts.

"John."

He stopped fidgeting about the room.

"You know I do love you, right?"

He stared at me for a beat before answering. "I know," he said before saying, "I love you too, Punkin."

He left, and I rolled onto my back staring at the ceiling while Bailey and Baxter, our two teacup Yorkies, nuzzled next to my face.

I burrowed my nose in their fur, drinking in their puppy smell for what I knew would be the last time.

It was 6 a.m.

✶ ✶ ✶ ✶ ✶

My flight was at 2:45 that afternoon, and there was so much to do before then.

My heart was pounding. I was actually doing it. After five years of threatening to leave, I was finally doing it. I was finally leaving my husband, this marriage, this place I've made my home.

My phone buzzed. It was a text from Emily.

"I hope you know how strong you are."

My phone buzzed again.

It was Chuck sending me encouraging words.

Emily and Chuck were the only two friends I'd been able to hold on to as tightly as I did. Emily became acceptable to John as a potential friend during bobsled season when she helped me cope with the political fuckery that ran rampant through the halls of the Lake Placid Olympic Training Center. She was currently studying to be a lawyer. She could not give me legal advice yet, but she could tell me what her textbooks and professors said on the subject of any questions I'd had. Chuck had been my best friend since the universe dropped him into my orbit 12 years earlier. Even during long spells, when I'd disappear and stop speaking to him, when I did resurface, we always picked up where we left off. Both Emily and Chuck had been invaluable support for me during the last two months of planning. Emily held copies of my will. Chuck held incorporation papers and banking documents. And, although it was me who had to put one foot in front of the other, I could not have gotten as far as I had without them.

I went over my to-do list. I wrote it down over and over, tearing the copies, and flushing them or burning them each time.

Step one: Grab your Diamond League Trophies and your Olympic Medals and take them to the storage unit. That was the tricky part. Once I'd done that, I couldn't come back home. The rest of my errands would happen outside of Avila. Once I removed the medals and trophies from the mantle, my housekeeper Rosa would absolutely call John and ask about them. At that point, John would call me, or come right home. I had to be long gone by the time that happened.

I had a second phone. Before that my only phone was a part of a family plan that included John, his parents, and his employees on AT&T. So, I got a T-Mobile phone. Too scared to bring it in the house in secret in case John or the housekeeper discovered it later, I told John that T-Mobile would save us money because data was unlimited, even internationally. The best part about that was that it was true. So, I was *allowed* to keep the phone. I blocked John's phone numbers in my T-Mobile phone in advance. I planned to leave my AT&T phone behind. I didn't pay for it, and I wanted to be careful not to be seen as overly malicious in my departure. I was already struggling with how mean it was to do this to a person and how awful I was to lie to his face day after day. I felt equally monstrous to continue to have sex with a person I now hated more than anything while pretending that all was still well in paradise. I had become a manipulative, sneaky, and deceptive person. I was worried about my karma and the consequences of the actions I'd taken to survive.

I walked around to every TV in the house. I had an Apple TV for each of them. I logged out of each one and changed my Apple ID password. Bailey and Baxter, the teacup yorkies, were following me around the house sensing a shift in the atmosphere. Bailey, old and tired of all the pacing I was doing, returned to her bag in the closet. Baxter, a puppy John purchased for me and to give Bailey a companion, was my good little boy and stayed close to my ankles. I crouched down to take his little face in both my hands. I kissed his cold little nose and hugged his warm squirming body to my chest. I couldn't do it. I couldn't leave him. I called Chuck. "I can't leave my dog," I said.

"Bring him then," Chuck said. "As much as I hate dogs, a dog cannot be the reason you don't get the fuck up out of that house." I thought about it, and then I thought about Bailey and how she seemed to come back to life after she got used to Baxter. I couldn't split them up, and I had never once seen John do anything even remotely close to harmful to either of them. He was tender with them and I believed he would remain so. I told Baxter I was sorry I had to leave him. Baxter raised his leg and peed on my foot. He knew.

I had just enough time to wipe the pee off my foot, pile my trophies and medals into a plastic storage container, and get out of there before the housekeeper arrived. I had forgotten about my Olympic Rings! I ran back into the house and threw them both into the box, but I removed the one I'd earned from 2012 and put it back on the mantle. That one had John's initials on it too. I didn't want it. I would never wear it.

I left my cell phone on the table along with a note explaining where he could find the car, my Walt Disney World Annual pass (which I'll be honest was harder for me to part with than I'd expected), my American Express black card, and my fake wedding rings. I kissed my dogs goodbye for the last time, took one last look at the home that on my very first visit was my vision board in real life but quickly turned into my gilded cage, shut the door behind me, and left.

I passed the housekeeper in the car on the way out. I only had one minute before she pulled into the driveway, maybe another minute before she discovered the note, and one minute more, max, before she'd call John. I had to move.

The security gate at the storage unit was moving slow as molasses that day. I was preparing to ram it with the car when it finally opened. I swerved into the lot and to the door nearest my unit. My hands were shaking, and it took me three attempts to open the door. I slid the door open, placed my tub of trophies and medals inside, and grabbed my luggage, important documents, and my "go bag." I learned about the importance of having a go bag from domestic violence support websites. My go bag held a change of clothes, gift cards and a small amount of cash because they were untraceable, photo copies of my birth certificate, passport, and social security card, and toiletries. My go bag had been hidden in the house for some time. But I relocated it to the storage unit as I grew more and more paranoid that I'd be found out; instead, I kept the storage unit keys in a jewelry box in my nightstand. If I did have to run, I'd only have to run the 5 miles to the storage unit with the keys. I closed the door, reattached the lock, and got out of there as fast as I could.

Step Two: Close all accounts at Regions Bank

As soon as I did this Dennis would know, and within seconds he'd have John on the phone, and they'd panic and work each other up. And if they found me...I shudder to think about it. I pulled into the bank's parking lot. My phone rang; it was John. I dropped my T-Mobile phone, a new iPhone, and shattered the glass on the back completely. Bad omen. The personal banker was kind but talked too much, I wanted to get in and out. They explained how I needed to leave some money in the account for any pending transactions to go through. *Sure, no problem, let's wrap this up!*

"Have fun in Europe!" they shouted at the back of my head, as I sprinted back to the car.

I couldn't take it anymore. I felt like a sitting duck...if one could be both on the run and a sitting duck at the same time. I had originally planned to eat an actual meal at one of the nice restaurants near the airport, but now I wouldn't feel safe until I was past the security checkpoint at the airport. I'd eat there.

I floored it to the airport on the Veteran's Expressway, parked the car where John always parked it, and dropped the key in the mail. I had already prepared a priority express package addressed to his office. I did not want him reporting the car stolen before I could ditch it so I made it a point to tell him where it would be. He still could have reported it stolen, but in a crazy twist of irony I would have been able to show the police officer my "freedom/ travel papers." A laminated letter placed in the glove compartment of the BMW John "bought" for me for my birthday in Club 360 Management's name (another way of saying "with Tianna's money") said something to the effect, "I, John Bartoletta have granted permission for my wife, Tianna Bartoletta to drive this BMW owned by Club 360 Management of which I am the sole owner."

I flew through security and up into the Delta lounge. I could hardly sit still, and I had three hours until my flight to Atlanta. I tried to sit. I had emails to schedule for delivery. Dennis would get an email directing him, as my former CPA, to turn over any documents he had regarding me to my new accountants. Paul, my agent, would finally be told what was happening.

Nike would be directed to redirect my next payment to a new company. While drafting these emails, new emails were coming through. Apple ID password reset request, Delta Forgotten Password Request. USADA (the US Anti-Doping Agency that MUST know where I am at all times) Password reset requests. They were systematically looking for me. Dan, the IT guy at John's financial office had set up my email, and even though I had changed the password they owned the domain. It was only a matter of time.

I jumped out of my seat after changing my passwords again to be sure and sprinted to the help desk.

"Is there any way I can get on an earlier flight to Atlanta? Please?" I was fidgeting badly. The two women behind the desk didn't ask questions but flashed me a knowing and reassuring smile.

"Go now, they're boarding!" I thanked them and told them that this was the first day of the rest of my life. They shouted their congratulations as I sprinted down the stairs, out of the club, and to the gate.

I was in the last seat in the last row. I had it to myself and once I buckled the seat belt, once the safety protocols had been read, once we began to taxi, and once the plane's wheels finally lifted away from the ground, I cried.

I wiped my tears as a male flight attendant servicing the back of the plane asked for my drink order and placed a handful of Biscoff cookies on my tray table. I sat sipping Jack Honey, eating cookies, silent tears streaming down my face. I had done it. There was a small part of me that wasn't convinced I was brave enough, strong enough, or bold enough to go through with it. But here I was. I had looked at my life and all of its gold and illusions and demanded better. I had reached down into the abyss and pulled myself out. I had found one sliver of life left in me and resuscitated it. I had done it.

ON THE RUN

Chuck scooped me up in a huge hug when I arrived in Montgomery, Alabama. He couldn't stop telling me how proud he was of me; he couldn't stop asking if I was proud of myself. None of it seemed real. I think I was in shock. I was going back and forth between pride, relief, guilt, anguish, fear, and terror. I put my phone in airplane mode when I boarded the flight in Atlanta and never looked at it again. I handed my phone to Chuck in baggage claim, as he handed me yet another new phone with a new number. Over dinner, although I did not need to, I kept looking over my shoulder eventually needing to switch seats so that my back could be against the wall and I could see the entire restaurant. Chuck, who was screening my messages and emails, created a filter that sent emails from John, Dennis, George, and any other of his minions, to a folder I did not have access to. Nothing good would come of me reading those emails, so Chuck made that impossible.

It took me a moment after blinking my eyes open to remember where I was the morning after. Once I was aware of my new surroundings and my new reality, I ran a gamut of emotions from guilt to glee in a matter of moments.

"What do you want for breakfast kid?" Chuck asked. "I don't know, what do you want?" I replied. "It's up to you," he said. *Up to me?* That was going to take some getting used to.

I was only in Montgomery for a few days when I tagged along with Chuck to the SWAC Conference Championships. He had gotten permission from his head coach, Ritchie Beene, for me to attend after telling him what had happened. As much as I loved being alone, I needed to be around people— especially black people. My last five years had been a life controlled by white males, and they were who I was running from. John and friends would be easy to spot at the SWAC Championships if they figured out where I was. I was certain I had more than a few allies willing to protect me from them. Finally.

I only needed to make it to May 9. My flight to Shanghai was out of Atlanta. I couldn't bring myself to steal or destroy John's passport so that he wouldn't be able follow me, but I hid it pretty damn good in the house to buy myself more time. I also knew that he was afraid of flying. I usually held his hand and distracted him with ridiculous stories, or movies during takeoff and landing. But I had learned to never underestimate what he was willing to do when he was angry. The meet I was most worried about was the

Prefontaine Classic in Eugene, Oregon. John was in possession of my entire meet schedule, and that was the only meet, besides nationals, I had on U.S. soil. He didn't need his passport to travel to those competitions. If he wanted to drag me back to Tampa, it would have to be from one of those two places. Outside of the meets, he didn't know where I was. Chuck had already told me he couldn't make it because the Prefontaine Classic conflicted with the NCAA regional meet which he needed to attend with his team.

That left me with only one choice. I picked up the phone and called my dad.

THE PRODIGAL DAUGHTER, PART 2

My dad picked up the phone and I said, "Hey dad, it's T." I could hear him thanking the Lord under his breath. I wasn't sure how I'd be received, but I was relieved that this was the reception. "I'm calling from China. I've left John, and I'm scared. I'm on the run. Can you meet me at Prefontaine? I'm too scared to return to the U.S. alone. I need someone there to watch my back please," I was begging.

"Of course, me and your mom will be there," he said. I remained silent. My mom. There was a lot of water under that bridge. He put her on the phone. Her reception was far less warm than my father's. I told her what I had just told him, that I needed backup. I was scared. She assured me that they'd be there.

In return, I assured them that we could talk about the last five years after the meet. The meet organizers were dubbing this year's Prefontaine Classic as the "Olympic rematch" between Brittany Reese and me. I could not afford to be any more of an emotional wreck than I was already. They agreed.

I lost to Brittany, but I jumped 6.83—a distance I could live with, considering the stress I was under. Afraid to be a sitting duck at the meet hotel, I rented an Airbnb and my own car so that I would never have to be anywhere I couldn't control access to. What a time to be alive.

My parents sat together across the room from me on the couch back in the AirBnB after the competition. I sat in an armchair against the wall.

"Where do we start?" I said in an attempt to break the ice. *Where do you start after being estranged for so long, after so much hurt had been inflicted on all parties?* I was shocked at how much anger I felt toward them, listening to them explain why they sued me.

"Our attorney said that we could depose you alone, away from John, and talk to you. We thought that was the only way to get to you." I tried to articulate the layers of damage that move caused, especially since we all knew the truth. I told them my best guess of what it cost me in financial losses and the depression it threw me into. I told them that every time they gave an interview or made a public post on Facebook, every single time I had paid for it with my body.

"What do you mean?" my dad asked.

"What do you think I mean, Dad? What could I possibly mean?" He bit his lip and buried his face in his hands.

"He's evil," my mother said.

"Maybe," I said, shocking them. "But what he won't be is a scapegoat. We had real issues between us as a family that left me primed and ready to be a mark for a man like that. Do you understand what I'm saying to you? You don't get to sit here and place the full blame on him. The three of us set that up long before I became Tianna Bartoletta."

"The family has been torn apart, your uncle, my own brother, Adrianne..." I stopped him. He had it all wrong when it came to my older sister.

"Adrianne was the only one of you all who was willing to play the game in order to keep her finger on me—the only one. She did that for me because my big sister was looking out for me. And look at the thanks she got for being the only person in the whole damn family not ready to write me out of her life completely. All of you owe her."

I was fuming. There was a lot of blame swirling in the room from all sides and none of it was productive. Even I was letting my anger get the best of me, when we all wanted the same thing—to be family again.

"T, the scripture says we must forgive," my dad said before I cut him off.

"I'm not a Christian. You're free to tell me what the Bible says, but one, I already know what it says, and two, as a non-Christian, I don't have to do anything your Bible says."

"But it's what we believe," he said in response.

"And you're free to believe it, and I'm free to be unmoved by the appeal."

"I was so hurt," my mom said beginning to tear up. She explained how after a lifetime of believing prayer was sufficient for problems, she had to seek out a therapist. John had tried to get her fired by sending accusations to her bosses about theft and breaches of fiduciary responsibility. She was in pain, and my heart hurt for her. But my temper would not to be squelched. I had been in therapy, largely about her, for 12 years!

"I understand that you're hurting," I said softly, "but none of you get to be more hurt than me." But pain isn't a competition. It's a highly individualized experience. I struggled to appreciate their experience of the last five years through the lens of my own. My pain wouldn't have been diminished by acknowledging theirs. The last five years were hard on each of us, in very different ways. But there the three of us were. Perhaps having the first real and honest conversation we'd ever had. I took advantage.

"Mom, why were you a different parent to me than you were to Christina?" I'd wanted to ask that forever and the question seemed to float to the center of the room and lay over us like a blanket of fog. Mom cleared her throat.

"I'd always known you'd be okay." she said.

Unsatisfied, I asked a follow-up question, "What does that even mean? I wasn't born with a post-it note on my forehead that said 'hey, this one can handle herself.'" She went on to explain that it's just something she knew, intuitively.

Not one to argue about the validity of people's perspectives, I had to accept her answer, but not before saying, "What you believed to be giving me space because I could handle myself, I interpreted as neglect. Just so you know."

It felt good to get that off my chest. I had always looked at my mom's relationship with my little sister and wondered why I didn't deserve that. I had spent my entire life, with the exception of the last five years, trying to earn my way into that kind of relationship with her. I had hated myself for so long for needing that from her and never getting it. But now I had a different need.

"Dad, why didn't you come for me?" I asked. "Why didn't you get on a plane and drag my ass out of that house. Daddy, you know me. Don't you?" This was the deepest hurt I had been carrying all that time. I thought of *all* people my father would know I needed him. Ever since the release of the movie, Taken, I believed my father was just like Liam Neeson's character. For the entire first year of our estrangement, I still wrote my father's name and details into the Emergency Contact Information line when I traveled. After the phone call at the 2012 Olympic Trials, where I'd heard him say that he didn't want to know the woman I'd become, I stopped believing. I stopped listing him as my emergency contact.

"Thank you for being here for me," I said, taking a break from my anger to express my genuine gratitude. I really hadn't been sure that they would want to. I was happy to be wrong. We all wanted to move forward, but no one knew how. I was the first to speak, "I no longer need a mother, that ship sailed a long time ago. But I do need my family. I don't need to be parented. But I do need my family. We can't go back, and I don't want to go back to the way things were. But I want my family."

"We want that too," my parents said in unison.

"Okay," I said.

"Okay."

We decided to wrap it up for the evening. We would drive to Multnomah Falls together on the way to Portland the following day and hike up to the waterfall. Our time in nature together was healing for us. We had a long road of healing ahead of us, and the wounds were fresh; but there was one thing I was sure of after that, that I wasn't sure of before, they loved me.

BYE BYE BYE

I had a bye to the World Championships, so I simply needed to show up and compete in *something* at the USATF Outdoor National Championships. We had a celebratory air about us. Me, Chuck, my parents, and Chuck's mom Gina all showed up. My parents could not stop thanking Chuck for being there for me when they weren't. For saving me. He corrected them by saying that I had saved myself. They thanked him anyway; my mother did what could only be described as a slow-motion Baywatch beach run into his arms to give him a giant hug; my dad, keeping his cool a bit more, shook his hand and pulled him in for a half embrace.

"Wow. We've come a long way since the last time y'all met 13 years ago, huh?"

My mom shot me an intense look; my dad flashed an embarrassed smile. Thirteen years ago, my parents decided they had to meet "this boy" I was spending so much time with. They questioned the two of us and our "activities." During that "interrogation," my parents had learned that not only was their daughter sleeping over at a boy's house (a sin), that boy was also a proud atheist (the worst sin)! Thirteen years ago they told us we were both going to hell; my parents cut me off financially and took my car, driving my hard-earned Saturn back to Ohio from Tennessee; Chuck thought it was funny; I was mortified. And now, 13 years later, the tables had turned. I enjoyed that moment of pettiness. But honestly, I was elated that they all were there. Together.

The day before the competition during our pre-meet workout, Chuck and I had spotted Tracy Sundlun taking pictures and videos of me in the warmup area. Because I knew how close he had become to John, I knew those images weren't for anything good. To make matters worse, John had just been announced as the newest member of the USATF Foundation's Board of Directors. This worried me. I was afraid he would haunt me for the rest of my time in the sport and suspected that, after being turned off by them in the Bahamas, my leaving was exactly why he accepted.

I hopped in the 100 as a warmup for the long jump and to have my name on the start list so that the coaches would consider me for the relay pool. I made the semifinal and ran an easy 11.35, which obviously did not make the final, and turned my attention to the long jump. I had quite the series, jumping over 23 feet, three times. Brittany jumped 6.98 for second. Shake ela

Saunders 6.92 for third. And because I had a bye, the fourth-place jumper Quanesha Burks also made the team.

At team processing, where we get our uniforms and handle logistics for training camps and the upcoming World Championships, I was extended an invitation for the relay pool and as a result was invited to relay camp in Monaco. Three of the four members of our Rio Olympics winning 4x100-meter team had returned for relay camp. But public opinion was largely that we did not deserve to be there. English and Allyson had placed sixth and eighth in the final respectively and I didn't "even make the final." The personal coaches and agents of the young sprinters that had "outperformed" us at nationals cried foul and were pressured by Orin Richburg, the relay coach to sit us out and give the young ones a chance.

I told Orin I was happy to race for my spot, that I'd race any woman who wanted to run the first leg head-to-head, from blocks the entire turn, no problem. He said that wouldn't be necessary.

"Well in case it is, I'm willing," I said to him before leaving him to sit in his misery in the hotel lobby in Monaco.

I was on USA Red Team which was basically our Rio team with Aaliyah Brown as the anchor. Everything was going well until the last exchange. Aaliyah left early, which meant by the time English caught up to pass the baton, they'd be out of the zone, and we'd be disqualified. Aware she was approaching the end of the zone Aaliyah "slammed on the brakes" which forced English to "slam on the brakes." English made the pass, but she tore her ACL to do it. Allyson and I ran to English who was inconsolable. As much as some people questioned why we were there, English is the perfect example why. English didn't have to sacrifice herself to make that pass. It was just a Diamond League meet. She had been through relay mishaps and knew how to handle herself and did so admirably. We were all there because of our experience. We were there because we had earned the right to be.

But I knew it wasn't going to be a smooth ride to be selected for that relay team. I returned home to the Netherlands to train, spend time with Andrey and Anthony, my Airbnb hosts turned family I would kill for, and wait for word on the relay. Team USA would be staging in Birmingham before bussing to London and checking in to the team hotel. Team USA staging camps were optional but gave us time and inexpensive ways to acclimate to the new country; however, relay camp was not optional. I was packing my car to head to the Amsterdam airport to meet the relay team in Birmingham when Orin told me not to come.

"Not at all?" I asked. Not at all. I was out of the relay. "I can't race for it? Prove fitness? Nothing?" I asked. No, nothing. Not at all. Do not come. Lawrence Johnson another coach assisting Orin with the relays texted me and asked me to come anyway, basically saying he wouldn't turn me away if I was already there. This sounded extra shady. Rana and I decided that I would just focus on the long jump. I had a title to defend.

There was a lot on the line. Winning here would give me a bye to the next World Championships in Doha, Qatar. I'm getting older and byes are gifts from above. My contract would expire December 31, and Nike would determine if they were resigning me based on my performance here. There was a lot on the line, and the emotional toil the relay was taking on me was not worth it.

I arrived in London and the Grange Hotel to find Orin in the lobby. He was the last person I wanted to see, and definitely the last person I wanted to see first. He looked troubled. I shot him a look I hoped would discourage him from speaking to me. I failed. He walked over and said hello, patted me on the shoulder, and then whispered, "I think we may need you."

ALL THAT REMAINS

I could hardly stand it, being around Team USA at this point. Nearly all of my interactions felt forced.

Everyone knew where Team USA was staying. Which meant that I'd be easy to find if John decided to come. I had heard through the grapevine that he'd been telling people he'd "see them in London." I had no idea what type of access he'd have as a member of the USATF Foundation's Board of Directors. I mentioned my concern to the team manager, who had our security team reach out to me. We couldn't stop John from attending a public event, but we could be on the lookout for him. I had a room at the meet hotel. But I also had an AirBnB flat near the second meet hotel—a small studio condo near the Tower Bridge in an area I was quite familiar with. I felt most relaxed and at ease there. The main door required a code to enter, and only the Team Managers, Chuck, and the anti-doping agencies knew my whereabouts.

When I needed to get away, when I needed my space, I disappeared to this condo. I made myself dinner, and I unwound slowly to Netflix on the television. I could feel that I was barely hanging on. I was shocked at my fragility. I thought the hardest thing I'd have to do, I had already done months before. But I was wrong. I didn't understand what I was feeling. Some people think (and I had been one of them) that, once you remove yourself from a bad situation, your turnaround is immediate. And sure, there are some things you experience sudden relief from. But your new reality, and the feelings that arise in response to it, ebbs and flows like the tides of Calm Lake one day and a tempestuous sea the next.

I'm an angry person but not an inherently mean one, and I was dealing with how mean it was to have left in the manner that I did. It bothered me every day that I could not say that I had acted in a way worthy of my beliefs of ahimsa: a yogic principle meaning: do no harm. The guilt of this weighed heavily on me.

Then there was the fact that this was a championship. I'd been to five global championships in the last five years and at each of them my husband either sat in the coach's box next to my coach at the pit, near the start if I was running a relay, or near the finish for an open sprint.

In those years, before initiating my jump, I would look at him. I don't know why. He didn't signal me. I wasn't communicating with him. Perhaps it was my needing to remind myself I wasn't alone before initiating a jump that may or may not get me on the podium.

And at London 2017, I did the same. I looked over at the stands. Both looking and not looking for his face. Sometimes seeing Rana, sometimes seeing Chuck, sometimes seeing a random but familiar friendly face.

John may not have been present, but his voice still was—I could hear him reviewing a timeline he made of my accomplishments, "before John" and "with John." I was still replaying a scene between us from two years prior in a hotel room ahead of the Diamond League Final in Zurich ; When John stormed out of the hotel room in a fit of rage and returned with computer printer paper. Scribbled on the page was a horizontal line, a nearly perfect stroke written in the tell-tale flourish of a Sharpie pen. A hash mark split the horizontal line. The words "before John," and "with John" marked the newly created segments on what I understood to be a timeline. The "before John" segment listed two medals: 2005's World Championship gold medal in Helsinki, Finland, and 2006's upgraded Indoor World Championship gold. The "with John" column was hefty: 2012's Indoor World Championship bronze medal in the 60-meter dash. London's Olympic Gold, the 4x100-meter relay world record. The 2014's Indoor World Championship bronze medal in the 60-meter dash, another Diamond League Champion title, National Championship title in the 100-meter dash, and 2015's Diamond League Championship and World Championship gold. The point he was making was clear: I was more successful with him.

Now I was back in London, but this time "without John," and hearing his voice in my head, jeering me, teasing me, essentially saying that when I miss the podium this time I'd know exactly why. I'd know then that it wasn't worth it, my leaving him—that I was stupid, naive, and just as ungrateful as he believed I was.

Psychologists say one way to combat negative thoughts is to replace them with the exact opposite thought, like a positivity swap. So, for the duration of the event, I was working on this. I couldn't focus on my execution checklist as I usually would because I needed that space to overwhelm my mind with positive thoughts so that when it was time for my next attempt, I would possess enough self-belief to take the first step. I was struggling, and I could feel it manifesting in my body language, in the clench of my fists, and jaw. At one point, both Chuck and Jimmy (who had made the trip from Oslo) signaled me over to talk to me at different times.

"Are you okay?" Chuck asked me.

I hate talking during a long jump competition, even to my coach. I hardly ever walk over to the wall to converse with my coach after jumps. It's not because I feel like they aren't useful. Long-winded talks take me out of the moment and give my adrenaline time to settle. I only need to know two things in competition:

1. If my foot was on the board for takeoff, and if not where was it?

2. Did I drive my right knee?

Usually, I can get both those answers by watching the replay on the large in-stadium screen if they have it. So, the two of them coming over to speak to me only highlighted how far out of the ordinary this performance was for me.

No, I was not okay.

I had one jump left, and I was not in podium position. I had just one more chance to get there.

I took a deep breath.

I begged myself to commit to the run.

I reminded myself that physics doesn't give a fuck about any of this, that it was me holding myself back. All I needed to do was step out of the way and execute.

I took the first step, then the second. Then autopilot kicked in.

I took off.

I landed.

I didn't fly out of the back of the pit like I usually do. This means I got every bit I could out of that jump. I let not one centimeter of momentum go to waste.

I stood up.

I took a moment with my eyes closed, still standing in the center of the pit. I took that moment to thank myself. I knew that jump had been my best jump of the day. I said to myself, *no matter where it placed me, I gave it all that I had.*

I looked at the performance board.

Third place overall.

In the immediate moment, I was relieved to have jumped to the podium. But the competition was far from over. Ivana Španović, a Serbian long jumper, prepared to take her final jump. I was on edge. She initiated her run, bounding the first part of her approach before reaching her top speed. She took off and extended her arms and legs beautifully, gracefully. She landed feet first, butt second, her back and ponytail following behind leaving a trail in the sand. She exited the pit. They measured her jump and she remained in fourth, which means I remained in third.

My jump held on—barely.

Ivana's coach and agent appealed the results which delayed the medal ceremony. Under the stadium, I watched as Brittany Reese and Darya Klishina, both in their podium suits, got fitted with the special adhesive bibs the championship's sponsor wants displayed. They did not fit me with mine. Because Ivana was appealing there was a possibility that I'd get booted from the podium altogether. They didn't want to waste an adhesive bib on me if it turned out I was actually in fourth place. Time stood still as I watched Brittany and Darya happily pace the podium staging area waiting for the moment they could stand proudly and receive their hard fought for and earned medals. I stayed seated on my chair, using all my remaining strength to silence the voice in my head telling me that Ivana will win her appeal, and I'll be escorted back out of the podium staging room, and out to the warmup track, as fourth place, with no medal.

A meet official, Rowena, a beautiful woman I'd met a few times before on the competition circuit, approached me with an adhesive bib.

"Does this mean…?" I couldn't even get my question out.

"Yes," Rowena said, smiling.

As we approached the podium to receive our medals, I lost my grip on my emotions and drowned into a sea of my own tears.

FREEDOM ISN'T FREE

My tears on the podium were largely misunderstood at the time. I fought to maintain my composure but the national anthem, particularly the words "O'r the land of the free, and the home of the brave" pierced my heart and soul so deeply I could no longer hold the dam of emotion. I was finally free, and I had been brave. And because my compatriot Brittney Reese won the competition, I still got to hear those words of the national anthem, exactly when I needed to.

I walked back through the warmup area with my medal in hand and scrolled through my social media mentions and saw comments that read, "It's okay champ, there's always next time" or "can't win 'em all!"

I decided to share with the public, with my newfound ability to do so, what my tears were actually about. It wasn't sadness about losing. But a release of all that I had been holding on to. They were tears of relief. That Instagram post was shared and liked thousands of times. That post caught the attention of the BBC and I sat down to speak with them about it.

I was afraid to speak so openly about what had been an extremely private struggle, and I was ashamed of myself too. Just a week before, one of my own training partners asked me how I could let myself get abused when I could power clean 200 pounds for reps? It hurt me to hear, because it was a question I had been grappling with myself. How much of this did I let happen? Am I a victim or am I a co-perpetrator? An enabler of my own abuse? I knew that talking about this would open me up to these sorts of questions from others. But I decided that if there was a chance that there was a single human being paying attention and wondering if they should choose themselves over the abuse they were currently tolerating, I needed to say something. If there was someone grappling with staying or leaving because the familiarity of the abuse is less terrifying than the unknown, I needed to say something.

The first time I actually "said something" was in Oslo, Norway, earlier in the season ahead of the Oslo Diamond League. I was waiting for my bags at the baggage claim when a tall man with a friendly face and a great head of hair struck up conversation. Tired, hungry, and not really interested in dealing with men, I decided to be polite and engage anyway. He told me his name was Jimmy and that he had dedicated his life to advocacy. He had done extensive work all over the world and was telling me that he was returning from interviewing some doctors in "Doctors Without Borders." His latest project, the Human Aspect Project featured a "Life Experience"

Library which captured my attention. On their website you could click on any "experience" and see video interviews of people who have gone through that experience. I wanted to be a part of it. And we made arrangements to meet the following day for the sit-down interview. It was in this interview that I told the secret of my marriage, and that I was running, and that I didn't know if the story had a happy ending, but I was working on it.

Off-camera Jimmy's mouth had fallen open. I gave him no indication, during our initial conversation in the baggage claim at the airport, that this was my life. He had expected to hear about the struggles of living life as a world-class athlete and instead he got...*that*. I was uncomfortable talking about it with Jimmy and Isabelle (who also was working on the project and helped with the video interview) but they were so open and willing to listen and hold space for me, that I pushed through the discomfort that vulnerability initially presents itself as. It helped me to know that this video would live on a website where someone could and would click "domestic violence," watch me speak to them, and hear me say, "It's okay to choose better."

But the BBC interview was different. It felt like I was opening a can of worms, a Pandora's box even. I had no idea what the consequences could or would be for speaking out. I was terrified. The only comfort I could glean from the experience was that it was the truth. As uncomfortable, gross, and dark as it was, it happened—it happened to me. And I was ready to own it.

It only took 24 hours from the time I agreed to sit for the interview with the BBC to go from being proud of myself about making it to the podium under all of that adversity, to beating myself up for not being able to pull off "the win." The win would have granted me a bye to the next World Championships in 2019 in Doha, Qatar. The win would have signaled to Nike that I was worth resigning. The win would have been absolute validation to me that it was MY effort that produced big time performances at the right time.

Instead, the bronze medal, left just enough of a fissure in my body armor for self-doubt to set in. And the voices in my head, my God, the voices! I had heard John's voice over and over both in my head and every single day for the previous five years. It was naïve of me to think I'd just be able to stop hearing that voice or replaying those shame tapes over and over and over.

Was John right? Is the reason I didn't win? Because I left? Would I have won if I had stayed? If he were here? Was he really the x-factor? Do I mean nothing in this equation? Could he make a winner of anyone? Am I not elite or world class?

I continued to beat myself up with those questions. And then I'd beat myself up further for asking those questions. And then beat myself up further still for not being able to stop replaying those questions on a loop or hearing that voice when I no longer needed to.

Intellectually I knew how bogus that line of thinking was, but I was an emotional wreck. It didn't help that my line of thinking was being validated constantly by the nature of the sport I'm in.

My salary at the time that I won the bronze medal was over $200,000 due to my successes as both a sprinter and jumper. Until July 1st, 2017, my earnings went directly to John. But because I left my marriage in May, I was able to keep half of my salary for that year. Getting that July 2017 check was the first time in six years that money that I had earned, was in my account, for me to do with what I chose to.

But it wasn't a windfall, and I didn't treat it as such either. My divorce was only just beginning and my attorney's fees were already sky high due to the amount of time she had to spend chasing down documents and begging for cooperation from the other side. Once again, unpaid taxes that I believed were being handled by Dennis and John fell to me to settle up. And the usual expenses related to training and competition: coaching fees, therapy (mental, physical, and massage), travel expenses, training camps, and all other living expenses were on me to handle. That's the nature of this sport; one has to invest in themselves upfront this way in order to put themselves in the best position to achieve their goals and perhaps get reimbursed or financially compensated as a reward. That wasn't a problem. It was just costly. And there were no guarantees.

Nike did offer to sign me again under a new contract. For a new salary of $75,000. For reasons they did not state, they decided that a salary cut was not only deserved—but indicative of my value to the company. Although I ended the 2017 season with the second longest jump in the world and a medal from the World Championships, I had also "earned" a nearly 70% pay cut.

I was devastated by this hit. And the "shame" tapes began to play on a loop in my head all over again. "See?" I heard John's voice say. "They know. Everybody knows. You're nothing without me."

The depressive state I was in was deep and dark. Feeling undeserving of a chance at a new beginning. I was struggling with feelings of self-worth and suicidal ideations. I wasn't just thinking suicidal thoughts, I was trying to figure out how to execute them. Fueling my increasing inability to control my thoughts and feelings were my opioid withdrawals. I had grabbed a handful of hydrocodone tablets, Percocet pills, and my prescription bottle for Xanax when I left home three months before. I had run out of them all not even a week after my arrival in Alabama. I tried, unsuccessfully, to get my Xanax prescription refilled. The prescription was classified as a controlled substance and could not be filled across state lines. There was no way, with the crack down on prescription drug abuse taking place across the country, that I was going to be able to find another doctor as willing as John's doctors to write scripts for those. I could no longer use drugs to escape and avoid feeling my feelings and had no respite from my withdrawals. I was in detox in every way one could detox.

My freedom was and still is an expensive endeavor. But once, while passing time at the airport, in a business lounge I overheard two men talking about their divorces. One said, "turns out it woulda' been cheaper to keep her." They both chuckled and took another swig of their amber beers. The other, set his glass back down on the table, leaned in close to his friend, and whispered, conspiratorially, "It's expensive...because it's worth it."

Freedom is not, has never been, and will never be...free.

THINGS FALL APART

Track and field has always been the vehicle I used to move my life forward. In middle school, it provided me friends at a confusing time. In high school, it opened the doors to college. In college, it opened the doors to the world as a professional athlete. So, it was only natural for me to turn to track, again, to deliver me out of my suffering.

Fall training 2017 was an opportunity for me, for the first time, to train without worrying about anyone or anything other than myself. I told Rana, prior to returning to The Netherlands to train, that I wanted…no, I needed to have an incredible indoor season. I wanted to prove to myself that it was *my* effort, discipline, and commitment that made me elite. I wanted to prove Nike wrong in their assessment of my worth.

My goal was to make the team for the Indoor World Championships that would take place in Birmingham, England. I wanted two medals, another 60-meter dash medal, and what would be my second long jump medal. But it didn't take me long after training began to start to question if my goals were attainable.

First, training was not the same. I understood that it was not practical or necessary to do the same thing all the time year after year—but I do know the type of training my body responds well to, and the work we were doing on the track, my body was NOT responding to. I wasn't getting faster or sharper. And for whatever reason, Rana was spending less and less time with me correcting my specific technical issues. I got nowhere close to the attention to detail I got in 2012, or 2016, and the 2017 seasons. My questions likely irritated Rana who probably felt he did not need to prove to me that he was a good coach. He insisted that all was well. But with such a drastic change in the training and in our interactions with each other—something had gone wrong. And I was uncomfortable that the alarm bells of my intuition were ringing so loudly about the person that I was now trusting with my career, a person who was essentially holding the key to unlocking a new start for me.

I'd spent five years ignoring the red flags and alarm bells my intuition tried to bring to my attention. The cost for casting those warnings aside and pressing forward was high, and I paid for it then with my body, soul, and spirit. But now, I was unwilling to trust him over myself. There were too many things happening around us that gave me pause. I thought back to previous training camps, and meets where I'd felt cast aside, ignored, or dismissed and decided that it was time for me to leave Rana and the training group. I did not leave my marriage and its constant belittling and diminishing of my worth and value, to then voluntarily subject myself to feeling the same way within my training group.

When someone I work with lets me down, I'm disappointed for a while but eventually I can decide to move beyond that and continue to work with them or go in another direction. But it's a different level of hurt when it's someone I love—Rana was one of the few people who knew what I was dealing with over the last several years. He was one of the only people who knew what it took for me to show up and give my best effort at training day after day. He was one of the only people who knew what I was going home to at night. He knew what every win and every loss meant for and to me.

The hug Rana gave me as I leaned over the rail after my final attempt in the long jump at the 2017 World Championships meant the world to me, because he truly knew the effort that that performance took. He knew how fragile, how broken, and how determined I was in that moment. He knew.

And because he knew that. He also knew what I was fighting for, and how the following indoor season could have done a lot for me emotionally and financially.

But I got the impression that that didn't matter to him like it mattered to me. I had learned, over the course of the previous five years, that a person can't make themselves matter to someone. Every day that I went to training, whether it was in The Netherlands, in Tenerife, or in Barcelona, it was as if Bonnie Raitt's ballad, "I Can't Make You Love Me" was the soundtrack.

That much I knew for sure, for my entire life so far to that point, I couldn't make anyone love me, and I couldn't make anyone care. Not unless they wanted to. And I was no longer willing to force it either, and so I let our coach/athlete relationship, and the friendship that developed alongside it, fall apart.

PERMISSION TO THRIVE

I don't have a crystal ball. So, I don't actually know how this story ends. But this is what I do know. I'm pretty hard to kill. I went into the 2018 track season trying to force success. Which is an approach that never works. I don't like making mistakes. But I do make them, it's part of being human. But I am *not* okay with making the same mistake twice. After all I had been through, I was *still* looking for things and people outside of myself to save me, which was the same thinking that got me into my mess of a life in the first place. I needed a change. And the change I made was to turn my attention inward, to focus on myself, and my healing.

First up on the agenda: a vacation. I never made it to Hawaii, but I did get to Costa Rica, thanks to Chuck and Brianna Glenn, a former training partner who now curates amazing vacations with her company Milk and Honey Travels. There in the rainforest, I slowed down long enough to listen to my own voice. At times it was difficult to hear through the white noise of doubt and sadness, but it was there; soft as a whisper, but it was there.

Slowly, my body started to unwind, settle, and understand that it no longer needed to be in fight or flight mode. It was safe. I was safe. I had survived.

There was just one last thing weighing me down: my sport. My entire identity was wrapped up in it. Not only was track and field what I did, it was also who I was. And this was a huge problem for me.

My 2018 season was disappointing. I hadn't been running fast or jumping far. I was embarrassed and ashamed of myself and my performances every time I set foot on the track or the runway. The only exception was when I received an upgraded medal at the Birmingham Indoor World Championships, because the previous title holder, Tatyana Kotova was banned and subsequently stripped of her titles from the indoor championship 12 years earlier in Moscow, Russia. That moment was bittersweet, but I did allow myself to be proud. And although it's impossible to know just how much my life would have been different if I had won the gold back then, I did know that things would have been different. It's impossible to recuperate the financial loss, and repercussions when an athlete cheats us out of our rightful medals.

What's more, my joints were starting to give me trouble, my period was being weird, and my depression was kicking my ass too. I was without a coach, having opted instead to train with and consult with people I looked up to, respected, or trusted. Among them were Chuck, my best friend of nearly 18 years, Italian strength and conditioning coach, Carlo Buzzichelli whom I'd met at the 2017 World Champs, Dutch coach Bart Bennema who I was fond of after spending so much time around him and his group when training in The Netherlands.

By the end of that season, I fully believed that I was done with track. Actually, it felt more like track was done with me. I'd gone to one of my favorite physical therapists and doctors at The St. Vincent's Sports Performance Clinic, in Indiana, for a physical, and x-rays showed that I had 9 stress fractures in my left leg, the one that I used to jump off of in the long jump. When I asked the doctor if I could just switch legs, he x-ray'd the right. The right leg had 7 stress fractures too. He told me that I was on borrowed time, that any of my 16 fractures could become a clean break at anytime, and that the only cure was rest and time. Time away from track and field was not something I wanted. I was still struggling to answer the question: who am I outside of track and field? The answer was: nobody. And so, I did not rest. I continued to jump. It was a season-ending ankle sprain that forced me to take the time and rest my body needed. It was almost as if my body was overriding my mind. My body had decided for me that it was done. If my body was too broken to continue training and competing in track and field, then it was urgent for me to find out who I was without it. So, I did what I always do, I ran away. I ran fast and far, all the way to Bali. I turned to yoga to reconnect me to my true self. Yoga, the practice of linking breath and movement to still the mind, slowed my inner talk down enough for me to see my emotions. My yoga and meditation practice allowed me to observe my innermost self, and then act from a place of clarity—rather than chaos and confusion.

In the summer of 2018, I attended yoga teacher training at Love Story Yoga in San Francisco. I crashed on Chuck's mom's couch for six weeks while I dove deep into yoga philosophy led by Stephanie Snyder. I never intended to teach it, I just wanted to better understand why the practice was so powerful, and how it continued to save my life. Gina's attention, and being immersed in bhakti yoga (the yoga of devotion characterized by chanting) set me back on a healing road.

My spirit began to heal, but my body continued to fail me. It started with my period changing. I rationalized those changes. Maybe it's stress? maybe I'm not eating enough? After all everything around me was changing, my diet, my surroundings, my lifestyle, everything. Why not my period too? So, I ignored it.

Still going back and forth to divorce court in what had become a very contentious ordeal, I was doing a good job of not letting the mudslinging bring me down. And even though I had to hire yet *another* attorney because John sued me for defamation, I still tried to stay focused on all that was ahead of me to achieve and attain.

That's not to say that I never went to bed at night crying tears of sorrow for all the money I've earned and had stolen from me, or the idea that I'd wasted the best years of my life on the wrong person. And the best seasons of my life completely unable to enjoy the fruits of my labor. What would my perceived value to brands have been if I had been able to utilize social media while winning 7 global championship medals? I've gone down those rabbit holes plenty. But I was now fully equipped to pull myself back out of them.

I went into the 2019 track season hopeful. I was in a much better space. Track and field was something I did. Not who I was. Making the distinction was life changing for me. But one thing wasn't changing. My performances. My sprained ankle from the year before would not heal. Even though it was stronger than it had been, I still could not jump off of it. And so I made the decision to attempt to switch jump legs rather than sit out of yet another season. I jumped off the opposite leg at the national championship and placed 17th out of 17. I tried to put on a strong face, but the divorce was dragging on, the bills were pilling high, and I was struggling to see the "why" of it all. Maybe it really was time to quit?

But before I did, I made some calls and flew to the Olympic Training Center in Colorado Springs so they could look at my ankle. I needed to be sure that my body was really incapable of continuing in the sport before calling it quits for good. But shortly after I spoke with the receptionist to check in, I passed out in the lobby, which triggered a lot of tests, and monitoring. I was severely anemic. And although I had been made aware of my low iron a month before, I had no concept of how severe it was. At the same time, I got PRP on my ankle, a treatment that uses your own plasma injected directly into the site of pain to promote a healing response. I also received the first of many iron infusions.

But slowly, over the next several months my health deteriorated further. I could no longer kill workouts that were easy for me. I'd lie down for a nap and be almost impossible to arouse. At night my legs would jump and twitch involuntarily making sleep impossible. Sleep deprived, in pain, sinking into despair, and growing increasingly desperate, I told Chuck I was afraid to see a doctor because if they offered me painkillers I was not sure that I'd say no. I had not touched a narcotic since I ran through my final stash over two years before, but since then I had yet to make it through a single day without the *thought* of having one. I was not confident that if it were just the doctor and I, alone in the examination room, that I would turn down a new prescription to relieve the pain. But Chuck said he believed in me, and that he was confident that I would say no. I begged him not to force me to put myself in that position. I knew what the cravings were like and that I still had them—the pull was strong. But the pain was greater than the fear, and I returned to Colorado Springs.

The team doctor stared at me in disbelief as I told him that we either figured out what was wrong with my body or I was retiring on his watch as the reigning Olympic Champion. After pounding my fist on the desk, I was able to see a gynecologist, Dr. Charles LaLonde. I begged him to give me a transvaginal ultrasound. I was convinced my uterus was trying to kill me, I had been blogging about my ordeal and, as a result, other women told me to request one. He was able to squeeze me in at the last minute before my return flight back to California. On the table, legs in stirrups, I looked over my right shoulder at the monitor and saw it, a fibroid tumor filling my uterus and the cause of my current suffering. I underwent emergency surgery a little over three hours later. In recovery, Dr. LaLonde told me that the surgery went well, and that, although he had diagnosed it as a benign fibroid tumor, he sent it off for a biopsy anyway. Those tests would eventually return negative for cancer screening. But the doctor informed me that the blood loss combined with the iron deficiency was so severe that had it not been for the surgery, he wasn't sure I would have survived another week before my organs began to fail me.

My body began to heal but not fast enough with the Tokyo 2020 Olympics approaching. After much prodding, and a final go ahead from the World Anti-Doping Agency and World Athletics, I got a much needed blood transfusion to help jumpstart my body back to health. My body had been working extremely hard to create more blood and to store iron, but it was too far behind. I finally started to feel better toward the end of February 2020, just as the world shut down to protect itself from the Novel Corona Virus.

The postponement of the games gave me an extra year to heal, and although the body will heal on its own timeline, I was grateful for the gift of more time. It was a challenging year, but I'm grateful to have gotten through it with my physical and mental health intact.

On December 31st, 2020, my contract with Nike expired. They did not exercise the option to keep me under contract with the same terms or offer to sign me to a new contract at a lower rate, they did not say "hey, the last 15 years were great, and thanks for seven medals." I wasn't actually expecting that, but it's kind of like leaving a job you've worked for nearly two decades with zero acknowledgement. It was strange. And no other shoe or apparel company made an offer to sponsor me either.

And so, I go into a new year, scarred with the lingering fingerprint of a lifetime of trauma and pain. So much suffering behind me, yet so much hope propelling me onward. I'm bruised but not broken. Unsponsored but not unsupported. More free than I have ever been. And looking forward to my future both on and off the track.

I have survived.

Now it's time to thrive.

RESOURCES

You are not alone. Below I've included resources that I've leaned on myself to fight my way back to the light. The organizations, websites, or services included on this list are limited to the United States. I encourage you to take the time to locate any additional resources you may need, or help available to you in your state, city, or country of residence.

Domestic Violence
    The National Domestic Violence Hotline
        Thehotline.org
        1.800.799.SAFE
        TTY: 1.800.787.3224

    National Coalition Against Domestic Violence
        NCADV.org

Sexual Assault
    National Sexual Assault Hotline
        800.656.4673
    RAINN (Rape, Abuse, & Incest National Network)
        rainn.org

Suicide Prevention
    National Suicide Prevention Lifeline
        800.273.8255
    Crisis Text Line
    text TALK to 741741

Eating Disorder Support
    The Alliance for Eating Disorders Awareness
        Allianceforeatingdisorders.com

Fibroid Awareness
    The Fibroid Foundation
        www.fibroidfoundation.org

ACKNOWLEDGMENTS

I have always wanted to be and I have always been a writer; and yet, nothing has made this seem more real to me than this process. And just like on a podium when I'm receiving a medal, it appears that I've done it alone, but I assure you, wholeheartedly, that that is not at all the case. The same is true of this book.

This book would not be in your hands if it weren't for the encouragement, love, and support of my best friend Charles Ryan. He'll tell you that I saved myself. But I'll tell you I wouldn't have bothered if he hadn't been there constantly reminding me of who I was. He is the reason this book is as gritty, vivid, and as honest as it is. Believe me, there were memories I did not want to write or relive and dark places I did not want to revisit. But he urged me forward, and on more than one occasion, helped me piece myself back together when I came undone all over again while writing. I don't believe in unconditional love, but I think this is as close as I'll ever get.

Speaking of love, I want to thank my parents Robert and Jo Ann Madison. The conversations we've had over the last few years have been life affirming. My mom used to quote a scripture from Joel. It says, "So I will restore to you the years that locusts have eaten." I have asked myself over the years how I'll ever get back that time. But now I know that our time together as a family has not only been restored it has been made plenty. I'd go through that hell over and over again if I knew it would lead us to this. I know I am loved, I hope you know how much I love you too.

To my big sister Adrianne. I have and always will adored you. You taught me what it means to be a big sister, to nurture, and to love fiercely. The lover in me, started with you.

To my little sister Christina Madison. There aren't really words for "us." But I'm honored to be your big sister. Thank you for all you've taught me and are still teaching me.

To my niece Mikayla and nephews Jaelon and Sol. Little loves of my life. I don't necessarily need you to read this book, but it's here for you if you need a reminder of the type of fight, resolve, and determination you have in your DNA.

To Justin Allen, my high-performance coach. You are one of my not-so-secret weapons. Only you and I truly know what shape I was in when we first started working together. Thanks for all the homework you gave me, all the time, all the calls, all the resources. I hope you're proud.

To Cejih Yung, founder of The CG Sports Company, who read one sample of my writing and said, "Hell, yeah, we're publishing your book!" To Matt Amerlan, who fields my questions and big ideas, keeps me on deadline, and has exceeded all of my expectations. To Rachel Draffen, who takes my ideas and sprinkles them with her marketing magic. To Tony DiPasquale, who knocked out my book cover photo shoot and hype reel in one afternoon, and to Nicole Wurtele, for her amazing work taking those photos and turning them into beautiful covers.

To Mike Nicloy. I am so grateful that it was him I got to navigate the world of publishing with. I was terrified when I submitted my manuscript the first time and was even more terrified to answer the phone when he called after he had finished reading it. But his first words were, "I want to give you a hug," and since then he has answered every question I had about the publishing process (I even asked about the texture of the paper and how many shades of white I'd have to choose from). He's as diligent with commas as he is with deadlines.

To my editor Marla. You did such a fantastic job on a manuscript that I'd considered to be an affront of the laws of grammar. Somehow you were able to keep my voice while keeping me in line. To my editor Lyda, you must have read this memoir with the eyes of God. I have never been so impressed by someone whose job it is to point out my mistakes as I am with you. Thank you for your eye.

To everyone who has joined me on this journey since 2017. Thank you for reading my posts and sharing my blogs. You helped me become a better writer. You helped me push this memoir across the finish line.

There are so many more that I'd love to thank by name but don't have the time and space to do so here. I'll tell you in person.

I believe we learn something from everyone we encounter. Some lessons are painful. Some lessons are painless. Others are priceless. All are valuable. Thank you for it all.

ABOUT THE AUTHOR

Tianna Bartoletta was born in Elyria, Ohio. Her successes in Track and Field have been her passport to the world, granting her the opportunity to live in different countries and learn multiple languages.

However, she believes that her resume as a track and field athlete is the least interesting thing about her. In addition to her nine global championship medals, she's the writer of a well-read blog at tiannabee.com, and the author of the popular eBook, *Why You're Not a Track Star*, a short read that helps young athletes level up their performances by avoiding the mistakes she made.

Tianna is also a certified yoga instructor, an avid reader, a dedicated meditator, and a fierce competitor.

She is currently still training and resides in the Bay Area, California.

CPSIA information can be obtained
at www.ICGtesting.com
Printed in the USA
BVHW040931190621
609910BV00003B/807